MAY 2 8 2010

DISCARDED

D1455588

# A PATH OF NORTHERN LIGHTS

# UNE TRAÎNÉE D'AURORES BORÉALES

NORFOLK COUNTY PUBLIC LIBRARY

TORCH RELAY
RELAIS DE LA FLAMME
vancouver 2010

The Story of the Vancouver 2010 Olympic Torch Relay
*L'histoire du relais de la flamme olympique de Vancouver 2010*

In loving memory of
Jack Poole, the
eternal flame keeper
of Vancouver 2010

April 14, 1933 – October 23, 2009

*À la douce mémoire de
Jack Poole, éternel
gardien de la flamme
de Vancouver 2010*

*14 avril 1933 – 23 octobre 2009*

He taught us things not known to kings.
— *Irish song lyric*

*Il nous a appris des choses inconnues des rois.*
— *paroles d'une chanson irlandaise*

™ Trademark © Copyright 2010, Vancouver Organizing Committee
for the 2010 Olympic and Paralympic Winter Games. All Rights Reserved.

ᴹᶜ Marque de commerce © Copyright 2010, Comité d'organisation
des Jeux olympiques et paralympiques d'hiver de 2010 à Vancouver.
Tous droits réservés.

All rights reserved. No part of this work covered by the copyright herein
may be reproduced or used in any form or by any means — graphic,
electronic or mechanical — without the prior written permission of the
publisher. Any request for photocopying, recording, taping or information
storage and retrieval systems of any part of this book shall be directed
in writing to The Canadian Copyright Licensing Agency (Access Copyright).
For an Access Copyright licence, visit www.accesscopyright.ca or call
toll free 1-800-893-5777.

Tous droits réservés. Toute reproduction ou tout usage, sous quelque
forme ou selon quelque procédé que ce soit (graphique, électronique
ou mécanique), de tout extrait de la présente publication couverte par
les droits d'auteurs, est interdite sans l'autorisation écrite de la maison
d'édition. Toute demande de photocopie ou autre reproduction graphique
de tout extrait de la présente publication doit être faite par écrit auprès
de The Canadian Copyright Licensing Agency (Access Copyright). Pour
obtenir une licence Access Copyright, visitez www.accesscopyright.ca
ou composez le numéro sans frais 1-800-893-5777.

Library and Archives Canada Cataloguing in Publication

A PATH OF NORTHERN LIGHTS:
The Story of the Vancouver 2010 Olympic Torch Relay

ISBN 978-0-470-16152-4

1. Olympic Torch Relay (2010 : Canada).
I. Vancouver Organizing Committee for the 2010
   Olympic and Paralympic Winter Games

GV721.92.P38 2009          796.980971
C2009-905918-5

Bibliothèque et Archives Canada Programme
de catalogage avant publication

UNE TRAÎNÉE D'AURORES BORÉALES :
L'histoire du relais de la flamme olympique de
Vancouver 2010

ISBN 978-0-470-16152-4

1. Relais de la flamme olympique (2010 : Canada).
I. Comité d'organisation des Jeux olympiques et
   paralympiques d'hiver de 2010 à Vancouver

GV721.92.P38 2009          796.980971
C2009-905918-5

John Wiley & Sons Canada, Ltd.
6045 Freemont Blvd.
Mississauga, Ontario
L5R 4J3

Printed in Canada
Imprimé au Canada

1 2 3 4 5 FP 14 13 12 11 10

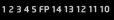

Mixed Sources
Cert no. SW-COC-001271
© 1996 FSC

 **WILEY**

# A PATH OF NORTHERN LIGHTS
### The Story of the Vancouver 2010 Olympic Torch Relay

# UNE TRAÎNÉE D'AURORES BORÉALES
### L'histoire du relais de la flamme olympique de Vancouver 2010

At Panathinaiko Stadium in Athens, Greece, John Furlong carries the Olympic Flame that, in 107 days, will officially open the Vancouver 2010 Olympic Winter Games.

*Au stade Panathinaiko à Athènes, en Grèce, M. John Furlong porte la flamme olympique qui, 107 jours plus tard, marquera le début des Jeux olympiques d'hiver de 2010 à Vancouver.*

# At the starting line
## *Un pied sur la ligne de départ*

With less than a week before the torch relay begins, there's a growing sense of anticipation for everyone involved. After 106 days travelling across Canada, the Olympic Flame will arrive at BC Place, marking the start of the Vancouver 2010 Olympic Winter Games. The 60,000 fans at the stadium, like the projected three billion television viewers around the world, will wait with excitement as the flame travels its final steps — a truly memorable moment for all.

When the Olympic Flame arrives inside BC Place, I hope every Canadian will feel like they've given it a push to get there.

I hope every Canadian feels they've contributed to that great moment, that they are part owner of what's about to unfold. And I also hope they feel pride — that they say to themselves, "This was something we all did together."

The Vancouver 2010 Olympic Torch Relay embodies a vision of our Games that we've held from the earliest days: that the 2010 Winter Games are truly "Canada's Games." At Vancouver 2010, we've always wanted these Games to be about the entire nation — to let everyone in, from every single corner of this huge, extraordinary country. We want these Games to bring Canadians together, igniting something in our hearts and souls that makes us better.

Somehow, the Olympic Flame has the power to do this.

The Olympic Flame gives people a chance to hope, and to believe that when we give our best we can achieve anything. There are days when something seems impossible, or that change will never come. And then the Olympic Flame comes along … and it completely lifts people's hearts. It reminds us that there really is greatness inside all of us and that, together, there's no stopping us. There couldn't be a more perfect way to start the Olympic Games.

Like all torch relays, ours will have its own life and its own story. At this moment, we don't know how our story will unfold — what will challenge us, surprise us, or take our breath away. What we do know is that it will be good. A story of dreams and spirit and a country standing shoulder to shoulder as one.

John A. Furlong

Chief Executive Officer, Vancouver Organizing Committee for the 2010 Olympic and Paralympic Winter Games (VANOC)

October 16, 2009

*Moins de une semaine avant le début du relais de la flamme, on sent monter l'enthousiasme des participants aux Jeux. Après un voyage pancanadien de 106 jours, la flamme olympique arrivera à BC Place pour souligner le début des Jeux olympiques d'hiver de 2010 à Vancouver. Les 60 000 spectateurs présents, tout comme les trois milliards de téléspectateurs de par le monde, attendront avec impatience les derniers pas de l'ultime porteur du flambeau — un moment qui sera mémorable pour tous.*

*Lorsque la flamme olympique entrera à BC Place, j'espère que tous les Canadiens et Canadiennes auront l'impression d'avoir aidé la flamme à faire son chemin vers le stade.*

*J'espère aussi que tous sentiront qu'ils ont contribué à ce moment extraordinaire et qu'ils sont partiellement responsables des événements que l'on s'apprête à dévoiler. Je souhaite que la fierté anime chaque individu, que tout le monde se dise : « Voici ce que nous avons accompli, tous ensemble ».*

*Le relais de la flamme olympique de Vancouver 2010 est à l'image d'une vision des Jeux à laquelle nous avons tenu mordicus depuis le tout début : les Jeux d'hiver de 2010 sont véritablement Des Jeux pour tout le Canada. Au COVAN, nous avons toujours souhaité que ces Jeux s'inspirent de la nation dans sa totalité; nous avons voulu intégrer tout un chacun, tous les résidants de toutes les collectivités de ce vaste et merveilleux pays. Nous avons eu le désir de voir ces Jeux rassembler tous les Canadiens et toutes les Canadiennes et allumer dans le cœur et l'esprit de chaque personne une étincelle faisant de nous tous de meilleures personnes.*

*D'une manière qui demeure inconnue, la flamme olympique a le pouvoir de réaliser un tel exploit.*

*Elle donne aux gens une raison d'espérer et de croire que lorsqu'on fait de son mieux, on peut surmonter tous les obstacles. Certains jours, les défis peuvent paraître irréalisables ou les changements peuvent tarder à se manifester. Puis, arrive la flamme olympique et on sent son cœur devenir plus léger. Elle nous rappelle qu'en chacun de nous se trouve un être extraordinaire et qu'ensemble, rien ne peut nous arrêter. Une telle introduction aux Jeux olympiques n'a pas d'égal.*

*Comme tous les relais de la flamme, le nôtre aura une personnalité distincte et son histoire sera unique. À ce jour, la fin de cette histoire demeure inconnue; qu'est-ce qui nous mettra au défi, nous surprendra ou nous éblouira? Nous serons assurément heureux du dénouement d'une histoire qui parle de rêves, d'esprit olympique et d'un pays où les gens sont unis.*

*John A. Furlong*

*Directeur général, Comité d'organisation des Jeux olympiques et paralympiques d'hiver de 2010 à Vancouver (COVAN)*

*Le 16 octobre 2009*

I

# SPARKS BECOME FLAMES

Relay Beginnings

# *DE L'ÉTINCELLE NAÎT LA FLAMME*

*Rétrospective du relais*

*Steeped in tradition: amid ancient ruins, a high priestess in Olympia, Greece harnesses the sun's power to light the Olympic Flame.*

*Au cours d'une cérémonie ancrée dans la tradition grecque et au sein des magnifiques ruines d'Olympie, en Grèce, la grande prêtresse capte l'énergie du soleil pour allumer la flamme olympique.*

# A Sacred Fire, A Call for Peace
## *Un feu sacré, un appel à la paix*

### THE ORIGINS OF THE OLYMPIC TORCH RELAY

With the passing of a flame, the world comes together. This is what the Olympic Torch Relay represents, a tradition rooted in history dating back to the ancient Games of Olympia, Greece. As in most cultures, fire was a sacred element to the Greek people, who maintained perpetual fires in front of their principal temples. In the sanctuary of Olympia, a permanent flame burned on the altar of the goddess Hestia. This fire was lit using the sun's rays to guarantee its purity.

In those times, prior to the staging of the Games, messengers wearing olive crowns left for other cities to announce the competition dates and invite citizens to the event. This marked the start of the sacred truce (known as *ekecheiria*) — a period of peace when athletes and spectators could travel safely to and from the Games.

In modern times, the Olympic Flame was reintroduced for the Amsterdam 1928 Olympic Games. Carl Diem, an Olympic historian and philosopher, introduced the first torch relay for the Berlin 1936 Olympic Games. The first Olympic Torch Relay celebrating a winter games occurred in 1952 in Oslo, Norway. Since then, the relay has become a powerful, unifying event that ignites the spirit of the Host Country, and the world, in the lead-up to the Games.

### *LES ORIGINES DU RELAIS DE LA FLAMME OLYMPIQUE*

*Grâce au transfert de la flamme, le monde se rassemble. C'est ce que représente le relais de la flamme olympique, une tradition ancrée dans l'histoire qui remonte aux Jeux anciens d'Olympie, en Grèce. Comme dans la majorité des cultures, le feu était un élément sacré pour le peuple grec. En effet, les Grecs alimentaient des feux perpétuels devant leurs principaux temples. Au sanctuaire d'Olympie, une flamme brûlait en permanence sur l'autel de la déesse Hestia. Afin d'assurer sa pureté, ce feu prenait naissance des rayons du soleil.*

*À cette époque, avant l'organisation des Jeux, des messagers qui portaient des couronnes d'oliviers se rendaient dans les villes voisines pour annoncer les dates des compétitions et inviter les citoyens à l'événement. Ces messagers ont marqué le début de la trêve sacrée (appelée ekecheiria), soit une période de paix pendant laquelle les athlètes et les spectateurs pouvaient voyager de façon sécuritaire vers et depuis les Jeux.*

*À l'époque moderne, on a fait revivre la flamme olympique pour les Jeux olympiques de 1928 à Amsterdam. Carl Diem, historien olympique et philosophe, a présenté le premier relais de la flamme à l'occasion des Jeux olympiques de 1936 à Berlin. Le premier relais de la flamme célébrant des Jeux olympiques d'hiver a eu lieu en 1952, à Oslo, en Norvège. Depuis ce temps, le relais est devenu un événement puissant et unificateur qui enflamme l'esprit du pays hôte, et du monde, jusqu'au début des Jeux.*

How can we bring people together? What stories can we tell? What can we share?

— Jim Richards, Vancouver 2010
  Torch Relay Director

*Comment rassembler les gens? Quelles sont les histoires à raconter et les choses à communiquer?*

*— Jim Richards, directeur, relais de la flamme de Vancouver 2010*

# Lighting the Land
## *Illuminer la terre*

PLANNING THE VANCOUVER 2010 OLYMPIC TORCH RELAY

*PLANIFIER LE RELAIS DE LA FLAMME OLYMPIQUE DE VANCOUVER 2010*

The team that organized the Vancouver 2010 Torch Relay knew the Olympic Flame had enormous power to inspire. According to Jim Richards, torch relay director, "It's a privilege to be involved with the relay . . . because of its potential impact. But with that, there's a huge responsibility. We like to keep things lighthearted and fun on the surface, but deep down inside, all of us understand the complexity of the task and the expectations that the nation, and the Olympic community, have for us."

Knowing this, the torch relay team set out to connect people in a way that left a lasting impression. The team wanted the relay to reach as many Canadians as possible while celebrating all that was unique and wonderful about Canada. Our heritage and history. Our magnificent land. Our small towns and big cities. Our cultural diversity. Our everyday heroes. And most of all, our spirit.

And this had to be achieved within approximately 100 days (according to International Olympic Committee guidelines), in the second-largest country in the world, during a Canadian winter.

For this, the team needed much help. Sponsors, government partners, communities and volunteers enthusiastically joined the family. In the end, it would be the longest domestic Olympic Torch Relay in history, at 106 days long, covering 45,000 kilometres and involving 12,000 torchbearers.

*L'équipe responsable de l'organisation du relais de la flamme de Vancouver 2010 savait que la flamme olympique avait un immense pouvoir, celui d'inspirer les gens. Selon Jim Richards, directeur, relais de la flamme, « c'est un privilège de prendre part à l'organisation du relais en raison des répercussions possibles d'un tel événement. D'importantes responsabilités accompagnent toutefois cette tâche. Nous aimons que les choses paraissent simples et amusantes même si, en réalité, chacun de nous sait que la tâche est complexe et qu'il faut satisfaire aux attentes de la nation et la communauté olympique. »*

*En ne perdant pas cela de vue, l'équipe du relais de la flamme s'est donnée comme mission de rassembler les gens de façon à créer des souvenirs durables. Elle voulait qu'autant de Canadiens que possible profitent du relais de la flamme tout en célébrant les caractéristiques uniques et extraordinaires du pays, notamment notre patrimoine et notre histoire, les paysages époustouflants, les petites et grandes villes, la diversité culturelle, les héros du quotidien et surtout, l'esprit de la nation.*

*Selon les directives du Comité international olympique, nous avions environ 100 jours pour atteindre tous ces objectifs... dans le deuxième plus grand pays du monde et en plein cœur de l'hiver canadien.*

*À cet effet, l'équipe avait besoin de beaucoup d'aide. Des commanditaires, des partenaires gouvernementaux et des bénévoles ont été ravis de se joindre à la famille. En somme, il s'agirait du plus long relais de l'histoire des Jeux olympiques à se dérouler au sein d'un même pays; la flamme aura parcouru 45 000 kilomètres, le relais aura duré 106 jours et 12 000 porteurs de flambeau y auront participé.*

Aboriginal youth, athletes and elders play a special role in these Games, including paddling across Victoria's Inner Harbour with the Olympic Flame on its first day in Canada. Once there, the First Nations chiefs follow the traditional custom of asking local First Nations for permission to come ashore.

*Les jeunes, les athlètes et les aînés autochtones ont participé à ces Jeux de façon toute spéciale, y compris comme accompagnateurs de la flamme olympique, lorsqu'elle est arrivée au port de Victoria. Après avoir amarré, les chefs des Premières nations ont demandé la permission aux Premières nations locales de monter sur la rive, selon la coutume traditionnelle.*

# Route Selection
## *Choix du parcours*

In 2003, when Vancouver won the right to host the 2010 Winter Games, communities began making impassioned pleas to be part of the torch relay. It was an early sign that Canada would be at its best when it hosted the Games. For the team tasked with developing the route, this nationwide excitement was both energizing and daunting as the team considered how to bring the relay to as many Canadians as possible.

In the end, the route was planned so it would come within a one-hour drive of 90 per cent of all Canadians. It would be an epic journey — one that would ultimately see the flame travel by more than 100 modes of transportation and begin, very close to its end point, on the West Coast of British Columbia.

"We debated all kinds of options for the starting point. Everyone had a strong opinion and a good case for one place or another. But then we ended up stepping back for a moment and thinking about what the relay was all about, at its core," recounted Jim Richards. "We went back to the relay's roots in the ancient Games, and the heralds that left the province of Elis, where Olympia is located. These heralds travelled to surrounding states to announce the Olympic festival and to invite their citizens to come and take part."

From this perspective, the choice was clear. Starting in Victoria, the torchbearers would circle the nation like the ancient heralds, inviting all Canadians to share in the Games.

*En 2003, lorsqu'on a nommé Vancouver ville hôte des Jeux d'hiver de 2010, des communautés ont soumis des demandes passionnées afin d'être sélectionnées comme communautés du parcours pour le relais de la flamme. C'était un signe avant-coureur qui indiquait que le Canada serait à son meilleur pendant les Jeux. Pour l'équipe chargée de l'élaboration du parcours, l'enthousiasme qui devait se répandre à l'échelle du pays était tout aussi stimulant que déconcertant puisqu'il fallait veiller à ce que le plus grand nombre de Canadiens possible puissent profiter de ce relais.*

*Finalement, on a planifié le parcours pour que 90 p. cent des Canadiens se trouvent à moins de une heure de conduite d'un point de passage du relais. L'aventure se révélerait mémorable et la flamme allait être transportée à l'aide de plus de 100 moyens de transport différents avant de revenir tout près de son point de départ, sur la côte Ouest britanno-colombienne.*

*« En ce qui concerne le point de départ, nous avons envisagé toutes sortes de possibilités. Tout le monde était bien déterminé à faire valoir son opinion, avec de bonnes raisons à l'appui. Nous avons ensuite décidé de prendre un répit et de nous pencher sur ce qui représentait l'essence même du relais », a expliqué M. Richards. « Nous avons retracé la route jusqu'aux Jeux anciens, en des temps où les hérauts quittaient la province d'Elis, là où se trouve Olympie. Ces hérauts se rendaient dans les états environnants afin d'annoncer le festival olympique et de lancer l'invitation à leurs citoyens. »*

*Dans ce contexte, la voie à suivre était claire. À partir de Victoria, les porteurs de flambeau feraient le tour du pays, tout comme les hérauts d'autrefois, afin d'inviter tous les Canadiens à participer aux Jeux.*

*All my life I've been third place. Today I was first.*

— Torchbearer Paul Toth, Atlanta 1996 Olympic Torch Relay

*J'ai occupé la troisième place toute ma vie. Aujourd'hui, j'étais en première position.*

— Paul Toth, porteur du flambeau pour le relais de la flamme olympique d'Atlanta 1996

# Torchbearer Selection
## *Sélection des porteurs de flambeau*

The unprecedented participation and spirit of the Calgary 1988 Olympic Torch Relay inspired the torchbearer selection process for Vancouver 2010. In 1988, the torch relay was open to anyone who wanted to take part. Children and seniors alike submitted entries, sometimes dozens or even hundreds at a time — sparking "torch-relay frenzy" long before the flame arrived in Canada.

Organizers of the Vancouver 2010 torch relay loved the inclusiveness of this approach. They wanted a relay that was open to anyone who dreamed of participating. They wanted everyone to feel worthy of carrying the flame.

Canadians who committed to live more active, environmentally friendly lives or who were inspired to create a better Canada could win the once-in-a-lifetime opportunity to carry the Olympic Flame through 2010 Olympic Torchbearer programs run by Games sponsors, and torch relay presenting partners, Coca-Cola and RBC.

Within nine months, hundreds of thousands of people from every corner of the country had applied to be part of the relay. When selected, their reactions were often as emotional as those of the athletes who would be chosen to represent their country on the field of competition at Games time.

*La participation et l'enthousiasme sans précédent qu'a suscités le relais de la flamme olympique de Calgary 1988 ont inspiré la création du processus de sélection des porteurs de flambeau de Vancouver 2010. En 1988, tous ceux qui le désiraient ont pu postuler pour prendre part au relais de la flamme. Petits et grands ont soumis leur candidature, voire des douzaines ou des centaines de formulaires à la fois. C'est ainsi qu'on a vu naître la « folie du relais » bien avant l'arrivée de la flamme en sol canadien.*

*Les organisateurs du relais de la flamme olympique de Vancouver 2010 ont aimé l'inclusivité de ce processus de sélection. Ils avaient envie de mettre sur pied un relais auquel pouvaient participer les gens qui rêvaient de le faire; ils voulaient que tout un chacun se sente apte et à la hauteur de porter la flamme olympique.*

*Grâce aux programmes de sélection des porteurs de flambeau qu'ont mis sur pied des commanditaires des Jeux ainsi que les partenaires principaux du relais, Coca-Cola et RBC, les Canadiens qui se sont engagés à adopter un mode de vie plus actif ainsi que des habitudes plus écologiques ou encore qui ont été inspirés à contribuer à un Canada meilleur ont couru la chance unique de porter la flamme olympique.*

*En neuf mois, des centaines de milliers de personnes de différents endroits au pays avaient posé leur candidature afin de participer au relais. La réaction des candidats choisis était souvent aussi émouvante que celle des athlètes qu'on allait choisir pour représenter leur pays pendant les Jeux.*

# The Torch
## *Le flambeau*

In many ways, the creation of the Vancouver 2010 torch reflected the vision of the relay — a project that would bring people from across the country together for a once-in-a-lifetime collaboration to shine a light on Canada's land and spirit.

Over the course of a year, the torch was developed by a team from VANOC and Bombardier, a Games sponsor and Canadian transportation and aerospace success story. All told, Bombardier produced 12,000 Olympic torches in addition to six community celebration cauldrons and eight safety lanterns (used to keep backup Olympic Flames).

"The team faced many complexities when designing the torch. The torch had to work in every winter weather condition — from the mild West Coast climate, to potentially extreme cold, snow and wind in other parts of the country. It had to be easy to carry for people of all ages and sizes, and the flame had to be easy to transfer from one torch to the next," said Bruno Comtois, a Bombardier engineer. The torch also had to maintain a visible flame for 12 to 15 minutes in all light and weather conditions.

The torch had to be beautiful, timeless and uniquely Canadian. The final design takes its inspiration from the fluid lines and curves of winter sport, and the beauty of icicles and snowdrifts. The torch's large size represents the vastness of Canada and the limitless potential of its people. When lit, the torch is designed to carry a large, dramatic Olympic Flame — that unfurls like a banner in the wind.

"The Vancouver 2010 Olympic Torch design is like Canada — young, exciting, innovative, and welcoming to everyone who sees and holds it," said Jacques Rogge, President of the International Olympic Committee.

*De nombreuses façons, la conception du flambeau de Vancouver 2010 traduisait la vision du relais, soit un projet qui unissait les gens des quatre coins du pays dans une collaboration unique afin de faire briller la terre et l'esprit du Canada.*

*Durant toute une année, une équipe du COVAN et de Bombardier, commanditaire des Jeux et entreprise canadienne reconnue pour ses innovations en transport et dans le domaine aérospatial, a conçu le flambeau. En tout, Bombardier a produit 12 000 flambeaux olympiques, en plus des six vasques communautaires et des huit lanternes de sécurité (utilisées pour conserver la flamme olympique de secours).*

*« L'équipe a dû relever plusieurs défis lors de la conception du flambeau puisqu'il était appelé à fonctionner dans des conditions climatiques hivernales très variées, allant de la douceur de la côte Ouest au froid extrême, à la neige et au vent dans d'autres parties du pays. Facilement portable par des gens de tous âges et de toutes tailles, la flamme devait également être facilement transférée d'un flambeau à l'autre »,
a mentionné Bruno Comtois, ingénieur pour Bombardier. Le flambeau devait également alimenter une flamme visible pendant une période de 12 à 15 minutes, peu importe la luminosité ou les conditions météorologiques.*

*Le flambeau devait être magnifique, intemporel et purement canadien. Le concept final du flambeau s'inspire des lignes fluides et des courbes qu'on laisse après avoir pratiqué un sport d'hiver, et de la beauté des glaçons et des amoncellements de neige. La taille imposante du flambeau traduit la grandeur du Canada et le potentiel sans bornes de son peuple. Lorsqu'il brûle, le flambeau porte une flamme olympique haute et saisissante qui s'élance telle une banderole dans le vent.*

*« Le concept du flambeau olympique de Vancouver 2010 est comme le Canada : il est jeune, captivant, innovateur et accueillant pour tout le monde qui le regardera et le portera », a dit Jacques Rogge, président du Comité international olympique.*

When they hold it in their hands,
I want them to be proud.
— *Leo Obstbaum, Vancouver 2010 Design Director*

*Lorsqu'ils le tiendront dans leurs mains,
je veux qu'ils soient fiers.*
— *Leo Obstbaum, directeur de la conception de Vancouver 2010*

VANCOUVER 2010 OLYMPIC TORCH

**Height:** 94.5 centimetres
**Weight:** 1.6 kilograms
**Operational temperature:** -50° C to +40° C
**Materials:** white composite finish, stainless steel burner, aluminum core

*FLAMBEAU OLYMPIQUE DE VANCOUVER 2010*

***Hauteur :*** *94,5 centimètres*
***Poids :*** *1,6 kilogramme*
***Température d'emploi :*** *de -50 ℃ à +40 ℃*
***Matières :*** *fini composite blanc, brûleur en acier inoxydable, cœur en aluminium*

Small design touches on the 2010 Olympic Torch make it truly Canadian. A maple leaf on the back is not only symbolic, but plays an important functional role — an air intake hole to ensure the Olympic Flame always burns brightly. The Vancouver 2010 motto *With Glowing Hearts/Des plus brillants exploits*, is engraved on the torch, opposite where the flame burns.

*De fines touches ajoutées au concept du flambeau olympique de Vancouver 2010 en font un élément purement canadien. Une feuille d'érable à l'arrière du flambeau constitue non seulement un élément symbolique, mais elle joue un rôle fonctionnel important : elle sert d'entrée d'air afin que la flamme olympique brûle de façon flamboyante en tout temps. Le slogan des Jeux d'hiver de 2010 « With Glowing Hearts / Des plus brillants exploits », est gravé sur le flambeau, du côté opposé à l'endroit où brûle la flamme.*

# The Lighting Ceremony
## *La cérémonie d'allumage*

Olympia, Greece — Sanctuary of Zeus. Site of the Ancient Olympic Games. Home of the Olympic Flame.

Amid the serenity and beauty of the ruins of the temple of Hera (goddess of love and marriage), the lighting ceremony that began the Vancouver 2010 Olympic Torch Relay was steeped in Greek tradition. After a prayer to Apollo (god of the sun), an actor playing the role of a high priestess lit the Olympic Flame, holding a torch in a parabolic mirror and harnessing the power of the sun's rays according to an ancient tradition. The flame was then placed in an urn and carried into the ancient stadium, where the high priestess lit the torch of the first runner of the 2010 Olympic Torch Relay. The final presentation of an olive branch and the release of a dove sent a message of peace — the ultimate goal of the torch relay and the Olympic Games.

*Olympie, Grèce — Sanctuaire de Zeus. Site des Jeux olympiques de l'Antiquité. Domicile de la flamme olympique.*

*En toute tranquillité, au sein des magnifiques ruines du temple d'Héra (déesse de l'amour et du mariage), on a marqué le début du relais de la flamme olympique de Vancouver 2010 au cours d'une cérémonie d'allumage, ancrée dans la tradition grecque. Après avoir récité une prière à Apollo (dieu du soleil), une actrice incarnant le rôle de la grande prêtresse a allumé la flamme olympique en captant l'énergie du soleil à l'aide d'un miroir parabolique, selon la tradition ancienne. On a ensuite placé la flamme dans une urne et on l'a portée au stade ancien où la grande prêtresse a allumé le flambeau du premier porteur du flambeau du relais de la flamme olympique de Vancouver 2010. La cérémonie s'est terminée par la présentation d'une branche d'olivier et l'envol d'une colombe — le véritable message de paix que visent à exprimer le relais de la flamme et les Jeux olympiques.*

Greek skier Vassilis Dimitriadis ran out of Olympia's ancient stadium to begin the eight-day Greek leg of the Vancouver 2010 Olympic Torch Relay.

*Vassilis Dimitriadis, skieur grec, sort du stade d'Olympie en courant pour marquer le début du segment grec du relais de la flamme olympique de Vancouver 2010, qui a duré huit jours.*

# The Handover Ceremony
## *La cérémonie de transfert*

On the evening of October 29, 2009, with the eight-day Greek portion of the Vancouver 2010 torch relay concluded, in a moving handover ceremony at the Panathinaiko Stadium in Athens, Greek officials entrusted the Olympic Flame to Canada. VANOC Chief Executive Officer John Furlong enthusiastically accepted the flame, stating, "On behalf of all Canadians, we accept the Olympic Flame with humility and respect . . . we take with us the knowledge that the flame represents much more than a sporting event. It embodies the values of peace, friendship and respect, and has the power to unite, inspire and bring harmony to the world."

*Le 29 octobre 2009, en soirée, le segment grec du relais de la flamme olympique de Vancouver 2010 s'est terminé au stade Panathinaiko d'Athènes, en Grèce. Au cours d'une cérémonie de transfert émouvante, des représentants officiels grecs ont confié la flamme olympique au Canada. M. John Furlong, directeur général du Comité d'organisation des Jeux olympiques et paralympiques d'hiver de 2010 à Vancouver (COVAN), a accepté la flamme avec enthousiasme. « Au nom de tous les Canadiens, j'accepte la flamme olympique en toute humilité et avec le plus grand respect. Nous comprenons que la flamme représente beaucoup plus qu'un événement sportif. Elle est un symbole de paix, d'amitié et de respect qui a le pouvoir d'unir, d'inspirer les gens et de faire valoir l'harmonie dans le monde entier », a-t-il affirmé.*

Eight safety lanterns transported the Olympic Flame from Greece to Canada on the aptly named Canadian Forces Flight 2010, with the flight and an enthusiastic team arriving in Victoria on the morning of October 30, ready to kick off the flame's pan-Canadian journey.

*En tout, on a transporté huit lanternes de sécurité contenant la flamme olympique, de la Grèce au Canada, à bord d'un avion des Forces canadiennes que l'on a nommé le vol 2010 des Forces canadiennes. L'avion et l'équipe enthousiaste sont arrivés à Victoria le 30 octobre, en matinée, prêts à commencer le voyage pancanadien de la flamme olympique.*

II

30 MILLION
FLAMES
The Canadian Journey

*30 MILLIONS
DE FLAMMES*
*Le voyage canadien*

(Above) Olympians Simon Whitfield and Catriona Le May Doan, the relay's first two torchbearers in Canada, perform the first transfer between torchbearers as they touch torches with fellow Olympians Silken Laumann and Alexandre Despatie.

*(Ci-dessus) Les olympiens Simon Whitfield et Catriona Le May Doan, les deux premiers porteurs de flambeau au Canada, effectuent le premier transfert de la flamme en touchant le flambeau de deux autres olympiens, Silken Laumann et Alexandre Despatie.*

# The journey begins
## Le voyage commence

106 DAYS, 12,000 TORCHBEARERS, 1 FLAME.

On a mild, West Coast autumn day, thousands of spectators gathered on the lawn of the British Columbia Legislature in Victoria to welcome the flame that would ignite the Vancouver 2010 Olympic Torch Relay. Excitement and pride filled the air, with onlookers draped in Canadian flags standing alongside schoolchildren wearing bright toques and the signature Vancouver 2010 red mittens.

As spontaneous rounds of *O Canada* rang out, a procession of chiefs from the Four Host First Nations (Lil'wat, Musqueam, Squamish, Tsleil-Waututh), Songhees and Esquimalt slowly emerged, carrying the Olympic Flame in its safety lantern after entering the harbour in a flotilla of hand-carved, red cedar canoes.

Cheers and applause broke out like a wave, and continued as Darlene Poole, wife of VANOC's longtime champion and recently deceased chairman Jack Poole, transferred the flame to Victoria's Olympic Cauldron for the first of 189 community celebrations.

First to carry the torch were Canadian gold medallists Catriona Le May Doan and Simon Whitfield, who passed the flame to Olympic medallists Silken Laumann and Alexandre Despatie. They were followed by 143 others on foot and by airplane, by wheelchair and on bicycle, travelling north from the provincial capital to the peninsula's smaller coastal towns. As one torch dimmed, another burst into sight. And so it would go until the Olympic torch completed its 45,000-kilometre odyssey, shining a light on a vast northern nation ready to welcome the world.

In the moments before my run began, people were drawn to the torch . . . One elderly woman walked slowly towards me from across the street. With her eyes fixed upon the torch, she asked just to touch it. "By all means," I said and, after a moment, her eyes clouding with tears, she thanked me and walked away.

— Lloyd Robertson, CTV anchorman, Day 1, Parksville, BC

106 JOURS, 12 000 PORTEURS DE FLAMBEAU, 1 FLAMME

*Par une belle journée d'automne au temps doux de la côte Ouest, des milliers de spectateurs se sont rassemblés devant les édifices de l'assemblée législative de la Colombie-Britannique, à Victoria, pour accueillir la flamme et signaler le début du relais de la flamme olympique de Vancouver 2010. Dans l'ambiance de fête et de fierté, la foule brandissant des drapeaux canadiens, et des enfants, portant des tuques colorées et les fameuses mitaines rouges de Vancouver 2010, ont attendu la flamme.*

*Tandis que les spectateurs chantaient des bouts de l'hymne national, on a aperçu les chefs des quatre Premières nations hôtes (Lil'wat, Musqueam, Squamish et Tsleil-Waututh) et des Premières nations Songhees et Esquimalt, arriver au port à bord de canots de cèdre rouge taillés à la main, en portant la flamme olympique dans une lanterne de sécurité.*

*La foule s'est animée d'applaudissements et d'encouragements lorsque Mme Darlene Poole, épouse de feu M. Jack Poole, président du conseil d'administration et champion de longue date du COVAN, a allumé la vasque communautaire de Victoria pour marquer le début de la première des 189 célébrations communautaires.*

*Catriona Le May Doan et Simon Whitfield, Canadiens médaillés d'or, ont été les premiers à porter la flamme avant de la transférer au flambeau de Silken Laumann et d'Alexandre Despatie, médaillés olympiques. À pied, en avion, en fauteuil roulant et à bicyclette, 143 autres personnes ont porté la flamme olympique depuis la capitale provinciale aux petites communautés de la péninsule, sur la côte Nord. D'un flambeau à l'autre, on pouvait voir briller la lueur de la flamme. C'est ainsi que se déroulerait le relais de la flamme olympique au cours de son voyage de 45 000 kilomètres, une traînée d'aurores boréales pour illuminer ce vaste pays nordique prêt à accueillir le monde entier.*

*Avant de commencer mon segment du parcours, les gens étaient attirés par le flambeau... Une femme plus âgée a traversé la rue et s'est lentement approchée de moi. Ses yeux rivés sur le flambeau, elle m'a demandé si elle pouvait le toucher. « Je vous en prie », lui ai-je répondu. Après un moment, elle avait les larmes aux yeux. Elle m'a ensuite remercié et elle est partie.*

— Lloyd Robertson, chef d'antenne, CTV, jour 1, Parksville, C.-B.

### Day 1, British Columbia

From heroes to hopefuls: members of Canada's gold-medal-winning men's eight rowing team (Beijing 2008) stop mid-lake to pass the torch to the next generation of junior rowers and Olympic contenders.

### Jour 1, Colombie-Britannique

*Place à la relève : Les membres de l'équipe canadienne d'aviron de huit masculin, médaillée d'or olympique (Beijing 2008), s'arrêtent au milieu du lac pour passer la flamme à la prochaine génération de jeunes athlètes d'aviron et concurrents olympiques.*

It's definitely something I am never going to forget. It's absolutely incredible to meet my heroes, my role models, and [to be] able to row alongside them.

— *Junior coxswain Aimee Hawker, after members of Canada's gold-medal-winning men's eight rowing team (Beijing 2008) passed the torch to her junior rowing crew.*

*Il s'agit d'un souvenir que je n'oublierai jamais. Il est incroyable de rencontrer mes héros, mes modèles et d'avoir l'occasion de faire de l'aviron à leurs côtés.*

— *Aimee Hawker, barreuse junior, après que les membres de l'équipe canadienne d'aviron, médaillée d'or olympique (Beijing 2008), ont passé la flamme à son équipe junior d'aviron.*

**Day 1-2, British Columbia**

Fans and torchbearers soak in the Olympic spirit in small towns across Vancouver Island.

*Jour 1 et 2, Colombie-Britannique*

*Les partisans et les porteurs de flambeau s'imprègnent de l'esprit olympique dans les petites villes de l'île de Vancouver.*

**Day 2, British Columbia**

Along with the dignitaries and Olympic athletes, princesses, giraffes and Superman were among the colourful spectators on Halloween, the relay's second day.

*Jour 2, Colombie-Britannique*

*Le deuxième jour du relais, en plus des dignitaires et des athlètes olympiques, on trouvait des princesses, des girafes et Superman parmi les spectateurs colorés, à l'occasion de l'Halloween.*

It was an amazing feeling. It really set in, what I was doing, while I was running, even my little segment . . . was a big part of getting the flame back to Vancouver in February.

— 14-year-old torchbearer Adam Long,
   Day 2, Nanaimo, BC

*C'était un sentiment incroyable. J'ai vraiment pris connaissance de ce que j'étais en train de faire lorsque j'ai couru... même mon court segment a été une partie importante du voyage de la flamme, avant qu'elle ne revienne à Vancouver en février.*

— Adam Long, porteur du flambeau, 14 ans,
   Jour 2, Nanaimo, C.-B.

**Day 3, British Columbia**

Surf's up: Ruth Sadler, 72, wades into the chilly waters of Tofino, BC for a first-of-its-kind Olympic moment. After two attempts, Raphael Bruhwiler lit his torch and caught a wave to become the first surfing torchbearer in Olympic Torch Relay history.

*Jour 3, Colombie-Britannique*

*Place au surf : Mme Ruth Sadler, 72 ans, marche dans les eaux glacées de Tofino, en Colombie-Britannique, une première olympique. Après deux essais, M. Raphael Bruhwiler a allumé son flambeau et a trouvé une vague pour devenir le premier porteur du flambeau de l'histoire du relais de la flamme olympique à faire du surf avec la flamme.*

## Day 5, British Columbia

The torch travels by *Lootas* (meaning "Wave Eater" in Haida), a 15-metre war canoe carved from a single cedar log by renowned artist Bill Reid and other Haida carvers. The ceremonial boat is only put into the water for significant celebrations, and the upright paddles indicate the travellers come in peace.

## *Jour 5, Colombie-Britannique*

*Le flambeau se déplace en canot de guerre de 15 mètres que l'on appelle « Lootas » (qui signifie mangeur de vagues en haida). Il a été sculpté dans un seul billot de cèdre par l'artiste haïda renommé Bill Reid en collaboration avec plusieurs sculpteurs haïdas. On ne met le bateau cérémoniel à l'eau qu'à l'occasion de célébrations importantes; les pagaies qui pointent vers le haut signifient que les voyageurs arrivent en paix.*

Torchbearer Percy Williams at an Aboriginal flame blessing ceremony in Skidegate, BC, a place often considered the heart of Haida culture.

*Percy Williams, porteur du flambeau, assiste à une cérémonie de bénédiction de la flamme à Skidegate, en Colombie-Britannique, un endroit que l'on considère souvent le cœur de la culture haïda.*

## A FEAST OF COLOUR IN HAIDA GWAII

On Day Five, unbroken beams of amber sunlight streamed past the mist-covered mountains of the Queen Charlotte Islands, a stunning, diverse archipelago of 150 islets inhabited by 5,000 people. The people of Haida Gwaii — literally, Islands of the People — stood along its pebbly shores and atop driftwood logs, many draped in striking red and black button blankets decorated with the ravens, orcas and eagles that feature so prominently in Haida artwork.

Together, the group waited for another piece of Haida art, and a key part of Haida history, to appear on the clear waters. And it did, as elder Percy Williams rounded the corner in a treasured 15-metre war canoe created by Bill Reid, legendary Haida carver. The team of First Nations paddlers took graceful, measured strokes as Williams held his torch aloft, its flame contrasting starkly with the clear blue sky behind him. A canoe welcoming song was the first of many to mark the boat's arrival, as Williams and the flame were ushered ashore. "I thought torchbearing was something in a distant, foreign land," he said solemnly. "I didn't think I would ever get involved."

But that's the magic of canoe voyages, especially for the Haida people, who view extended canoe travel as a pathway to discovery and a powerful way to foster connections between people and cultures that might otherwise remain a mystery.

## UN FESTIN DE COULEURS À HAÏDA GWAII.

*Le jour 5, des rayons dorés couvraient les montagnes brumeuses des îles de la Reine-Charlotte, un archipel époustouflant et diversifié composé de 150 îlots où habitent 5 000 personnes. Les résidants de Haïda Gwaii, qui signifie « îles du peuple », se tenaient debout sur des billots de bois flotté près des rives de galets. Bon nombre étaient vêtus de superbes couvertures à boutons rouge et noire ornées du grand corbeau, de l'épaulard et de l'aigle; des motifs que l'on trouve souvent dans les œuvres d'art haïda.*

*Le groupe a attendu qu'une autre œuvre d'art haïda, un élément important de l'histoire des Haïdas, fasse son entrée sur les eaux claires. Peu de temps s'est écoulé avant que Percy Williams n'apparaisse au loin, à bord du canot de 15 mètres qu'a créé Bill Reid, sculpteur haïda légendaire. Les rameurs des Premières nations, gracieux et attentionnés, ont dirigé le canot vers la rive tandis que M. Williams tenait son flambeau bien droit et que la flamme dansait contre le ciel bleu. Pendant qu'on accompagnait M. Williams et la flamme, le premier d'une série de chant d'accueil s'est fait entendre. « J'ai toujours pensé que porter le flambeau était quelque chose que l'on fait dans des pays lointains », a-t-il affirmé. « Je n'aurais pu imaginer avoir l'occasion de le faire un jour. »*

*Voilà la magie du canotage, particulièrement chez les Haïdas pour qui les longs voyages en canot représentent un cheminement vers la découverte et un moyen puissant de nouer des liens entre peuples et cultures, des liens que l'on ne pourrait découvrir autrement.*

NORFOLK COUNTY PUBLIC LIBRARY

## Day 6, Yukon

Day Six and -36: The town of Old Crow's breath-stealing -36-degree temperature tests the propane-fuelled torch but not the spirit of the torchbearers who run atop gleaming, ice-covered roads and celebrate with caribou kebabs, chinook salmon, jig lessons and traditional throat singing.

## Jour 6, Yukon

*Jour 6, température -36 : Dans la communauté d'Old Crow, il fait -36 °C et on met à l'épreuve le mécanisme à propane du flambeau. Par contre, l'esprit des porteurs de flambeau continue d'illuminer les rues glacées tandis qu'ils célèbrent avec des brochettes de caribou, du saumon du Pacifique, des leçons de gigue et des spectacles de chant guttural.*

As each day goes by since the celebrations in Old Crow, I am embracing what truly took place, how very special that day was for our community and our visitors. These memories will be in our hearts forever.

— *Lorraine Netro, Old Crow, YT*

*Depuis les célébrations qui ont eu lieu à Old Crow, je continue de contempler ce qui s'est passé, l'importance de ce moment spécial pour notre communauté et nos visiteurs. Ces souvenirs demeureront à jamais gravés dans notre mémoire.*

— *Lorraine Netro, Old Crow, Yukon*

**Day 7, Nunavut**

Kugluktuk residents spanning all generations brave frosty conditions to live an Olympic moment in this remote Nunavut village, population 1,300.

*Jour 7, Nunavut*

*À Kugluktuk, petit village de 1 300 personnes au Nunavut, les résidants de toute génération sortent malgré le temps froid pour vivre le moment olympique.*

Day 11, Nunavut          *Jour 11, Nunavut*

A First Nations torchbearer is joined by marathon runner Chief Tammy Cook-Searson in traditional dress in La Ronge, SK. The Olympic Flame visited La Ronge after a hard-won campaign by Tammy.

*Après avoir travaillé très fort pour que la flamme visite sa communauté, Tammy Cook-Searson, chef et marathonienne, se joint, en costume traditionnel, à un porteur du flambeau autochtone à La Ronge, en Saskatchewan.*

I believe, or hope, it will ignite the flame that exists in each and every one of us.

— *Chief Tammy Cook-Searson, when describing why she fought so hard for the relay to visit her community.*

*Je crois, ou j'espère, qu'elle allumera le feu qui existe en chacun de nous.*

— *Chef Tammy Cook-Searson, pour décrire pourquoi elle s'est battue pour que le relais visite sa communauté.*

The Arctic's most famous icon — the polar bear — shares the spotlight in Churchill, MB, as locals, out-of-towners and the media shift their attention to the much-celebrated new visitor: the Olympic Flame. Being in the polar bear capital of the world, the torch took a tour on a Polar Rover.

*Jour 10, Manitoba*

*Le symbole le plus célèbre de l'Arctique, l'ours polaire, partage la vedette à Churchill, au Manitoba tandis que les résidants, les visiteurs et les médias accueillent leur invitée tant attendue : la flamme olympique. Puisqu'on se trouve dans la capitale mondiale de l'ours polaire, la flamme olympique fait un tour de Polar Rover.*

## Day 10, Nunavut

The Frozen Chosen: "We're almost doubling our population for 24 hours," jokes Major Sylvain Giguère, as the 56-person outpost in Alert, NU prepares to host the torch and its multitude of supporters. In Alert, the torch was carried by the "Frozen Chosen," the decade's-old nickname given to people living here, the world's most northern, permanently inhabited settlement.

## Jour 10, Nunavut

*Les choisis congelés : « Notre population a presque doublé en 24 heures », raconte le major Sylvain Giguère d'Alert au Nunavut, un avant-poste militaire où habitent 56 personnes qui ont accueilli la flamme olympique et ses nombreux partisans. Les « choisis congelés », nom que l'on donne aux résidants de la communauté depuis des décennies, ont porté la flamme à Alert, l'établissement habité en permanence le plus au nord du monde.*

## TORCHES ALONG THE TUNDRA

"On top of the world" not only describes the geographical reality of Canada's far north, but also the emotions it inspires. "I have been from coast to coast and to every province and territory, and this is my favourite place," says Meaghan Harris, now living in Alert, Nunavut.

After leaving Churchill, Manitoba, stopping briefly for an unsuspecting polar bear to cross its path, the torch flew by aircraft to Alert — a tiny Arctic outpost on the Lincoln Sea, a mere 800 kilometres from the North Pole. Alert represents the most northern place an Olympic Torch has ever travelled, an immense, remote region of Canada few ever get to experience. Those that do invariably find a study in contrasts. Either bathed in endless sunlight or plunged into 24-hour darkness, the country's Far North has an unforgiving climate but some of the warmest souls in the nation.

In Alert, Resolute and Iqaluit, spectators were bundled in fur and animal hides to protect from the extreme cold, huddling together on ice-encrusted roadways to welcome torchbearers travelling by snowshoes, dogsled and snowmobile. At a time of year when non-stop darkness normally reigns, a torch lit the way. On a frozen landscape where silence blankets in all directions, cheering and singing rang out. And for Canada's most isolated residents, an Olympic visit offered the rest of Canada and the world a rare glimpse into northern life and land.

*FLAMME DE LA TOUNDRA.*

*L'expression « au sommet du monde » décrit non seulement la réalité géographique du Nord canadien, mais aussi les émotions qu'il inspire. « J'ai voyagé d'un océan à l'autre et j'ai parcouru toutes les provinces et tous les territoires, et ici, c'est mon endroit préféré », affirme Meaghan Harris, qui vit actuellement à Alert, au Nunavut.*

*Après avoir quitté Churchill, au Manitoba, où on a dû s'arrêter pour laisser traverser un ours polaire insouciant, le relais s'est rendu en avion à Alert, un petit avant poste arctique dans la mer de Lincoln, à environ 800 kilomètres du pôle Nord. Il s'agit de l'endroit le plus au nord où a voyagé la flamme olympique et d'une vaste région isolée du Canada que peu de gens ont l'occasion de visiter. Les personnes qui ont la chance de se rendre à Alert y trouvent inévitablement une terre de contraste. Parfois sous le soleil de minuit, parfois plongé dans la noirceur, le Nord du pays présente un climat difficile où habitent certains des gens les plus chaleureux du Canada.*

*À Alert, Resolute et Iqaluit, les spectateurs, vêtus de fourrures et de peaux animales afin de se protéger du grand froid, se sont rassemblés le long des rues glacées pour accueillir les porteurs de flambeau qui se déplaçaient en raquettes, en traîneau à chiens et en motoneige. La flamme a illuminé le parcours puisque à cette période de l'année, il fait presque toujours noir. Dans ce paysage hivernal glacé et silencieux, les chants et les cris d'encouragement des gens de la communauté contrastaient. Pour les résidants des régions les plus isolées du Canada, la visite de la flamme olympique a représenté une occasion d'offrir aux autres Canadiens et au monde entier un rare aperçu de la vie dans le Nord.*

The hum of lively schoolchildren performing *O Canada* trickles through the grocery store doors in Kugluktuk, NU where Brenda Kolaohop surveys the energy from a distance. "I think it's wonderful that the torch is here," she says, smiling. "We sure aren't used to this kind of attention."

*La mélodie de l'hymne national, chanté par des enfants enthousiastes, se fait entendre derrière les portes de l'épicerie à Kugluktuk (au Nunavut), où Brenda Kolaohop contemple la scène. « Je suis ravie que la flamme soit ici », a-t-elle affirmé en souriant. « Nous ne sommes pas habitués à tant d'attention. »*

Day 11, Nunavut

Torchbearer Jason Qaapik in Ausuittuq,
Grise Fiord, NU.

*Jour 11, Nunavut*

*Le porteur du flambeau Jason Qaapik
à Ausuittuq, fjord Grise, au Nunavut.*

Day 13, Newfoundland and Labrador

*Jour 13, Terre-Neuve-et-Labrador*

(Above left) Veteran Henry Noseworthy at the Olympic Flame Welcoming Ceremony in Wabush, NL.

*(Ci-dessus) Henry Noseworthy, ancien combattant, à la cérémonie d'accueil de la flamme olympique à Wabush, T.-N.-L.*

Veterans across the country took part in the 2010 Olympic Torch Relay. (Above) One veteran pushes another who proudly holds the Olympic Flame in Sydney Mines, NS on Day 18.

*Des anciens combattants des quatre coins du pays ont participé au relais de la flamme olympique de Vancouver 2010. (Ci-dessus) Au jour 18, un ancien combattant pousse le fauteuil roulant d'un compatriote qui porte fièrement la flamme olympique, à Sydney Mines, en Nouvelle-Écosse.*

## A TORCH HELD HIGH

On Remembrance Day, November 11, the torch relay took on extra-special meaning during its travels through Newfoundland and Labrador. At an event at the Canadian Forces Base in Goose Bay, Newfoundland, Lieutenant Colonel Brian Bowerman, Wing Commander of 5 Wing remarked on the connection between honouring our war heroes and taking part in the torch relay. "We remember past veterans who have given their lives for a better future, and at the same time, the Olympic Spirit is about world peace."

A memorial in the small mining town of Wabush, Labrador brought together veteran Jim Adam and son Bruce on the steps of a recreation centre named after grandson Mike Adam, who won a gold medal in curling at the Torino 2006 Olympic Winter Games. Bruce Adam — a runner in the Calgary 1988 Torch Relay — recited a line from the famous World War I poem *In Flanders Fields* by Canadian Lieutenant Colonel John McCrae: "To you from failing hands we throw the torch; be yours to hold it high."

## UN FLAMBEAU PORTÉ BIEN HAUT

*Le 11 novembre, jour du Souvenir, le relais de la flamme a traduit un autre message très spécial durant son voyage à Terre-Neuve-et-Labrador. Au cours d'un événement organisé à la base des Forces canadiennes à Goose Bay, le lieutenant-colonel de la 5e Escadre, Brian Bowerman, a commenté sur la similitude entre le fait d'honorer les héros de la guerre et la participation au relais de la flamme. « On honore la mémoire des anciens combattants qui ont donné leur vie pour un avenir meilleur, et en même temps, l'esprit olympique lance un message de paix dans le monde. »*

*Une cérémonie commémorative dans la petite ville minière de Wabush, à Terre-Neuve-et-Labrador, a rassemblé Jim Adam, ancien combattant, et son fils Bruce sur les marches du Centre récréatif nommé en l'honneur de son petit-fils, Mike Adam, médaillé d'or à l'épreuve de curling aux Jeux olympiques d'hiver de 2006 à Turin. Bruce Adam, qui a porté le flambeau durant le relais de la flamme de Calgary en 1988, a cité un vers du célèbre poème sur la Première Guerre mondiale, Au champ d'honneur (adaptation du poème In Flanders Fields écrit par le lieutenant-colonel canadien John McCrae) : « À vous jeunes désabusés, à vous de porter l'oriflamme et de garder au fond de l'âme le goût de vivre en liberté ».*

And here we are in Wabush . . . and the torch will soon arrive. It is indeed our time to hold it high.

— *Torchbearer Bruce Adam, Calgary 1988 Olympic Torch Relay*

*Nous voici tous réunis ici, à Wabush. La flamme arrivera sous peu. C'est maintenant notre occasion de la porter bien haut.*

— *Bruce Adam, porteur du flambeau, relais de la flamme olympique de Calgary 1988*

## Day 17, Newfoundland and Labrador

Torrential rains don't dampen spirits one bit in Newfoundland. (Previous page) Children chase the relay on the streets of Kippens, and torchbearer Ashley Bishop's smile shines as brightly as the Olympic Flame as she enters the Kippens Community Celebration. (This page) In Channel-Port aux Basques, torchbearers run on the streets in ankle-deep water.

## Jour 17, Terre-Neuve-et-Labrador

*La pluie torrentielle n'attiédit aucunement les ardeurs à Terre-Neuve-et-Labrador. (Page précédente) Des enfants suivent le relais dans les rues de Kippens et le sourire de la porteuse du flambeau Ashley Bishop resplendit autant que la flamme olympique à son arrivée à la célébration communautaire de Kippens. (Cette page) À Channel-Port aux Basques, des porteurs de flambeau courent les pieds dans l'eau de pluie.*

## AN EDUCATION IN GENEROSITY

Thanks to his classmates, Chris Tremblett (above), a 15-year-old torchbearer from Newfoundland and Labrador knows a little something about the spirit of team required to pull off an Olympic dream.

As the Olympic Flame journeyed up the Avalon Peninsula toward his hometown of Gambo, the Grade 10 student from Smallwood Academy had yet to raise the $400 to buy his torch after completing his run.

But Chris was in for an unexpected surprise when the principal of his school announced that staff and students had each chipped in a loonie or a toonie to raise the necessary funds. "I found out on Friday and was very, very surprised," says Chris, adding that his torch would be on display at school afterwards — something he was more than happy to share.

On that glorious Saturday afternoon, Chris had his torch moment, inspired by cheering classmates who lined the narrow roadway, shouting words of encouragement and perhaps marvelling at how far $2 can go.

## *UNE LEÇON DE GÉNÉROSITÉ*

*Grâce à ses compagnons de classe, Chris Tremblett (ci-dessus), porteur du flambeau âgé de 15 ans et originaire de Terre-Neuve-et-Labrador, en a appris un peu plus sur l'esprit d'équipe nécessaire à la réalisation d'un rêve olympique.*

*Tandis que la flamme olympique faisait son chemin vers la presqu'île d'Avalon en direction de Gambo, sa villa natale, l'élève de 10e année de l'école Smallwood Academy n'avait pas encore réussi à amasser les 400 $ dont il avait besoin pour acheter son flambeau après sa participation au relais.*

*La surprise de Chris a été immense lorsque le directeur de son école a annoncé que le personnel et les élèves de l'école avaient tous fait don de un ou deux dollars afin de recueillir les fonds nécessaires. « On m'a transmis l'information vendredi et j'ai été très très surpris », a affirmé Chris, avant d'ajouter que son flambeau serait exposé à l'école et qu'il était bien heureux que les autres aient l'occasion de le voir.*

*Le samedi, par un après-midi enchanteur, Chris a participé au relais, inspiré par ses compagnons qui poussaient des cris d'encouragement le long de la route étroite tout en s'émerveillant probablement de ce qu'un simple don de deux dollars pouvait faire.*

## Day 18-19, Nova Scotia

Spectators of all ages gather to watch the torch relay. (Clockwise from top) Torchbearer Nick Morris joins his fans on the sidelines in Baddek, NS. Cheerleaders from Sydney Mines Junior High give a torchbearer a boost as he passes by Glace Bay. Children await the flame at the community firehall.

(Right) The Northside Vikings hockey team cheers on their beloved coach, Clint Lettice in Membertou, NS.

## Jours 18 et 19, Nouvelle-Écosse

*Des spectateurs de tous les âges se rassemblent pour assister au relais de la flamme. (De haut en bas dans le sens des aiguilles d'une montre) Le porteur du flambeau Nick Morris retrouve ses partisans en bordure de la rue, à Baddek, en Nouvelle-Écosse. Des meneuses de claques de l'école Sydney Mines Junior High encouragent un porteur du flambeau à son passage à Glace Bay en Nouvelle-Écosse. Des enfants attendent la flamme à la caserne de pompier de la communauté.*

*(À droite) Les membres de l'équipe de hockey Northside Vikings encouragent leur cher entraîneur, Clint Lettice, à Membertou, en Nouvelle-Écosse.*

### Day 20, Nova Scotia

Crosby-Mania: Bathing in the rosy glow of the city's streetlamps and nonstop pops from camera flashes, tens of thousands of vocal spectators compete for space in Halifax, NS to watch hockey phenom Sidney Crosby carry the torch. (Left, middle) Torchbearer Kirk Boudreau, who has a rare neurological disease that prevents him from seeing or speaking, lights the torch of hockey star Sidney Crosby, his sporting hero. (Above) In a 300-metre run that became more of a trot thanks to the giant turnout, Crosby meandered through the pack and extended a mitten-covered hand to light the torch of snowboarder

### Jour 20, Nouvelle-Écosse

La folie Crosby : Baignés par les lueurs rosées des lampadaires de la ville et les flashs incessants des appareils photo, des dizaines de milliers de spectateurs bruyants jouent du coude afin de trouver une place pour regarder le joueur de hockey phénomène, Sidney Crosby, porter le flambeau à Halifax, en Nouvelle-Écosse. (À gauche, au centre) Le porteur du flambeau Kirk Boudreau, atteint d'une affection neurologique rare qui l'empêche de parler et de voir, a transféré la flamme au joueur étoile de hockey, Sidney Crosby, son héros sportif. (Ci-dessus) La course de 300 mètres s'est plutôt transformée en une marche rapide en raison de l'immense foule présente. M. Crosby a réussi à se frayer un chemin dans la foule et a tendu une main gantée d'une mitaine rouge pour allumer le flambeau de la surfeuse des

Day 22, Nova Scotia

*Jour 22, Nouvelle-Écosse*

Day 24, Prince Edward Island

(Top) Two Canadian heroines: A young actress portraying Anne of Green Gables enjoys a buggy ride with three-time Olympic medallist and hockey legend Cassie Campbell-Pascall on the grounds of the fabled Cavendish, PEI house.

*Jour 24, Île-du-Prince-Édouard*

*(Haut) Deux héroïnes canadiennes : Une jeune actrice qui incarne Anne aux pignons verts profite des joies d'une balade en carriole en compagnie de la triple médaillée olympique et légende du hockey Cassie Campbell-Pascall sur les lieux de la fameuse maison « aux pignons verts », située à Cavendish, à l'Île-du-Prince-Édouard.*

(Top) Torchbearer Stephane Richard grins from ear to ear as he runs through a boisterous crowd of schoolchildren. (Below) A midday celebration of confetti, music and Acadian-style dance in Shediac, NB.

*(Haut) C'est avec un sourire fendu jusqu'aux oreilles que le porteur du flambeau Stephane Richard court à travers une foule déchaînée d'écoliers. (Dessous) Des confettis, de la musique et des danses acadiennes donnent le ton à une célébration du midi, à Shediac, au Nouveau-Brunswick.*

**Day 26, New Brunswick**

The world's highest tides recede, allowing
Brazilian gold-medal swimmer César Cielo
to run atop the Bay of Fundy's ocean floor
and through the Hopewell Rocks.

*Jour 26, Nouveau-Brunswick*

*La décrue de la plus haute marée du monde permet à
César Cielo, médaillé d'or brésilien en natation, de courir
sur le plancher océanique de la baie de Fundy et entre
les formations rocheuses de Hopewell Rocks.*

## KEEPING THE FIRES BURNING

With all the pageantry of the Olympic Torch Relay, its fascinating people, emotion-charged celebrations and non-stop natural wonders on display, it might be challenging to keep your eyes on just one thing. Not so for Dina Ouellette (above), whose gaze never drifts far from the Olympic Flame she has pledged to protect.

Recognizing the Aboriginal tradition of fire keepers, Ouellette is one of 10 young people selected to be a relay flame attendant. "It's such an honour," says Ouellette, a member of the Madawaska Maliseet First Nation in New Brunswick, "And it's a big responsibility. The Olympic Flame is so symbolic that it's important to [ensure] it's part of an unbroken chain, passed from person to person, all the way across the country. I'm one of the lucky people who make sure it always stays lit."

Ouellette and Aronhiaies Herne were the two flame attendants who helped VANOC CEO John Furlong transfer the flame directly from the Olympic Cauldron in Greece into the protective miners' lamps, which were then transported via Canadian Forces jet to Victoria, British Columbia to begin the relay. Ouellette did not leave the lanterns for a second, keeping them fuelled mid-flight, and standing guard to protect them through every step of the journey — a role that has evolved to escorting torchbearers as the flame gets transferred from torchbearer to torchbearer.

## VEILLER À LA FLAMME

*Avec l'éclat du relais de la flamme olympique, les gens fascinants que l'on rencontre le long du parcours, les célébrations chargées d'émotions et le superbe paysage, il peut parfois être difficile de garder l'œil sur une seule chose. Cela n'est pas le cas pour Dina Ouellette (ci-dessus), qui a toujours les yeux rivés sur la flamme olympique qu'elle s'est engagée à protéger.*

*Pour rendre hommage à la tradition autochtone des gardiens de la flamme, on a choisi 10 jeunes, dont Mme Ouellette, comme jeunes responsables de la flamme pendant le relais. « Il s'agit d'un grand honneur pour moi », a affirmé Mme Ouellette, membre de la Première nation de Madawaska Maliseet au Nouveau-Brunswick. « Il s'agit aussi d'une grande responsabilité. La flamme olympique est un symbole si important et il faut s'assurer qu'on ne brise pas la chaîne, qu'on passe la flamme, d'une personne à l'autre, en traversant le pays. Je fais partie des gens chanceux qui s'assurent que la flamme demeure toujours allumée. »*

*Dina Ouellette et Aronhiaies Herne ont été les deux responsables de la flamme qui ont aidé John Furlong, directeur général du COVAN, à prendre la flamme directement de la vasque olympique en Grèce et à la placer dans les lanternes de protection. On les a ensuite transportées dans un avion à réaction des Forces canadiennes vers Victoria, en Colombie-Britannique, pour commencer le relais. Mme Ouellette n'a jamais quitté la flamme et n'a cessé de la protéger en veillant à ce qu'elle brûle pendant le vol et en restant à ses côtés au cours de son voyage. Son rôle a plus tard évolué et elle a eu l'occasion d'accompagner les porteurs de flambeau lorsque la flamme se passait d'une personne à l'autre.*

## Day 29, New Brunswick

Community celebrations bring out all aspects of Canadian culture — from makeshift hockey stick flagpoles to a troupe of young Highland dancers, ready to take the stage in front of a sea of spectators.

## *Jour 29, Nouveau-Brunswick*

*Les célébrations communautaires mettent en valeur tous les aspects de la culture canadienne, y compris des porte-drapeaux improvisés à l'aide de bâtons de hockey et une troupe de jeunes danseuses écossaises, prêtes à monter sur scène devant une mer de spectateurs.*

**Day 31, Québec**

Canadian short track speed skater Guillaume
Bastille carries the torch to a community
celebration in Rivière-du-Loup, QC.

*Jour 31, Québec*

*Le patineur de vitesse canadien sur piste courte,
Guillaume Bastille, porte le flambeau à la célébration
communautaire de Rivière-du-Loup, au Québec.*

## A VERY LONG JOURNEY

To make his 6:00 am call time just before his run in Bathurst,
New Brunswick, Wilson Lau, a torchbearer from Toronto, planned
to fly into New Brunswick the night before. Unfortunately, high
winds redirected his flight to Montréal, with no chance of flying
to New Brunswick in time for his run. But high winds were not
enough to prevent Lau from his Olympic experience. He hailed a
cab from the airport and stunned the driver with his request to
go to Bathurst — a trip that would cost Lau $1,000 in addition to
the expense of his grounded flight. To top it off, the driver was
nearing the end of his shift and could not stay awake for the
entire trip, so Lau ended up driving the cab himself to ensure his
safe arrival and his turn with the Olympic Flame.

## *UN TRÈS LONG VOYAGE*

*Afin d'arriver à temps pour son heure de rencontre prévue à 6 h 00,
juste avant son segment à Bathurst, au Nouveau-Brunswick, Wilson
Lau, un porteur du flambeau de Toronto, avait prévu prendre un vol
à destination du Nouveau-Brunswick la veille. Malheureusement, de
forts vents ont forcé l'avion à atterrir à Montréal et éliminé toutes ses
chances d'arriver à temps pour son segment au Nouveau-Brunswick.
Les vents n'ont tout de même pas soufflé assez fort pour empêcher
M. Lau de vivre son expérience olympique. Il a hélé un taxi à l'aéroport
et a prié le chauffeur, ahuri par sa demande, de le conduire jusqu'à
Bathurst, un voyage qui lui a coûté 1 000 $, en plus du coût du billet
d'avion. Pour couronner le tout, le chauffeur allait bientôt terminer son
quart de travail et avait peine à rester éveillé... M. Lau a donc pris le
volant du véhicule et a conduit lui même afin d'arriver en toute sécurité
et de pouvoir porter la flamme olympique.*

**Day 35, Québec**

In Ville de Québec, the iconic Château Frontenac hotel looms large in the distance as a torchbearer lights up the night.

*Jour 35, Québec*

*Dans la ville de Québec, au loin, le grandiose Château Frontenac illuminé sert de toile de fond tandis qu'un porteur du flambeau illumine la nuit.*

**Day 36, Québec**

More than 4,000 people pack the Polyvalente Benoît-Vachon high school parking lot to celebrate with musical acts Les Jarrets Noirs and Taylor Made Fable.

*Jour 36, Québec*

*Plus de 4 000 personnes se sont entassées à la polyvalente Benoît-Vachon afin de célébrer le relais en regardant Les Jarrets Noirs et Taylor Made Fable.*

A small flame that will warm my soul for a long time!

— *Yann Benoit, torchbearer,*
  *Day 38, Drummondville, QC*

*Une petite flamme qui réchauffera longtemps mon esprit!*

— *Yann Benoit, porteur du flambeau,*
  *Jour 38, Drummondville, QC*

## VIVE LA FLAMME

As the Olympic Torch journeyed into Québec, first up were the tiny villages of Dégelis, Notre-Dame-du-Lac, Cabano and Saint-Louis-du-Ha!-Ha! — a town whose playful-sounding name (and lively exclamation marks!) practically forecast the enthusiasm that would come from every corner of "La Belle Province," 195 communities in all.

The torch illuminated Montréal's famous Notre-Dame Basilica, site of the funerals for hockey legend Maurice "the Rocket" Richard and Pierre Trudeau, just as it travelled through Montmagny, the accordion capital of Canada, and Saint-Prime, best known for a tasty cheese sampled by British nobility as well as its Cheddar Cheese Museum. Torchbearers jogged across the frosty cobblestone streets of historic Ville de Québec; they also stopped by the town of Drummondville, birthplace of Québec's gift to gastronomy — poutine.

From barn dances to massive outdoor concerts, through quaint villages with their signature church spires to burgeoning metropolises, the entire province of Québec seemed enchanted with snowflakes, holiday lights and the Olympic Spirit. In tiny Saint-Cœur-de-Marie, Mayor Marc Asselin compared the importance of the torch relay to witnessing the space shuttle take off. A teenager on an Innu reserve called the whole Olympic experience "bigger than Britney Spears."

In Sherbrooke, Nathalie Lavois marvelled at the celebration, as tambourines clacked away and the entire crowd swayed in unison holding Canadian flags. "This is a marvelous occasion. We will never see this flame again, at least not in my lifetime," said Nathalie. "I think part of the magic of these celebrations is that [they] make us all feel like kids."

## *VIVE LA FLAMME*

*À l'occasion de son passage au Québec, la flamme olympique a d'abord visité les petites communautés de Dégelis, de Notre-Dame-du-Lac, de Cabano et de Saint-Louis-du-Ha!-Ha!, une ville dont le nom amusant et les points d'exclamation colorés sont presque un reflet de l'enthousiasme qui a émergé des 195 communautés visitées dans « la belle province ».*

*La flamme a illuminé la célèbre basilique Notre-Dame de Montréal, lieu des funérailles de la légende du hockey Maurice « le Rocket » Richard et de Pierre Elliott Trudeau, avant de se rendre à Montmagny, capitale canadienne de l'accordéon, et à Saint-Prime, une ville mieux connue pour son fromage savoureux goûté par la noblesse britannique ainsi que pour son Musée du fromage cheddar. Les porteurs de flambeau ont couru sur les rues de pierres gelées de la vieille ville de Québec. Ils se sont aussi arrêtés à Drummondville, lieu de création de ce que le Québec a ajouté à la gastronomie mondiale, la poutine.*

*Des soirées de danse campagnarde aux impressionnants concerts extérieurs, des villages charmants avec leur clocher d'église typique aux métropoles bourgeonnantes, tout le Québec a semblé une province enchantée parsemée de flocons blancs et de lumières estivales et habitée par l'esprit olympique. Le maire de la petite ville de Saint-Cœur-de-Marie, Marc Asselin, a comparé l'importance du relais de la flamme au décollage d'une navette spatiale, et un adolescent d'une réserve innue a qualifié l'expérience olympique de « plus prisée que Britney Spears ».*

*Par ailleurs, à Sherbrooke, Nathalie Langlois a été émerveillée par la célébration tandis qu'on pouvait entendre le son de tambours de basque et que la foule se balançait arcs, drapeaux canadiens à la main. « C'est une occasion remarquable. Nous n'aurons plus la chance de voir cette flamme, du moins pas de mon vivant », a déclaré Mme Langlois. « Je pense qu'une partie de la magie de ces célébrations vient du fait qu'elles nous rappellent notre enfance. »*

### Day 39, Québec

Cardboard and aluminum, duct tape and plastic pipe are materials of choice for torches of the homemade variety, held high by kids in Sorel-Tracy, QC.

### Jour 39, Québec

*Du carton, de l'aluminium, du ruban adhésif et des tuyaux en plastique sont les matériaux de choix que des enfants de Sorel-Tracy, au Québec, ont utilisés pour fabriquer des flambeaux « maison ».*

### Day 40. Québec

(Right) In record time, local Olympic hero Alwyn Morris covers his 300-metre jog from the grocery store to Karonhianonhnha School in Kahnawá:ke, the Mohawk community south of Montréal. Afterwards, Alwyn stands with elder Joe Jacobs for a blessing. "I encourage all the young people here to one day go to the Olympics and bring home more gold than Alwyn," said elder Jacobs.

### Jour 40. Québec

*(À droite) Le héros olympique local Alwyn Morris a parcouru son segment de 300 mètres, en un temps record, de l'épicerie à l'école Karonhianonhnha, à Kahnawá:ke, communauté Mohawk au sud de Montréal. Après sa course, il s'est tenu aux côtés de l'aîné Joe Jacobs pendant une bénédiction. « J'encourage tous les jeunes ici présents à se rendre un jour aux Jeux olympiques et à rapporter chez eux encore plus de médailles d'or qu'Alwyn », a dit l'aîné M. Jacobs.*

## Day 42, Québec

A light dusting of snow kicks off Day 42 in Montréal, ultimately turning into the relay's first bona fide winter storm. Swirling flakes fell on many of the 206 torchbearers, who inched through intersections, and criss-crossed swarms of spectators, adding to the electricity of an already bustling urban core.

## Jour 42, Québec

*Une mince couche de neige donne le coup d'envoi au jour 42, à Montréal, avant de se transformer en une tempête de neige, la première vraie tempête hivernale du relais. Les flocons dansants se sont posés sur un grand nombre des 206 porteurs de flambeau qui ont progressé d'une intersection à l'autre et se sont frayé un chemin dans la foule, pour accentuer l'ambiance déjà survoltée dans le cœur de la ville.*

## Days 41–48

Winter announces itself in Québec and eastern Ontario, testing the relay team's precision logistics and its physical hardiness. As the mercury drops and snow piles up, shovels, fur-trimmed boots and layered clothing make their appearance, as does the occasional roadside hockey game, making the most of the season's icy streets.

## Jours 41–48

L'hiver est bel et bien arrivé au Québec et dans l'est de l'Ontario, ce qui a servi d'épreuve de logistique au sein de l'équipe du relais qui a dû relever un défi de taille. Au fur et à mesure que la température dégringole et que la neige s'accumule, les pelles, les bottes doublées de fourrure et les épaisseurs de vêtements s'ajoutent au décor, tout comme les parties de hockey de rue; tout pour profiter au maximum des conditions hivernales dans les rues glacées.

**Day 41, Québec**

Olympic short track speed skater
Jean-François Monette runs with the
torch in front of Montréal's Olympic
Stadium — principal venue of the
1976 Olympic Games.

*Jour 41, Québec*

*Le patineur de vitesse sur piste courte
olympique Jean-François Monette court
avec le flambeau devant le Stade
olympique de Montréal, site principal
des Jeux olympiques de 1976.*

## TO SOOT OR NOT TO SOOT

For all the camaraderie among torchbearers, it may
be surprising to learn that one issue divides them into
two distinct camps: those who keep the soot and
those who don't. Torches that have already carried the
flame bear a distinct black residue that coats the top —
a residue that can be easily wiped away. Some feel the
darkened, sooty tip adds to the magic of the torch,
while others want a torch that's as sparkly and clean
as the first time they held it. Soot or no soot? For
thousands of torchbearers, that was the question . . .

### AVEC OU SANS SUIE

*Malgré la camaraderie qui se développe entre les
porteurs de flambeau, il peut être surprenant
d'apprendre qu'un élément les divise en deux camps
distincts : ceux qui conservent la suie sur leur flambeau
et ceux qui ne la conserve pas. Les flambeaux qui
ont déjà servi à faire brûler la flamme portent une
marque visible de résidu noir à l'extrémité. Toutefois,
ce résidu se nettoie facilement. Certains croient que
l'extrémité noire et couverte de suie contribue à la
magie du flambeau, tandis que d'autres souhaitent
tenir un flambeau aussi étincelant et propre que
la première fois qu'il a servi. Avec ou sans suie?
Pour des milliers de porteurs de flambeau, là était
la question...*

## Day 42 and 44, Ontario

(Top) Olympic gold medallist Barbara Ann Scott-King parades though the House of Commons to chants of "Go Canada Go!" from Members of Parliament. (Bottom left) Peter Masson holds his extinguished torch while visiting the National Aboriginal Veterans monument. (Bottom right) Perhaps best known for his role commanding the United Nations Assistance Mission for Rwanda in 1994, Canadian hero, senator and retired lieutenant-general Roméo Dallaire carries the flame in Ottawa, ON at the Governor General's residence.

## Day 42 et 44, Ontario

(Haut) La médaillée d'or olympique Barbara Ann Scott-King défile dans la Chambre des communes devant des députés qui lancent des « Allez, Canada! ». (En bas, à gauche) Peter Masson tient son flambeau éteint au cours d'une visite du Monument aux anciens combattants autochtones. (En bas, à droite) Probablement mieux connu pour avoir commandé la Mission des Nations Unies pour l'assistance au Rwanda en 1994, le héros canadien, sénateur et ancien lieutenant-général Roméo Dallaire porte la flamme à Ottawa, en Ontario, à la résidence de la gouverneure générale.

### Day 45, Ontario

Twenty torchbearing soldiers, civilians and military family members from CFB Petawawa, ON pause for photographs after their 11-minute procession with the Olympic Flame, anchored by Master Cpl. Mike Trauner, who lost both legs in Afghanistan.

### Jour 45, Ontario

*Vingt soldats porteurs de flambeau ainsi que des civils et des membres de la famille des militaires de la base des Forces canadiennes Petawawa en Ontario s'arrêtent le temps de quelques photos, après avoir marché pendant 11 minutes avec la flamme olympique guidés par le caporal chef Mike Trauner, qui a perdu ses deux jambes en Afghanistan.*

## Day 47, Ontario

(Below) Making sure he looks his best for the Olympic Flame, Gus Dellapa gets a trim at Peter's Barber Shop in Cobourg, ON, while, outside, his wife tries to find the best viewing spot.

## Jour 47, Ontario

(Ci-dessous) Afin d'être à son meilleur pour porter la flamme olympique, Gus Dellapa se fait couper les cheveux au salon de coiffure pour hommes Peter's Barber Shop à Cobourg, en Ontario, tandis qu'à l'extérieur, sa femme tente de trouver le point d'observation idéal.

## Days 49-51, Ontario

Bright Lights, Big City: The Olympic Torch joins flashing billboards and a galaxy of lights scattered across the Toronto skyline. Hundreds of thousands of spirited Torontonians came out to cheer on an array of torchbearers including Bollywood superstar Akshay Kumar and Canadian filmmakers Jason and Ivan Reitman. (Top left) Young patients experience the magic of the Olympic Flame in the atrium of The Hospital for Sick Children in Toronto. (Top right) South Korean figure skater and 2010 gold-medal hopeful Yu Na Kim basks in the media spotlight.

## Jours 49–51, Ontario

*Lumières vives, grande ville : La flamme olympique se joint à des panneaux d'affichage clignotants et une galaxie de lumières dispersées à travers la ligne d'horizon de Toronto. Des centaines de milliers de Torontois enthousiastes sont venus encourager les porteurs de flambeau, y compris l'acteur bollywoodien Akshay Kumar et les réalisateurs de films Jason et Ivan Reitman. (En haut à gauche) De jeunes patients vivent la magie de la flamme olympique dans l'atrium du Hospital for Sick Children à Toronto. (En haut à droite) La patineuse artistique sud-coréenne et espoir de médaille d'or en 2010 Yu Na Kim attire l'attention des médias.*

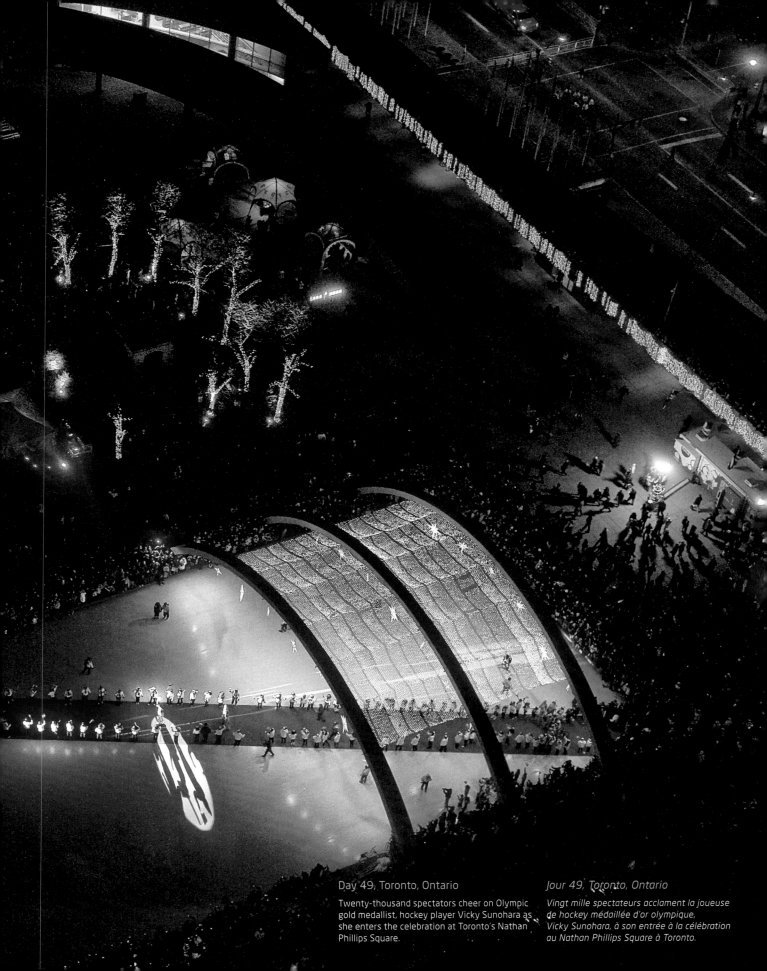

Day 49, Toronto, Ontario

Twenty-thousand spectators cheer on Olympic gold medallist, hockey player Vicky Sunohara as she enters the celebration at Toronto's Nathan Phillips Square.

Jour 49, Toronto, Ontario

Vingt mille spectateurs acclament la joueuse de hockey médaillée d'or olympique, Vicky Sunohara, à son entrée à la célébration au Nathan Phillips Square à Toronto.

You know this torch has already been through the hands of over 5,000 people, and while I may have represented Canada and the Olympics, today I'm just another Canadian.

— *Kurt Browning, torchbearer, Day 51, Mississauga, ON*

*Vous savez, plus de 5 000 personnes ont déjà porté le flambeau et même si j'ai représenté le Canada aux Jeux olympiques, aujourd'hui je ne suis pas différent de tout autre Canadien.*

— *Kurt Browning, porteur du flambeau, Jour 51, Mississauga, ON*

(Above) Hari Sihvo follows up his torch run by visiting his twin daughters' elementary school classroom.

(Ci-dessus) Après sa course avec le flambeau, Hari Sihvo rend visite à la classe de niveau élémentaire de ses filles jumelles.

## THE RUN OF HIS LIFE

For many torchbearers, their 300-metre segment is not only part of an epic relay across Canada. Their time with the flame is also part of a much larger personal journey and these journeys, lit for a moment by the Olympic Flame, remind the rest of us that there are heroes in our midst.

Hari Sihvo's run with the torch highlighted one of those journeys. His ongoing battle with Hodgkin's lymphoma has resulted in the amputation of nine fingers and all his toes, but he held the torch proudly as if it weighed nothing, and his infectious grin made it seem as if he was running swiftly, effortlessly.

"As I was running, I'd hear people scream my name or I'd see signs cheering me on, and my mind was totally preoccupied," he said. "It's like sheer joy was blocking out the pain."

For Hari, the changes to his life over the past five years had been non-stop and life-altering cancer. Twin baby girls. A stem cell transplant. A severe case of streptococcus pneumonia. Finger and toe amputations that left him on the athletic sideline and unable to grip a guitar, the instrument that had sustained him since childhood.

Years of painful trial and error with different instruments eventually led him to a custom-made bouzouki — an instrument similar to a mandolin — returning music to his life. But it wasn't until he took hold of the torch to run 300 metres on feet that were once bandaged and raw, and had confined him to a wheelchair for months on end, that Hari finally felt whole.

"I figured out how to live with my hands and still play music. But the fact that I ran with the torch . . ." he says incredulously, his voice trailing off. "The fact that I didn't walk — that I ran — makes me feel like I've come full circle."

## UNE COURSE UNIQUE

Pour de nombreux porteurs de flambeau, le segment de 300 mètres ne représente pas qu'une simple partie du relais historique qui traverse le Canada. Il s'agit également d'un moment spécial que l'on vit au cours d'un cheminement personnel. Éclairé pendant un moment par la flamme olympique, le cheminement de ces personnes nous rappelle tous qu'il y a des héros parmi nous.

Le segment d'Hari Sihvo, porteur du flambeau, a mis en lumière l'un de ces cheminements. En raison d'un lymphome hodgkinien, on a dû amputer neuf des dix doigts de M. Sihvo et tous ses orteils. Malgré cela, il a fièrement porté le flambeau comme s'il ne pesait rien du tout, et son sourire contagieux lui donnait l'air d'être au septième ciel.

« Pendant que je courais, j'entendais les gens crier mon nom ou je remarquais des affiches d'encouragement et mon esprit était complètement absorbé », a-t-il affirmé. « C'est comme si cette grande joie arrivait à apaiser la douleur. »

Pour M. Sihvo, les changements ont été nombreux au cours des cinq dernières années et ils ont changé sa vie. Le cancer, la naissance de ses jumelles, une greffe de cellules souches, un cas grave de pneumonie streptocoque, une amputation des doigts et des orteils qui l'a obligé à se retirer de la scène sportive et qui l'empêche de tenir une guitare, l'instrument qu'il chérit depuis son enfance : voilà ce qu'il a surmonté.

Après des années pénibles d'essai en vain de divers instruments, il s'est tourné vers un buzuki spécialement conçu pour lui. Cet instrument semblable à la mandoline lui a permis de renouer avec la musique. Mais ce n'est qu'en tenant le flambeau pendant son segment de 300 mètres qu'il a parcouru à la course, lui qui un jour avait eu les pieds pansés et vifs et avait été contraint à se déplacer en fauteuil roulant pendant des mois, que M. Sihvo s'est senti accompli.

« J'ai appris à vivre avec mes mains et je joue encore de la musique. Mais le fait de courir avec le flambeau... Le fait que je n'ai pas marché, mais bien couru, m'a fait comprendre que j'avais bouclé la boucle », a-t-il mentionné, épaté.

**Day 53, Ontario**

A soft glow pierces the
dusky backdrop of Niagara
Falls, North America's most
famous waterfall.

*Jour 53, Ontario*

*Au crépuscule, une lueur douce
perce la toile de fond des chutes
Niagara, les plus célèbres chutes
d'eau en Amérique du Nord.*

**Day 54, Ontario**

Sunlight bathes torchbearers-in-waiting through the windows of the Canada Southern Railway station in St. Thomas, ON.

*Jour 54, Ontario*

*Les porteurs de flambeau en attente baignent dans la lumière du soleil à travers les fenêtres de la Canada Southern Railway Station à St. Thomas, en Ontario.*

Inside the torch relay command car, Vidar Eilertsen (director, torch relay operations) follows the progress of the relay on GPS while staying in touch with the rest of the team by radio, keeping the relay on track and on time. Vidar and the rest of the 20-member operations team spend an average of 18 hours a day managing hundreds of details — everything from scheduling, to navigation, to crowd control.

"This is one of the few jobs where you can cry every day for a good reason," says Vidar, who counts the 2010 torch relay as the seventh of his career. "This is the ultimate project to work on. You see the best in people, the best of the country, the best of the human spirit. To be part of that is just a fantastic gift."

À l'intérieur du véhicule de commandement, Vidar Eilertsen (directeur, exploitation du relais de la flamme) suit le progrès du relais sur GPS tout en restant en contact avec le reste de l'équipe par radio, pour que le relais poursuive la bonne route, à l'heure. M. Eilertsen et le reste de l'équipe d'exploitation qui compte 20 membres passent environ 18 heures par jour à gérer des centaines de détails – de l'établissement des horaires au contrôle de la foule en passant par la navigation.

« Il s'agit d'un des rares emplois où il est possible de pleurer tous les jours pour de bonnes raisons », a expliqué M. Eilertsen, qui souligne que le relais de la flamme olympique de Vancouver 2010 est le septième relais de sa carrière. « Il est exceptionnel de travailler à ce projet. On peut voir le meilleur des gens et du pays. C'est une occasion tout simplement remarquable. »

## Day 55 and 60, Ontario

(Top) Surprise torchbearer and legendary Hockey Hall of Famer Gordie Howe finishes his run with the flame, but not before a fellow torchbearer throws him an elbow in honour of one of "Mr. Hockey's" signature moves.

(Bottom Right) As the relay travels through the country's residential neighborhoods, spirits lift at the sight of houses dressed up for the occasion. In Kincardine, ON, Connie Ross lit her own replica cauldron and set up a giant bobsledding penguin to mark the occasion. "We did it because we're excited about the Olympics and we're just so proud of Canada."

## Jours 55 et 60, Ontario

(Haut) Gordie Howe, porteur de flambeau surprise et membre du Temple de la renommée du hockey, court avec la flamme, mais pas avant qu'un autre porteur du flambeau lui donne du coude en l'honneur de l'une des manœuvres caractéristiques de « M. Hockey ».

(En bas, à droite) Au gré des déplacements du relais dans les quartiers résidentiels du pays, l'atmosphère s'embrase à la vue des maisons décorées pour l'occasion. À Kincardine, en Ontario, Connie Ross a allumé sa propre réplique de la vasque et a installé un pingouin qui fait du bobsleigh afin de souligner ce moment. « Nous avons fait ce montage parce que nous sommes emballés par les Jeux olympiques et nous sommes si fiers du Canada. »

## FROM HAND TO HAND AND HEART TO HEART

There they stand in bunches, bonding over a few nervous jokes or some shared astonishment at the heft or smoothness of the Olympic Torch. Some quietly discuss how they're going to carry it, or practice "kissing" the tips of their torches to get the flame transfer just right. Still others are teased for fussing with their uniforms, adjusting their toques or checking and re-checking the knots on their shoelaces for the umpteenth time.

For thousands of Olympic Torchbearers, no one else can appreciate what these fleeting, shared moments are like, or how they have a way of uniting people despite vast differences in geography, age, background, athleticism and inspiration. "You can tell torchbearers have a bond almost instantly," remarks Dave Doroghy, an Olympic shuttle host who's witnessed first-hand the intensity and immediacy of countless torchbearer connections.

"Before torchbearers run, I hand out pre-assigned stickers that show people who they'll pass their flame to. One time, I put stickers 152 and 153 on the jackets of two old friends who'd been laughing it up, joking around and having a great time since I picked them up in the bus. Seeing their numbers, and realizing they'd be passing off to one another, they burst out laughing, incredulous. Turns out they weren't longtime friends at all. One was from Salt Lake City, one was from Toronto, and they'd met only 10 minutes earlier on the street."

But you'd never know it from the warmth of their relationship, says Dave. "They know they're about to do something for the first time and, probably, the only time in their lives. That's an incredible thing to share with someone, even if you've just met."

## DE MAIN À MAIN ET DE CŒUR À CŒUR

*Ils sont tous là, en groupes, à faire connaissance en se racontant des blagues, avec une certaine nervosité, pendant que d'autres décrivent leur surprise au sujet du poids ou du profil du flambeau olympique. Certains discutent paisiblement de la façon dont ils porteront le flambeau, ou encore pratiquent la technique de transfert de la flamme avec la pointe des flambeaux, afin de bien la réussir durant leur segment. Dans d'autres cas, on taquine des porteurs de flambeau occupés à ajuster leur uniforme; ils replacent leur tuque ou vérifient pour la énième fois si leurs lacets de chaussures sont bien attachés.*

*Pour des milliers de porteurs de flambeau olympique, personne d'autre ne peut apprécier davantage ces moments futiles et communs ou imaginer à quel point ils ont un pouvoir unificateur malgré les immenses différences géographiques, d'âge, de milieux, de conditions physiques ou d'inspiration. « On voit que les porteurs de flambeau nouent des liens presque immédiatement », constate Dave Doroghy, hôte de la navette olympique qui a eu la chance de témoigner sur place de l'intensité et de la rapidité des nombreux liens qui se nouent entre les porteurs de flambeau.*

*« Avant le segment des porteurs de flambeau, je remets des autocollants préassignés qui indiquent aux gens à qui ils transféreront la flamme. Dans un certain cas, j'ai apposé les autocollants 152 et 153 sur le manteau de deux amis de longue date qui riaient, blaguaient et passaient réellement du bon temps depuis le moment où ils avaient monté dans l'autobus. En voyant leur numéro, ils se sont rendus compte qu'ils se transféreraient la flamme et ont éclaté de rire, incrédules. Finalement, ils n'étaient pas des amis de longue date du tout. L'un était de Salt Lake City et l'autre de Toronto. Ils s'étaient rencontrés dix minutes plus tôt dans la rue. »*

*« On n'aurait jamais pu le deviner à la chaleur de leur relation », a mentionné Dave Doroghy. « Ils savent qu'ils s'apprêtent à vivre une expérience unique pour la première fois, et probablement la dernière fois de leur vie. C'est un moment incroyable à partager avec quelqu'un, même après s'être tout juste rencontré. »*

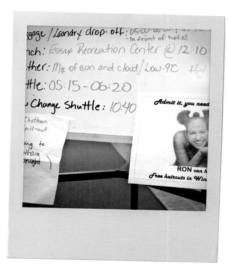

Tending to 250 to 300 travelling staff members on this cross-country odyssey means managing a mountain of details as big as the team's own laundry pile. "We average 100 bags of washing every three days — and we need it cleaned in less than 24 hours. It's craziness," says Jessie Grant, Rest Overnight Manager. While the logistical ballet of feeding, housing and transporting this pack through 1,036 cities over 106 days can be frenzied (especially in smaller towns where the team is spread over three or four different hotels), Jessie and her 12-person crew find ways to lighten the mood. Organizing free on-site haircuts does the trick. So does arranging guest speakers and local band nights, or offering survival gift packs filled with red mittens, extra toothpaste and other portable necessities for the long, eventful home stretch.

*La prise en charge de 250 à 300 employés en voyage pendant cette odyssée à travers le pays signifie qu'il faut gérer une montagne de détails aussi grande que la pile de lessive de l'équipe. « En moyenne, nous accumulons 100 sacs de lessive tous les trois jours — et elle doit être lavée dans un délai de 24 heures. C'est fou », dit Jessie Grant, gestionnaire de l'hébergement et de la logistique. Bien que le ballet logistique qui consiste à nourrir, héberger et transporter cette équipe vers 1 036 villes en 106 jours puisse être frénétique (plus particulièrement dans les villages où l'équipe est dispersée dans plus de trois ou quatre hôtels différents), Mme Grant et son équipe de 12 personnes trouvent des façons d'alléger l'atmosphère. On offre des coupes de cheveux gratuites sur place, on présente des conférenciers invités et des groupes locaux en soirée ou encore on offre des sacs-cadeaux remplis de mitaines rouges, de pâte dentifrice supplémentaire et autres nécessités de voyage pour « assurer la survie » durant l'étape finale qui sera longue et mémorable.*

## CHRISTMAS FOR THE CREW

Now at the relay's halfway mark, its weary, nomadic 250-person team savours a two-day break after watching Santa Claus — the one person with a busier agenda, perhaps — raise the torch and a red velvet sleeve on Christmas Eve. For the next 48 hours, the crew relaxed with a spirited video game marathon, unwrapped Secret Santa gifts, enjoyed a leisurely pyjama breakfast on Christmas morning and, for many, reunited with a special friend or relative who, travelled to Ontario to ring in the holidays.

## NOËL POUR L'ÉQUIPE

*Le relais maintenant à mi-chemin, son équipe fatiguée et nomade de 250 personnes profite d'une pause de deux jours après avoir regardé le père Noël — la seule autre personne ayant un horaire plus occupé sans doute — lever le flambeau d'un bras recouvert d'une manche de velours rouge la veille de Noël. Pendant les 48 heures suivantes, l'équipe s'est reposée en participant à un marathon de jeux vidéo animé, a déballé les cadeaux apportés par un père Noël secret et a profité d'un déjeuner tranquille en pyjamas le matin de Noël. Un grand nombre d'entre eux se sont réunis avec un ami ou un membre de la famille spécial qui s'est rendu en Ontario pour célébrer les Fêtes.*

### Day 59-60, Ontario

(Top) A spectacular community celebration in Orangeville, ON includes skating, ski and snowboard demonstrations on Murray's Mountain, youth singers, a kazoo band and even a precision snowmobile team on four metres of new, man-made snow. In all, the celebration drew 6,000 people and took 18 months to plan, with many events choreographed by Orangeville local Roland Kirouac, who also choreographed the opening of the Calgary 1988 Olympic Winter Games.

(Right middle) Famous for its annual Shakespeare Festival, the quaint town of Stratford, ON enjoys the spotlight during its early afternoon celebration.

### Jours 59 et 60, Ontario

(Haut) La célébration communautaire spectaculaire à Orangeville, en Ontario, présente des démonstrations de patinage, de ski et de surf des neiges sur Murray's Mountain, des jeunes chanteurs, un groupe « mirliton » et même une équipe de motoneige de précision sur quatre mètres de nouvelle neige artificielle. En tout, la célébration a attiré 6 000 personnes et a pris 18 mois à planifier. Roland Kirouac, résidant d'Orangeville, a chorégraphié bon nombre des spectacles. C'est aussi lui qui avait chorégraphié la cérémonie d'ouverture des Jeux olympiques d'hiver de 1988 à Calgary.

(À droite, au centre) Reconnu pour son Shakespeare Festival annuel, le charmant village de Stratford, en Ontario, est en vedette pendant sa célébration en début d'après-midi.

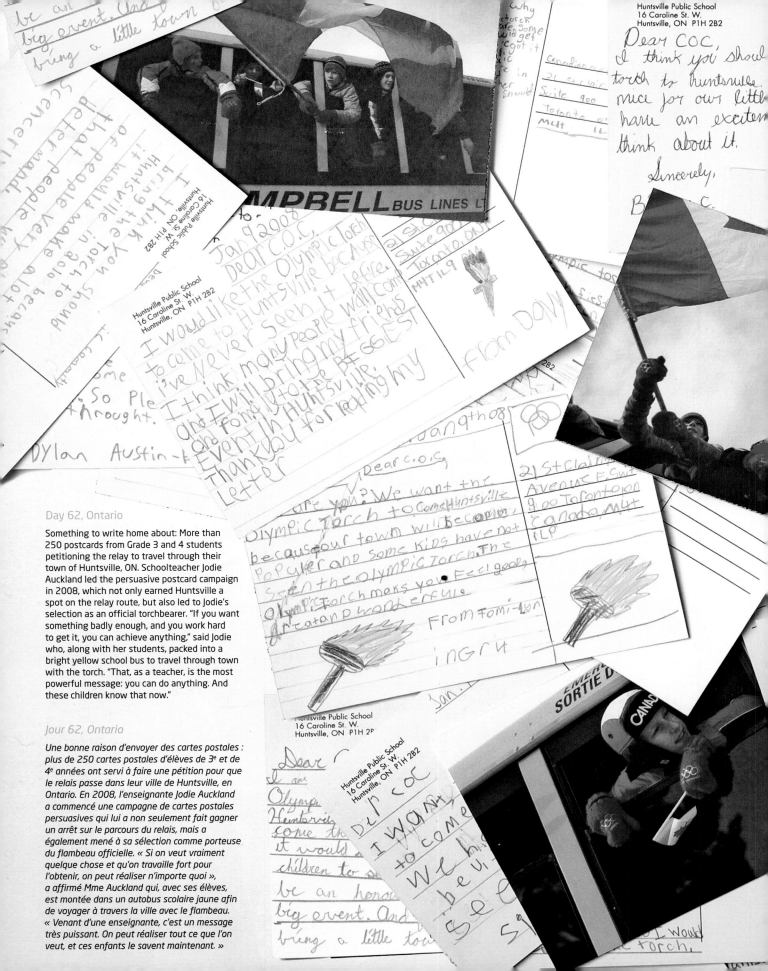

### Day 62, Ontario

Something to write home about: More than 250 postcards from Grade 3 and 4 students petitioning the relay to travel through their town of Huntsville, ON. Schoolteacher Jodie Auckland led the persuasive postcard campaign in 2008, which not only earned Huntsville a spot on the relay route, but also led to Jodie's selection as an official torchbearer. "If you want something badly enough, and you work hard to get it, you can achieve anything," said Jodie who, along with her students, packed into a bright yellow school bus to travel through town with the torch. "That, as a teacher, is the most powerful message: you can do anything. And these children know that now."

### Jour 62, Ontario

*Une bonne raison d'envoyer des cartes postales : plus de 250 cartes postales d'élèves de 3ᵉ et de 4ᵉ années ont servi à faire une pétition pour que le relais passe dans leur ville de Huntsville, en Ontario. En 2008, l'enseignante Jodie Auckland a commencé une campagne de cartes postales persuasives qui lui a non seulement fait gagner un arrêt sur le parcours du relais, mais a également mené à sa sélection comme porteuse du flambeau officielle. « Si on veut vraiment quelque chose et qu'on travaille fort pour l'obtenir, on peut réaliser n'importe quoi », a affirmé Mme Auckland qui, avec ses élèves, est montée dans un autobus scolaire jaune afin de voyager à travers la ville avec le flambeau. « Venant d'une enseignante, c'est un message très puissant. On peut réaliser tout ce que l'on veut, et ces enfants le savent maintenant. »*

### Day 64, Ontario

In -40 degree weather, country music superstar Shania Twain is welcomed by thousands of spectators in Hollinger Park, moments before lighting the Olympic Cauldron in her hometown of Timmins, ON. With fears of dropping the torch in mind, Shania added hockey tape to the bottom of her torch to ensure the best possible grip.

### Jour 64, Ontario

*À -40 degrés, des milliers de spectateurs acclament la grande vedette de musique country, Shania Twain, au Hollinger Park, quelques instants avant qu'elle allume la vasque olympique dans sa ville natale de Timmins, en Ontario. Craignant d'échapper son flambeau, Mme Twain a ajouté du ruban de hockey au bas de son flambeau afin d'assurer la meilleure prise possible.*

**Day 66, Ontario**

Bone-chilling temperatures cause the lunchtime celebration in Marathon, ON to move inside, where Guenther Wirtz, father of local Olympic figure skater Kris Wirtz, brings the glow of the flame — and an extra bit of heat — to the standing-room-only hockey arena.

*Jour 66, Ontario*

*La célébration du midi a lieu à l'intérieur en raison d'un froid glacial à Marathon, en Ontario, où Guenther Wirtz, père du patineur artistique olympique local Kris Wirtz, porte le flambeau en illuminant – et en réchauffant – l'aréna de hockey plein à craquer.*

### Day 66, Ontario

(Above) With slow, certain steps, St. Ignatius High School student Kailie Keast emerges from the crowd to honour her hero, Terry Fox. In Thunder Bay, ON, not far from where Fox's cross-country Marathon of Hope came to an early end, Keast pauses before the nine-foot statue as a determined young woman in remission from osteosarcoma — the very cancer Fox battled. "That's what Terry had, the exact same cancer, and I'm still here today. My school thought that was amazing and they nominated me. And I'm forever thankful."

### Jour 66, Ontario

(Haut) Lentement et d'un pas assuré, Kailie Keast, élève de l'école St. Ignatius High School, se dégage de la foule pour rendre hommage à son héros, Terry Fox. À Thunder Bay, en Ontario, près de l'endroit où s'est terminé le Marathon de l'Espoir de M. Fox, la jeune femme pleine de détermination s'arrête devant la statue de neuf pieds. Kailie est actuellement en rémission après un ostéosarcome, soit le même cancer contre lequel a lutté M. Fox. « Il s'agit du même cancer dont Terry souffrait, et je suis toujours ici. Les élèves de mon école ont pensé que cela était merveilleux et ils ont posé ma candidature. Je leur en serai toujours reconnaissante. »

Day 67, Ontario    *Jour 67, Ontario*

## PRAIRIE SPIRIT

Their infamous winter temperatures and frozen winds may have snapped audio cables and chilled relay spectators to their core, but the folks from Canada's heartland welcomed the torch with true Prairie grit, from 2,200 school kids lining the frigid roadways of Oak Bank, MB to the eight blocks of street hockey in Regina, SK. Festivities continued in Alberta where balmy zero-degree weather let observers strip down to one fleecy layer to enjoy pancake breakfasts, full-day BBQs, a festival of red and white and even the sight of horses from nearby farms trotting around with Olympic Rings painted on their flanks.

## L'ESPRIT DES PRAIRIES

*L'hiver rigoureux et les vents glacials des Prairies ont peut-être brisé des câbles audio et glacé les spectateurs du relais jusqu'aux os, mais les gens du cœur du Canada ont accueilli la flamme avec une détermination digne des Prairies, comme l'ont montré les 2 200 élèves qui se sont rassemblés dans les rues d'Oak Bank, au Manitoba, et les personnes qui ont occupé huit pâtés de maisons pour jouer au hockey de rue à Regina, en Saskatchewan. Les célébrations ont continué en Alberta, où il faisait zéro degré, ce qui a permis aux observateurs d'enlever quelques couches et de ne porter qu'une veste en laine polaire pour profiter des déjeuners de crêpes et des barbecues toute la journée ainsi que d'un festival de rouge et de blanc. Ils ont même pu voir des chevaux sur lesquels les anneaux olympiques étaient peints et qui trottaient autour des fermes avoisinantes.*

Day 72, Manitoba

Brady Hotin lights up the pre-dawn in
Sioux Valley, MB, accompanied by 28
First Nations Unity Riders, historically
known as warriors and protectors of
the Dakota people.

*Jour 72, Manitoba*

*Brady Hotin éclaire l'avant-aube à
Sioux Valley, au Manitoba, accompagné
de 28 cavaliers d'unité des Premières
nations, traditionnellement connus
comme les guerriers et les protecteurs
du peuple Dakota.*

Torchbearer Jason Taylor of the Sioux Valley First Nation stands before a fire lit by Mary Hall, a Dakota elder, from a home fire she kept burning for four days and four nights. This sacred number reappeared throughout the Sioux Valley ceremony as the Unity Riders circled the fire pit four times, and tapped the base of the lit Olympic Torch four times against the fire logs, allowing the smoke from each to intertwine, symbolically uniting the Dakota people with the torch relay's spirit of peace and friendship.

*Le porteur de flambeau Jason Taylor de la Première nation Sioux Valley se tient devant un feu allumé par Mary Hall, une aînée Dakota, à partir d'un feu qu'elle a allumé chez elle quatre jours et quatre nuits auparavant. Ce nombre sacré a réapparu tout au long de la cérémonie de Sioux Valley : les cavaliers d'unité ont encerclé le foyer quatre fois et ont tapé quatre fois la base du flambeau olympique allumé contre les bûches brûlantes pour permettre à la fumée de chaque bûche de s'entrelacer pour unir symboliquement le peuple Dakota à l'esprit de paix et d'amitié du relais de la flamme.*

## THE TORCH RELAY CONVOY

The relay's convoy rolls on to its next stop, stretching across the horizon under the endless Saskatchewan sky.

## LE CONVOI DU RELAIS DE LA FLAMME

*En route vers son prochain arrêt, le convoi s'étend à l'horizon sous le ciel sans fin de la Saskatchewan.*

## Day 73, Saskatchewan

(Top) Taryn Brandt cheers on her grandpa Bob Fahlman (middle) as he runs with the torch in Mortlach, SK. (Bottom) An emotional Darlene Poole runs in place of her husband, Jack Poole — who passed away just hours after the Olympic Flame was lit in Greece. Poole's leadership was an enormous force behind the Vancouver 2010 bid and Organizing Committee, and he had been looking forward to his hometown run in Mortlach.

*Jour 73, Saskatchewan*

*(Haut) Taryn Brandt encourage son grand-père Bob Fahlman (au centre) pendant qu'il court avec la flamme à Mortlach, en Saskatchewan. (En bas) Darlene Poole, très émue, court à la place de son mari, Jack Poole, qui est décédé quelques heures après que la flamme olympique a été allumée en Grèce. Le leadership de M. Poole a été d'une grande influence pour la candidature de Vancouver 2010 et le comité d'organisation. M. Poole attendait avec impatience de courir dans sa ville natale de Mortlach, en Saskatchewan.*

**Day 73, Saskatchewan**

(Above) A torchbearer appears in a quintessential prairie setting, crossing a set of frozen railroad tracks in Herbert, SK.

*Jour 73, Saskatchewan*

*(Ci-dessus) Dans un décor typique des Prairies, une porteuse de flambeau traverse les voies de chemin de fer gelées à Herbert, en Saskatchewan.*

(This page) Olympic speed skater Doreen Ryan runs through a crowd of thousands at Sir Winston Churchill Square for Edmonton's evening celebration. (Opposite page) During a special ceremony to honour Olympic athletes, the flame makes a guest appearance at a National Hockey League (NHL) match-up between the Edmonton Oilers and the Pittsburgh Penguins.

(Cette page) La patineuse de vitesse olympique Doreen Ryan court à travers une foule de milliers de personnes à Sir Winston Churchill Square pour la célébration en soirée à Edmonton. (Page opposée) Pendant une cérémonie spéciale pour honorer les athlètes olympiques, la flamme olympique fait une apparition à un match de la Ligue nationale de hockey (LNH) entre les Oilers d'Edmonton et les Penguins de Pittsburgh.

Day 79, Alberta

Medicine Hat, AB has the unique distinction of holding its celebration in the world's largest tepee — an impressive structure that once towered over the Olympic Cauldron at the Opening and Closing Ceremonies of the Calgary 1988 Olympic Winter Games before being relocated to Medicine Hat in 1991.

*Jour 79, Alberta*

*Medicine Hat, en Alberta, se distingue en tenant sa célébration dans le « plus grand tipi du monde », une structure impressionnante qui avait été élevée au-dessus de la vasque olympique durant les cérémonies d'ouverture et de clôture des Jeux olympiques d'hiver de 1988 à Calgary, avant d'être déplacée et installée à Medicine Hat en 1991.*

## IGNITING A CULTURAL CONNECTION

In the community of Tyendinaga, Ontario, Chief Don Maracle addressed the youthful, 200-person crowd outside the Mohawk Community Centre by connecting the symbolism of the Olympic Flame to the role of fire in many First Nations cultures. "Fire is one of the elements of creation," he said. "It gave us heat and warmth, but it's also a light that perpetuates hope, peace and unity."

Following Chief Don's message of harmony, the flame received a traditional First Nations blessing, just as it had from other Aboriginal communities across Canada, from K'ómoks in British Columbia, to Sheshatshiu in Newfoundland and Labrador. Although each flame blessing was unique, reflecting the diversity of Aboriginal cultures within Canada, each community's response seemed universal. Singing, sign-waving crowds welcomed the flame and represented just a few of the many moments where Canada's Aboriginal people played a central role in the 2010 Olympic Torch Relay.

In all, the flame would visit 119 Aboriginal communities and involve more than 300 First Nations, Inuit and Métis people as torchbearers, flame attendants and honorary elder fire keepers. Their participation offers a chance to celebrate the rich Aboriginal heritage that is such an integral part of Canada's national identity. For many Aboriginal Canadians, the relay has become a moving, meaningful way to kindle the dreams of their people — youth in particular — by showcasing the power of sport and the opportunity to dream big.

## CRÉÉR DES LIENS PAR LE FEU

*Dans la communauté de Tyendinaga, en Ontario, le chef Don Maracle s'adresse à la jeune foule de 200 personnes à l'extérieur du Mohawk Community Centre et fait le lien entre le symbolisme de la flamme olympique et le rôle du feu dans de nombreuses cultures des Premières nations. « Le feu est l'un des éléments de la création », a-t-il dit. « Il nous a donné la chaleur, mais il sert également de lumière qui permet de perpétuer l'espoir, la paix et l'unité. »*

*Après le message d'harmonie du chef Maracle, la flamme a reçu une bénédiction traditionnelle des Premières nations, tout comme dans les autres communautés autochtones partout au Canada; des Premières nations K'ómoks, en Colombie-Britannique, aux Premières nations Sheshatshiu, à Terre-Neuve-et-Labrador. Bien que chaque bénédiction de la flamme ait été unique et ait reflété la diversité des cultures autochtones au Canada, la réponse de chaque communauté a semblé universelle. Des foules qui chantaient et agitaient des pancartes ont accueilli la flamme et représenté quelques-uns des nombreux moments où le peuple autochtone du Canada a joué un rôle clé dans le relais de la flamme olympique de Vancouver 2010.*

*En tout et pour tout, la flamme aura visité 119 communautés autochtones. Plus de 300 personnes des Premières nations, inuites et métisses auront participé au relais comme porteurs de flambeau, responsables de la flamme et gardiens aînés honoraires du feu. Leur participation permet de célébrer leur patrimoine autochtone riche comme partie intégrante de l'identité du Canada. Pour de nombreux Canadiens autochtones, le relais est devenu un moyen émouvant et significatif d'inspirer les rêves de leur peuple, plus particulièrement les jeunes, en illustrant le pouvoir du sport et la possibilité d'avoir de grands rêves.*

A young girl in Nova Scotia wears her father's Calgary '88 torchbearer uniform, one of many of the vintage red and white suits seen on Vancouver 2010 torch relay spectators across the country.

*Une jeune fille en Nouvelle-Écosse porte l'uniforme de porteur de flambeau de Calgary 1988 de son père, l'un des nombreux ensembles rouge et blanc que les spectateurs du relais de la flamme de Vancouver 2010 ont porté partout au pays.*

## CALGARY'S OLYMPIC SPIRIT STILL SHINES

Whoever said you can't go home again didn't come from Calgary. Twenty-two years after the Olympic Flame ignited a giant cauldron in McMahon Stadium, marking the start of the Calgary 1988 Olympic Winter Games, its familiar glow made a triumphant return to the one-time Host City.

The red and white vintage jerseys and retro toques dotting the crowd might have been more vibrant 22 years ago, but the energy from the 6,000-plus spectators inside Canada Olympic Park was as electric as ever. Together, the group watched torchbearers race down the bobsled track and zigzag down the halfpipe, while tens of thousands of fans packed the Olympic Plaza to witness Robyn Ainsworth reprise her 1988 role to light the city's cauldron once again.

But the three-day celebration in and around Calgary did more than relive past moments of sporting glory; it also emphasized the legacy of those distant Olympic days.

Five world-class facilities built for the Calgary 1988 Olympic Winter Games are home to eight national teams and have hosted some 200 national and international competitions since 1987. Calgary's Olympic Park is now the second largest tourist attraction in Alberta, drawing upwards of one million people annually. Canada's record medal count in Torino 2006, Calgary's level of volunteerism, and the number of Calgary-area youth participating in winter sports can be linked to the momentum, facilities and programs of the 1988 Winter Games.

But on Day 83, as the flame's amber glow began to dim in Calgary, the city literally and figuratively passed the torch westward on to another Canadian city ready to create lasting legacies of its own.

## L'ESPRIT OLYMPIQUE DE CALGARY EST TOUJOURS VIVANT

*La personne qui a dit qu'il ne faut jamais retourner dans le passé n'est pas de Calgary. En 1988, la flamme olympique a allumé l'énorme vasque au McMahon Stadium pour marquer le début des Jeux olympiques d'hiver de 1988 à Calgary. Vingt-deux ans plus tard, sa lueur familière a fait un retour triomphal dans la ville qui, une fois, fût l'hôte des Jeux.*

*Les chandails rouge et blanc de l'époque et les tuques rétro colorant la foule étaient sûrement plus éclatants il y a 22 ans, mais l'énergie de plus de 6 000 spectateurs rassemblés à l'intérieur du Parc olympique du Canada était toujours aussi débordante. Ensemble, le groupe a regardé les porteurs de flambeau courir sur la piste de bobsleigh et zigzaguer à travers la demi-lune, tandis que des dizaines de milliers d'enthousiastes ont rempli la Place olympique pour voir Robyn Ainsworth allumer la vasque de la ville pour une deuxième fois; elle l'avait allumée pour la première fois en 1988.*

*La célébration de trois jours dans la ville de Calgary et ses environs a fait revivre beaucoup plus que les moments de gloire sportive du passé; elle a également permis de mettre en évidence le legs de Calgary 1988.*

*Huit équipes nationales jouent dans cinq installations de classe mondiale construites pour les Jeux olympiques d'hiver de 1988 à Calgary. Ces installations ont accueilli près de 200 compétitions nationales et internationales depuis 1987. Le Parc olympique de Calgary est désormais la deuxième plus grande attraction touristique en Alberta et attire environ un million de personnes chaque année. Le nombre record de médailles que le Canada a remportées à Turin 2006, le nombre de bénévoles à Calgary et le nombre de jeunes dans la région de Calgary qui pratiquent des sports d'hiver peuvent être liés à l'enthousiasme, aux installations et aux programmes des Jeux d'hiver de 1988.*

*Au jour 83 cependant, lorsque la lueur ambre de la flamme a commencé à diminuer à Calgary, la ville a passé le flambeau – littéralement et au sens figuré – à l'ouest, à une autre ville canadienne prête à créer ses propres héritages durables.*

## THE BIG AND QUIRKY SIDE OF CANADA

We like things large in Canada — our mountains, our forests and, even our man-made monuments — which is why the torch visited several of the world's biggest roadside attractions in Canada, including a 16.5-metre-high steel fiddle in Sydney, Nova Scotia, a massive pumpkin in Roland, Manitoba and a towering T-Rex in Drumheller, Alberta adorned with, what else, homemade, drawstring Red Mittens made of an astonishing 12 metres of fabric.

In keeping with these off-beat attractions is the relay's commitment to carry torchbearers and the flame in unexpected, culturally meaningful ways. Everything from a fishing boat, tundra buggy and high-flying gondola, to a horse-drawn stagecoach, antique fire truck and a small yellow dory that crossed Petty Harbour, Newfoundland and Labrador. Even athletes helped mix it up by carrying the torch as they surfed in Tofino, British Columbia, snowboarded in Calgary, Alberta and skied, skated, snowshoed, dog sledded, kayaked and cycled across the country.

For the torch — and the nation — it's been one wild ride, an unforgettable road trip that's showcased the biggest,

## LE CANADA : PAYS DE GRANDEUR ET D'ORIGINALITÉ

*Au Canada, nous aimons les grandes choses : nos montagnes, nos forêts et même nos monuments. C'est pourquoi la flamme a visité plusieurs des plus grandes attractions en bordure de route du monde au Canada, notamment un violon en acier de 16,5 mètres de haut à Sydney, en Nouvelle Écosse, une citrouille massive à Roland, au Manitoba, et un énorme tyrannosaure roi à Drumheller, en Alberta, paré d'une paire de mitaines rouges à cordonnet faite maison avec pas moins de 12 mètres de laine!*

*Le relais a aussi fait preuve d'originalité en transportant les porteurs de flambeau et la flamme à l'aide de moyens de transport inattendus et culturellement significatifs comme un bateau de pêche, un buggy de toundra, une télécabine haute dans les airs, une diligence, un ancien camion d'incendie et un petit doris jaune qui a traversé Petty Harbour, à Terre-Neuve-et-Labrador. Même les athlètes ont contribué à diversifier les moyens de transport utilisés lorsqu'ils ont porté le flambeau en faisant du surf à Tofino, en Colombie-Britannique, du surf des neiges à Calgary, en Alberta, du ski, de la raquette, du patin, du traîneau à chiens, du kayak et du vélo à travers le pays.*

*Pour la flamme — et la nation — le parcours a été des plus fous; une aventure inoubliable qui a montré les choses les plus grandes, les plus belles et les plus bizarres que le pays*

## COMING 'ROUND THE MOUNTAIN

The relay team was overwhelmed with joy after catching its first glimpse of the Rocky Mountains, and the breathtaking scenes that followed — including a game of shinny played on the frozen waters of Lake Louise, AB.

## À LA VUE DES MONTAGNES

*L'équipe du relais était folle de joie à la première vue des montagnes Rocheuses et des scènes magnifiques qui ont suive comme une partie de shinny sur les eaux glacées du lac Louise, en Alberta.*

When those massive peaks came into view there was such a huge surge of adrenaline that I got on the radio to tell the team behind us, "We can see mountains! We're almost there!" We were all so giggly, knowing how close we were — close to our families, close to our own beds. What a boost…We all knew that we were bringing the flame home.

— *Virginie Lamarche, torch relay staff member*

*Lorsque j'ai vu ces sommets massifs pour la première fois, j'ai eu une telle montée d'adrénaline que j'ai appelé l'équipe derrière nous par radio pour lui dire "Nous voyons les montagnes! Nous sommes presque rendus!" Nous avons beaucoup ricané parce que nous savions que nous étions près — près de nos familles, près de nos lits. Quel élan! Nous savions tous que nous rapportions la flamme chez nous. C'est un sentiment que je ne peux pas décrire.*

— Virginie Lamarche, équipe du relais de la flamme

## HOMECOMING

"British Columbia has been waiting to celebrate for eight years — and it shows," says Sarah Mulhall, the torch relay's regional route coordinator for BC. "The relay has drawn some great crowds across the country, but you can actually feel the anticipation here."

Wally Buono, long-time general manager and head coach of the Canadian Football League's BC Lions, carried the torch into the Host Province via Kicking Horse Pass. For the next 22 days, the flame's provincial homecoming is met by breathless fans in towns of every size, cheering, screaming, singing, crying and basking in moments almost a decade in the making.

### LE RETOUR

« La Colombie-Britannique attend cette célébration depuis huit ans et ça se voit! », a dit Sarah Mulhall, coordonnatrice régionale du parcours relais de la flamme pour la Colombie-Britannique. « Le relais a attiré de bonnes foules partout au pays, mais on peut vraiment sentir l'effervescence ici. »

Wally Buono, directeur général de longue date et entraîneur-chef des BC Lions de la Ligue canadienne de football, a porté le flambeau dans la province hôte en passant par Kicking Horse Pass. Pendant les 22 jours qui ont suivi, d'innombrables enthousiastes fébriles se sont rendus dans des villes de différentes tailles pour célébrer le retour de la flamme dans la province. Ils ont applaudi, crié, chanté, pleuré et savouré ce moment, qui a nécessité près d'une décennie à organiser.

CANADIAN PACIFIC RAILWAY

MOUNT STEPHEN

The flame enjoys a moment of calm at Lake Okanagan in the town of Peachland, BC. In British Columbia's semi-arid interior, the Okanagan is known for its rich agriculture, picturesque wineries and lakeside spots, but also for its devoted sport fans. Neighbouring cities Kelowna and Kamloops drew 10,000 and 15,000 spectators respectively to cheer on local sports heroes and to see their community cauldrons light the hearts of the communities.

*La flamme profite d'un moment de calme au lac Okanagan, à Peachland, en Colombie-Britannique. Dans l'intérieur semi-aride de la Colombie-Britannique, on connaît l'Okanagan pour son agriculture riche, ses vignobles pittoresques et ses endroits riverains, mais aussi pour ses fanatiques de sports. Les villes avoisinantes de Kelowna et de Kamloops ont attiré 10 000 et 15 000 spectateurs, respectivement, pour encourager les héros de sports de la région et pour voir leur vasque communautaire allumer les cœurs des communautés.*

Just as the torch relay unites a nation, so did the promise of a transcontinental railway. As if to celebrate that link, the flame travels on the Royal Canadian Pacific between Revelstoke and Canoe, BC, pausing at Craigellachie — home of the "Last Spike" — a historical location that marks the Canadian Pacific Railway's connection between British Columbia and central Canada.

*Tout comme le relais de la flamme a uni une nation, la promesse d'un chemin de fer transcontinental en a fait de même. Comme si l'on célébrait ce lien, la flamme voyage à bord du Royal Canadian Pacific entre Revelstoke et Canoe, en Colombie-Britannique, en arrêtant temporairement à Craigellachie — domicile de la « dernière attache de rails » — un endroit historique qui marque la liaison du Canadian Pacific Railway entre la Colombie-Britannique et le centre du Canada.*

## WEARING OUR HEARTS ON OUR HANDS

Canadian fingers feel as comfortable filling out a pair of mittens as they do tugging on hockey skate laces or reaching out to catch the first few winter snowflakes.

So when red mittens were announced as part of the official torchbearer uniform — and were made available to fans — sales were as red-hot as the mittens themselves. Simple and nostalgic, these maple leaf red tokens perfectly captured the magic of a Canadian childhood full of winter play and soft, knitted clothes to keep us warm.

As soon as the relay started, so did "mitten mania." Within days, retail tables once piled sky high with mittens were cleared entirely as stores worked feverishly to keep up with demand. By the time the Games officially began, the Vancouver 2010 Organizing Committee had sold approximately three million pairs — sheltering six million hands and 30 million fingers from the cold. Plus, all this patriotic hand-warming had a heart-warming component to it, with net proceeds going to support Canadian athletes.

"It's amazing to see a mass of red mittens waving during a torch relay celebration," said Andrew Greenlaw, Vancouver 2010 torch relay marketing manager. "But the other day, during a break from the relay, I saw an elderly woman holding onto her walker wearing red mittens just as a young jogger ran by wearing a pair too. It was surreal. The mittens have gone from being Olympic paraphernalia to an everyday item in our wardrobe. I just love that."

## *LE CŒUR SUR LES MAINS*

*Les mains des Canadiens se sentent aussi à l'aise dans une paire de mitaines que lorsqu'elles tirent sur des lacets de patins de hockey ou tendent la main pour attraper les premiers flocons de neige l'hiver.*

*Après qu'on a annoncé que des mitaines rouges feraient partie de l'uniforme officiel des porteurs de flambeau — et que les amateurs pourraient s'en procurer — les caisses enregistreuses n'ont pas dérougi. Simples et nostalgiques, ces mitaines-souvenirs rouges ornées de la feuille d'érable ont parfaitement capté la magie de l'enfance au Canada : pleine de jeux d'hiver et de vêtements doux tricotés qui nous gardent au chaud.*

*Puis, le relais de la flamme a commencé, et la folie des mitaines aussi. En quelques jours, les tables des détaillants, autrefois pleines à craquer de mitaines, étaient complètement vides tandis que les boutiques travaillaient très fort pour satisfaire à la demande. Lorsque les Jeux ont officiellement, commencé le Comité d'organisation des Jeux olympiques et paralympiques d'hiver de 2010 à Vancouver avait vendu environ trois millions de paires de mitaines pour garder au chaud six millions de mains et 30 millions de doigts. De plus, ce « réchauffage patriotique » a aussi réchauffé le cœur, puisque le produit net des ventes a servi à appuyer les athlètes canadiens.*

*« C'est incroyable de voir cette masse de mitaines rouges qui s'agitent pendant une célébration du relais de la flamme », a déclaré Andrew Greenlaw, gestionnaire de marketing du relais de la flamme de Vancouver 2010. « L'autre jour, pendant une pause du relais, j'ai vu une femme âgée qui tenait sa marchette et portait les mitaines rouges tandis qu'un jeune joggeur la dépassait en portant une paire aussi. C'était surréel. Les mitaines, qui ont été conçues comme article de promotion, font maintenant partie de la garde-robe de tous les jours. J'adore! »*

## FROM STREET SWEEPER TO TORCHBEARER

They are streets the legendary Dennis Baptiste, a long-time Quesnel, BC resident, knows well. A hard-working city employee for 36 years and a volunteer firefighter for over two decades, Dennis has spent more than half his life sweeping these roadways, shovelling them clear of snow and smiling to everyone who travels along them.

But on Day 92 of the torch relay, he ran these streets instead, one ecstatic metre after another, through two blocks of shoulder-to-shoulder spectators cheering on a man rendered speechless by the honour. Following the same course as Olympians and other nominated community heroes across the country, Dennis dipped his Olympic Torch into the Quesnel community cauldron, igniting flames to roars of excitement from the entire town.

## *DE BALAYEUR DE RUE À PORTEUR DU FLAMBEAU*

*Les rues de Quesnel en Colombie-Britannique, Dennis Baptiste les connaît bien. Résident de longue date, il est estimé dans sa collectivité. Employé exemplaire de la ville depuis 36 ans et pompier bénévole depuis plus de 20 ans, M. Baptiste a passé plus de la moitié de sa vie à balayer les chaussées de la ville et à les déneiger tout en souriant à tous les passants.*

*Mais au jour 92 du relais de la flamme, il a plutôt couru dans ces rues, euphorique, entre deux pâtés de maisons où s'étaient rassemblés, coude à coude, des spectateurs pour encourager un homme ému par un tel honneur. À l'instar d'olympiens et d'autres héros communautaires choisis partout au pays, M. Baptiste a allumé la vasque communautaire de Quesnel à l'aide de son flambeau olympique, ce qui a suscité les acclamations de toute la ville.*

## COMMUNITIES COMING TOGETHER

"Attendance has been mind-boggling," remarks Randy Ferguson, master of ceremonies for each of the 189 torch relay community celebrations. "It's like having a rock concert twice a day — a very emotional rock concert."

Setup for the first of two daily celebrations begins long before sunrise with a crew of 15 and volunteers braving the conditions before unloading rigs full of generators, a stage, a jumbo video screen and other essential equipment. Hours later, with the area transformed, community members step onstage to showcase performances they've spent nearly a year perfecting.

Local childrens' choirs, poetry readers, dancers, athletes and magicians step into the spotlight alongside entertainment sponsored by RBC and Coca-Cola. A few speeches are followed by the ceremony's emotional close, where a local hero nominated to carry the torch lights the community's official cauldron before hundreds — or more often thousands — of supporters.

When describing the celebrations' profound moments, Randy rattles off dozens, stopping only to choke back tears. "A father ran in place of his daughter who was killed a year earlier by a drunk driver. Kids from economically hard-hit towns told us they felt inspired to do more, be more, dream more. Aboriginal elders told us this was the biggest thing to happen to their town for as far back as they could remember . . . I could go on and on."

"Celebrations like this make people realize how many heroes are among us," said Randy. "People want to honour them, and they also want to come together to celebrate this great country and the fact we're living in such an amazing time."

## DES COLLECTIVITÉS QUI S'UNISSENT

*« Il est stupéfiant de voir tous ces gens », remarque Randy Ferguson, maître de cérémonie pour chacune des 189 célébrations communautaires du relais de la flamme. « C'est comme si l'on présentait un concert de rock deux fois par jour – un concert de rock très émouvant. »*

*La préparation de la première des deux célébrations quotidiennes commence bien avant le lever du soleil avec une équipe de 15 personnes et de bénévoles qui affrontent la grêle, la neige ou d'autres conditions pénibles avant de décharger des générateurs, une scène, un écran vidéo géant et d'autre équipement essentiel. Quelques heures plus tard, après que l'aire est transformée, les membres de la communauté montent sur la scène pour présenter des spectacles qui leur ont pris presque un an à perfectionner.*

*Des chœurs d'enfants régionaux, des lecteurs de poésie, des danseurs, des athlètes et des magiciens se trouvent sous les projecteurs, tout comme les divertissements commandités par RBC et Coca-Cola. On entend quelques allocutions suivies par la clôture émouvante de la cérémonie, lorsqu'un héros local nommé pour porter le flambeau allume la vasque officielle de la communauté devant une centaine – ou plus souvent des milliers – de fervents.*

*Lorsqu'il décrit les moments profonds des célébrations, M. Ferguson en raconte des dizaines, en s'arrêtant quelques fois pour refouler ses larmes. « Un père a couru à la place de sa fille qui s'est fait tuer il y a un an par un conducteur ivre. Des enfants provenant de villes très touchées par la situation économique nous ont dit qu'ils se sentaient inspirés d'en faire plus et de rêver plus. Des aînés autochtones nous a dit qu'il s'agissait de l'événement le plus important qui avait lieu dans leur ville de ce qu'ils se souviennent... Je pourrais continuer longtemps. »*

*« Des célébrations comme celles-là font que les gens se rendent compte du nombre de héros qui se trouvent parmi nous », a déclaré M. Ferguson. « Ils veulent les honorer et ils veulent également s'unir pour célébrer ce merveilleux pays et le fait que nous vivons dans une ère incroyable. »*

CAPE FAREWELL

## WHISTLER: FIVE DECADES IN THE MAKING

In the early 1960s, what's now known as Whistler was a series of gloriously snowy but unknown alpine bowls without roads, running water, electricity or any infrastructure. But that didn't stop a group of legendary skiers and Vancouver entrepreneurs to drum up a bid for Whistler to host the 1968 Olympic Winter Games.

A half-century later, this beloved mountain town is getting its chance. To celebrate, locals and tourists jammed into Whistler Olympic Park, gathered in Skiers Plaza and applauded for Steve Podborski, a member of the fabled Crazy Canucks downhill team, as he passed the flame to Julia Murray, ski-cross athlete and daughter of Steve's fellow Crazy Canuck teammate — the late Dave Murray.

## WHISTLER : CINQ DÉCENNIES DE PRÉPARATION

*Au début des années 1960, l'endroit qu'on appelle aujourd'hui Whistler se composait d'une série de vallées alpines magnifiquement enneigées, mais inconnues, sans rues, eau courante, électricité ou infrastructure. Mais cela n'a pas empêché un groupe de skieurs légendaires et d'entrepreneurs de Vancouver d'élaborer une soumission pour la candidature de Whistler en vue d'accueillir les Jeux olympiques d'hiver de 1968.*

*Cinquante ans plus tard, ce village de montagne chéri aura sa chance. Pour célébrer, les résidants et les touristes se sont entassés au Parc olympique de Whistler, se sont rassemblés à Skiers Plaza et ont applaudi Steve Podborski, membre de l'équipe de descente légendaire nommée les « Crazy Canucks », lorsqu'il a passé la flamme à Julia Murray, athlète de ski cross et fille d'un coéquipier de Steve aussi membre des Crazy Canucks, le défunt Dave Murray.*

(Above) Running in Ashcroft, BC, Surrey resident Jarnail Sahota carries the flame — trailed by friends who opted to wear red turbans as a nod to Canada's official colours. "I held the torch for my community, for multiculturalism in Canada and to show the world I'm proud to be a Canadian Sikh," said Jarnail.

(Ci-dessus) À Ashcroft, en Colombie-Britannique, Jarnail Sahota, résident de Surrey, court avec la flamme suivi d'amis qui ont choisi de porter des turbans rouges comme affirmation des couleurs officielles du Canada. « J'ai tenu le flambeau pour ma communauté, pour le multiculturalisme au Canada et pour montrer au monde que je suis fièr d'être sikhe canadien », a dit M. Sahota.

Day 103, British Columbia

To honour the special friendship between Canada and its neighbour to the south, the Olympic Flame crosses into the United States at the Peace Arch border crossing before Chamila Anthonypillai, a 19-year-old Sri Lankan-born resident of Surrey, BC, returns the flame to Canadian soil.

*Jour 103, Colombie-Britannique*

*Afin d'honorer l'amitié spéciale entre le Canada et son voisin du sud, la flamme olympique passe aux États-Unis par le poste frontalier Peace Arch avant que Chamila Anthonypillai, une résidante de Surrey, en Colombie-Britannique, née au Sri Lanka, ramène la flamme au sol canadien.*

## Day 104, British Columbia

Olympic snowboarder Justin Lamoureux "tram-surfs" atop the Grouse Mountain Skyride in North Vancouver, strapped in a harness with bungee cord attachments. Two more torchbearers run the flame on the mountain, followed by a Skyride descent with Olympic skier Kennedy Raine, daughter-in-law of Olympic gold medallist Nancy Greene Raine.

## Jour 104, Colombie-Britannique

*Le surfeur des neiges, Justin Lamoureux, fait du surf par tram en haut du Grouse Mountain Skyride à North Vancouver, attaché dans un baudrier avec des tendeurs élastiques. Deux autres porteurs de flambeau ont couru avec la flamme sur la montagne, suivi par une descente par Skyride avec la skieuse olympique Kennedy Raine, bru de la médaillée d'or olympique Nancy Greene Raine.*

## Day 106, British Columbia

A city cloaked in darkness begins to buzz in the early hours of Day 106, the torch relay's final day. As the sun rises in Vancouver's eastern sky, the flame's glow begins in the west, touring the city's iconic Stanley Park, and passing through its downtown core and surrounding neighbourhoods amidst deafening cheers and endless seas of people.

Welcome home, Olympic Flame. The city's been waiting for you.

## Jour 106, Colombie-Britannique

*Une ville enveloppée par le noir commence à s'agiter aux premières heures du jour 106, dernier jour du relais de la flamme. Tandis que le soleil se lève à l'est de Vancouver, la lueur de la flamme commence dans l'ouest et fait le tour de Stanley Park, parc iconique de la ville, et passe par le cœur du centre-ville et les quartiers avoisinants au son de cris assourdissants et de foules à perte de vue.*

*Bon retour, flamme olympique. Il y a longtemps que la ville t'attend.*

III

WITH
GLOWING
HEARTS
The Lighting of the
Olympic Cauldron

DES PLUS
BRILLANTS
EXPLOITS
*L'allumage de la
vasque olympique*

Day 106, British Columbia

Rick Hansen enters BC Place as the first of the
relay's final five torchbearers — a collection of
Canadian athletic heroes, including Catriona
Le May Doan, Steve Nash, Nancy Greene Raine
and the relay's top-secret final torchbearer:
hockey legend and national icon Wayne Gretzky.

*Jour 106, Colombie-Britannique*

*Rick Hansen entre dans BC Place; il est le premier
des cinq derniers porteurs de flambeau — un
ensemble de héros athlétiques canadiens,
notamment Catriona Le May Doan, Steve Nash,
Nancy Greene Raine et le porteur du flambeau
ultrasecret final : la légende de hockey et icône
nationale, Wayne Gretzky.*

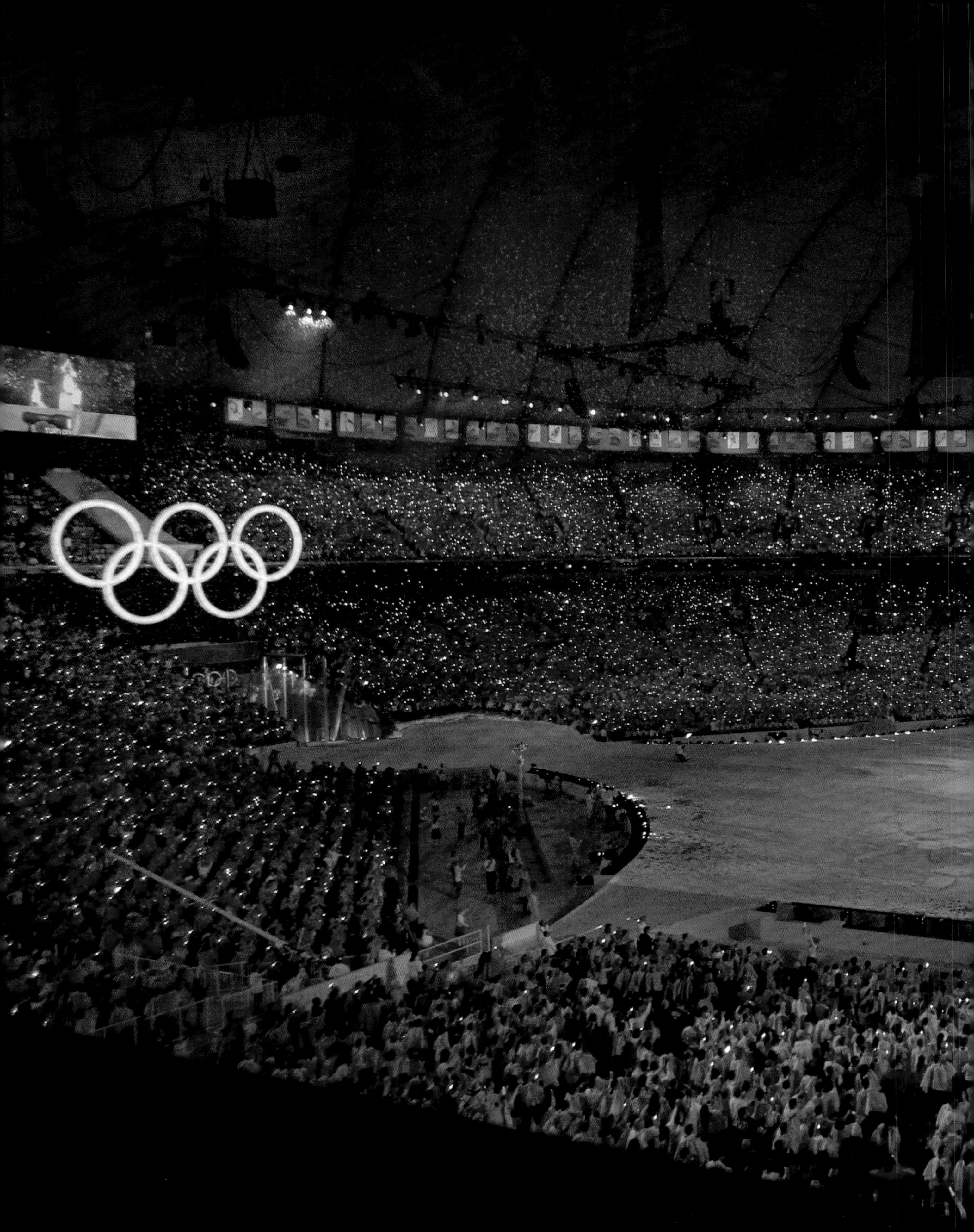

Day 106, British Columbia

The group-lit Olympic Cauldron illuminates the
sold-out stadium of 60,000 seats while billions of
television viewers tune in from around the world.

*Jour 106, Colombie-Britannique*

*La vasque olympique allumée par le groupe éclaire
le stade où se trouvaient 60 000 personnes, tandis
que des milliards de téléspectateurs étaient à
l'écoute de par le monde.*

**Day 106, British Columbia**

Wayne Gretzky stands before the external cauldron in Jack Poole Plaza after travelling from the indoor stadium by pickup truck and setting the cauldron alight as thunderous fireworks burst overhead. The Olympic Cauldron will burn for all 17 days of the Games and remain as a permanent landmark on the Vancouver waterfront.

*Jour 106, Colombie-Britannique*

*Wayne Gretzky, debout devant la vasque extérieure à Jack Poole Plaza, après avoir voyagé du stade par camionnette et allumé la vasque à la lumière de feux d'artifice éclatants dans le ciel. La vasque olympique brûlera pendant les 17 jours des Jeux et restera comme point d'intérêt permanent en bordure d'eau à Vancouver.*

IV

AFTERGLOW
The Spirit of the
Vancouver 2010
Torch Relay

DERNIÈRES
LUEURS
L'esprit du relais
de la flamme olympique
de Vancouver 2010

GOOD LUCK CANADA'S STARS! FROM ALL THE

FUTURE STARS AT LITTLE LIGHTS DAYCARE

# At the finish line
## *À la ligne d'arrivée*

Explaining the concept of a torch relay to children can prompt some interesting questions: "What if they drop it?" "Is it safe for them to run in the middle of the street?" "I thought we weren't supposed to play with fire." "Did someone swim it over from Athens? That's far." "Does the torch burn down like a matchstick?"

Even if all the relay's details aren't entirely clear to them, the relay's most curious, most fervent fans were often its smallest, with eyes the size of full moons and amazement that ricocheted between the cameras, the crowd, the vehicles, the torch bearers and, of course, the flame itself. It's fair to say the entire spectacle left an indelible mark on many of the country's littlest spectators — a phenomenon some nicknamed the "afterglow."

Parents were largely responsible for piquing torch relay excitement among their children. Bundling their little ones up and waiting for hours in often near-blizzard conditions, stenciling maple leafs on their toddlers' cheeks and kneeling down on wet, frosty sidewalks, they explained how the flame's message of hope and peace had touched the lives of people across the country.

"I took my daughter to watch the relay because it gave me a platform to get so many important messages to sink in," said Tiffany Haziza of North Vancouver, BC. "It's like, 'This is our community, Bella. And you live in an amazing country. And, also, you can do whatever you want in your life if you just believe. Just look around you . . .'"

Judging from the open-mouthed, wide-eyed reaction from kids everywhere, the children of this country are taking it all in — and giving it their own spin. "Oh, I get it," said Liam Labistour, who watched his dad run with the torch. "It's like . . . hope on a stick."

*Expliquer le concept d'un relais de la flamme aux enfants peut soulever des questions intéressantes : « Qu'arrive-t-il si on échappe le flambeau? » « Est-il sécuritaire de courir au milieu de la rue? » « Je pensais qu'on n'était pas censé jouer avec le feu. » « Quelqu'un l'a-t-il rapportée d'Athènes à la nage? C'est loin, non? » « Est-ce que la flamme brûle et s'éteint comme une allumette? ».*

*Même si les enfants ne comprennent pas bien la signification du relais, ce sont souvent eux, avec leurs yeux grands comme des vingt-cinq cents, les partisans les plus curieux et les plus fervents du relais de la flamme. Leur émerveillement s'est reflété sur les caméras, la foule, les véhicules, les porteurs de flambeau et, bien sûr, la flamme. Tout le spectacle a laissé une marque incontestablement indélébile sur bon nombre des plus jeunes spectateurs du pays; un phénomène que certaines personnes ont surnommé la « rémanence ».*

*Les parents, grandement responsables de susciter l'enthousiasme des enfants pour le relais de la flamme, avaient emmitouflé leurs petits et dessiné des feuilles d'érable sur leurs joues. Ils ont attendu pendant des heures dans des conditions de quasi-tempête de neige et se sont mis à genoux sur des trottoirs mouillés et froids pour leur expliquer comment le message d'espoir et de paix de la flamme a touché la vie de personnes partout au pays.*

*« J'ai emmené ma fille regarder le relais, car celui-ci m'a servi de base pour lui faire comprendre beaucoup de notions importantes, et je voulais m'assurer qu'elle les comprenait », a dit Tiffany Haziza de North Vancouver, en Colombie-Britannique. « C'était un peu comme lui dire : "Voici notre ville, Bella. Tu habites dans un pays incroyable. Tu peux atteindre tes buts si tu y crois. Regarde autour de toi..." ».*

*Les bouches ouvertes et les yeux écarquillés des petits Canadiens montrent qu'ils ne perdent pas une miette du relais même s'ils l'interprètent à leur façon. « Ah, je comprends maintenant », s'est exclamé Liam Labistour, qui a regardé son père courir avec le flambeau. « C'est comme... l'espoir sur un bâton. »*

Route Communities / *Communautés de parcours* 1 **BC** Arrival Ceremony in Victoria / *Cérémonie d'arrivée à Victoria* · Esquimalt · CFB/BFC Esquimalt · Esquimalt (FN/PN) · Songhees · View Royal · Sidney · North Saanich · Central Saanich · Saanich · Oak Bay · Victoria **2 BC** Sooke · T'sou-ke · Metchosin · Colwood · Fort Rodd Hill & Fisgard Lighthouse NHSC/LHNC · Langford · Mill Bay · Cowichan Bay · Khowutzun · Duncan · North Cowichan · Lake Cowichan · Ganges · Crofton · Chemainus · Ladysmith · Cedar · Snuneymuxw · Nanaimo **3 BC** Nanaimo · Lantzville · Nanoose Bay · Parksville · Coombs · Hilliers · Port Alberni · Hupacasath · Tseshaht · Ucluelet · Pacific Rim National Park (Long Beach) · Tla-o-qui-aht · Tofino 4 **BC** Qualicum Beach · Qualicum (FN/PN) · Qualicum Bay · Bowser · Fanny Bay · Union Bay · Royston · Cumberland · Courtenay · K'ómoks · Comox · CFB/BFC Comox · Black Creek · We Wai Kum · Campbell River **5 BC** Sandspit · Skidegate · Queen Charlotte · **YT** Whitehorse · Kwanlin Dun · **BC** Taku River Tlingit · Atlin **6 YT** Dawson City · Old Crow · **NT** Inuvik 7 **NU** Kugluktuk · **NT** Dettah · Ndilo · Yellowknife **8 AB** Grande Prairie · Fort McMurray · CFB/BFC Cold Lake · Cold Lake · 9 **SK** Lac La Ronge · La Ronge **MB** Thompson **10 MB** Churchill · **NU** CFS/SFC Alert **11 NU** Ausuittuq (Grise Fiord) · Qausuittuq (Resolute Bay) · Iqaluit 12 **QC** Kuujjuaq · Gaspé · Uashat Mak Mani-Utenam · Sept-Îles **13 NL** Wabush/Labrador City · CFB/BFC Goose Bay · Sheshatshiu · North West River · Happy Valley-Goose Bay **14 NL** Hopedale · L'Anse aux Meadows NHSC/LHNC · St. Anthony 15 **NL** Cape Spear NHSC/LHNC · Petty Harbour · Goulds · Conception Bay South · Manuels · Chamberlains · Topsail · Paradise · Mount Pearl · St. John's 16 **NL** Carbonear · Harbour Grace · Spaniard's Bay · Bay Roberts · Clarke's Beach · Cupids · Brigus · Clarenville · Glovertown · Gambo · Gander · Lewisporte · Bishop's Falls · Grand Falls-Windsor 17 **NL** Grand Falls-Windsor · Badger · Springdale · Deer Lake · Pasadena · Corner Brook · Port au Port · Kippens · Stephenville · Channel-Port aux Basques **18 NS** North Sydney · Sydney Mines · Membertou · Glace Bay · Dominion · Scotchtown · New Waterford · Sydney · Baddeck · Wagmatcook · Whycocomagh · Waycobah · Mabou · Port Hood · Judique · Port Hawkesbury **19 NS** Port Hawkesbury · Port Hastings · Tracadie · Paq'tnkek · Antigonish · New Glasgow · Trenton · Stellarton · Bible Hill · Truro 20 **NS** Truro · Millbrook · Stewiacke · Shubenacadie · Elmsdale · Enfield · Waverley · North Preston · Cherry Brook · Cole Harbour · Dartmouth · Beechville · Halifax **21 NS** Annapolis Royal · Bear River (FN/PN) · Yarmouth **22 NS** Halifax · Sackville · Windsor · Falmouth · Grand Pré · Wolfville · New Minas · Kentville · Kingston · CFB/BFC Greenwood · Middleton · New Germany · Bridgewater · Lunenburg 23 **NS** Amherst · **PE** Wood Islands · Belfast · Vernon Bridge · Cherry Valley · Pownal · Stratford · Charlottetown 24 **NS** Charlottetown · Cornwall · Winsloe · Hunter River · New Glasgow · Rusticoville · North Rustico · Cavendish · Stanley Bridge · New London · Clinton · Margate · Kensington · Lennox Island · Abram-Village · Wellington · Summerside 25 **NS** Summerside · Bedeque · Kinkora · Borden-Carleton · **NB** Port Elgin · Cap-Pelé · Shediac · Memramcook · Sackville · Dieppe · Moncton **26 NS** Moncton · Riverview · Lower Coverdale · Hillsborough · Hopewell Cape · Hopewell Rocks · Riverside-Albert · Alma · Fundy National Park · Sussex Corner · Sussex · Hampton · Quispamsis · Rothesay · Renforth · Saint John **27 NS** Saint John · Grand Bay-Westfield · Welsford · Oromocto (FN/PN) · Oromocto · CFB/BFC Gagetown · Lincoln · St. Mary's · Fredericton 28 Day off / Congé **29 NS** Fredericton · Taymouth · Boiestown · Doaktown · Blackville · Newcastle · Miramichi · Douglastown · Esgenoôpetitj · Neguac · Tracadie-Sheila · Shippagan · Caraquet · Grande-Anse · Bathurst **0 NS** Bathurst · Beresford · Oqpi'kanjik · Dalhousie · Campbellton · Atholville · Kedgwick · Saint-Quentin · Grand-Sault/Grand Falls · Saint-Léonard · Sainte-Anne-de-Madawaska · Rivière Verte · Madawaska · Edmundston 31 **NS** Edmundston · Saint-Jacques · **QC** Dégelis · Notre-Dame-du-Lac · Cabano · Saint-Louis-du-Ha! Ha! · Rivière-du-Loup · Cacouna · L'Isle-Verte · Trois-Pistoles · Saint-Simon · Saint-Fabien · Le Bic · Rimouski 32 **QC** Rimouski · Pointe-Au-Père · Sainte-Luce · Sainte-Flavie · Mont-Joli · Price · Métis-Sur-Mer · Baie-Des-Sables · Saint-Ulric · Matane · Baie-Comeau3 **QC** Baie-Comeau · Chute-aux-Outardes · Ragueneau · Pessamit · Forestville · Portneuf-sur-Mer · Longue-Rive · Les Escoumins · Essipit · Sacré-Coeur · Saint-Fulgence · Chicoutimi · Saguenay (Jonquière) **34 QC** Alma · Saint-Coeur-De-Marie · Sainte-Monique-De-Honfleur · Dolbeau-Mistassini · Saint-Félicien · Saint-Prime · Mashteuiatsh · Roberval · Chambord · Desbiens · Métabetchouan-Lac-à-la-Croix · Hébertville · Ville de Québec **35 QC** BFC/CFB Valcartier · Charlesbourg · Les Rivières · Limoilou · Beauport · Lac-Beauport · Wendake · La Haute-Saint-Charles · L'Ancienne-Lorette · Laurentien · Saint-Augustin-de-Desmaures · Sainte-Foy—Sillery · La Cité · Lévis 36 **QC** Montmagny · Lévis · Saint-Romuald · Saint-Jean-Chrysostome · Charny · Saint-Lambert-de-Lauzon · Scott · Sainte-Marie · Vallée-Jonction · Saint-Joseph-de-Beauce · Beauceville · Notre-Dame-des-Pins · Saint-Georges **37 QC** Saint-Prosper-de-Beauce · Saint-Georges · Saint-Benoît-Labre · Saint-Éphrem-de-Beauce · Sainte-Clotilde-de-Beauce · Robertsonville · Thetford Mines · Black Lake · Saint-Ferdinand · Plessisville · Princeville · Victoriaville · Warwick · Danville · Asbestos · Saint-Georges-de-Windsor · Windsor · Lennoxville · Sherbrooke **38 QC** Sherbrooke · Magog · Bromont · Cowansville · Granby · Saint-Dominique · Saint-Hyacinthe · Drummondville · Saint-Léonard-d'aston · Wôlinak · Bécancour · Trois-Rivières 39 **QC** Shawinigan · Nicolet · Odanak · Pierreville · Yamaska · Sorel-Tracy · Varennes · Sainte-Julie · Mont-Saint-Hilaire · Beloeil · Mcmasterville · Saint-Basile-le-Grand · Saint-Bruno-de-Montarville · Boucherville · Longueuil 40 **QC** Saint-Lambert · Greenfield Park · Longueuil · Brossard · Chambly · Iberville · Saint-Jean-sur-Richelieu · La Prairie · Candiac · Saint-Constant · Kahnawá:ke · Châteauguay · Mercier · Beauharnois · Salaberry-de-Valleyfield · Saint-Lazare · Hudson · Vaudreuil-Dorion · Pincourt · Sainte-Anne-de-Bellevue · Baie-d'urfé · Beaconsfield 41 **QC** Mont-Tremblant **42 QC** Montréal-Est · Mascouche · Terrebonne · Bois-des-Filion · Lorraine · Rosemère · Blainville · Sainte-Thérèse · Boisbriand · Sainte-Marthe-sur-le-Lac · Deux-Montagnes · Saint-Eustache · Laval · Dollard-des-Ormeaux · Kirkland · Pointe-Claire · Dorval · Montréal-Ouest · Côte-Saint-Luc · Hampstead · Mont-Royal · Westmount · Montréal **43 QC** Repentigny · L'Assomption · Joliette · Crabtree · Saint-Jacques · Saint-Lin-Laurentides · Sainte-Anne-des-Plaines · Mirabel · Saint-Jérôme · Lachute · Grenville · Hawkesbury · Montebello · Papineauville · Plaisance · Thurso · Masson-Angers · Buckingham · Gatineau 44 **QC** Aylmer · Hull · **ON** Ottawa · **45 ON** Ottawa · Kanata · Carleton Place · Almonte · Arnprior · Renfrew · Douglas · Eganville · Pikwàkanagàn · Golden Lake · CFB/BFC Petawawa · Petawawa · Pembroke **46 ON** Ottawa · Orleans · Rockland · Hammond · Limoges · Casselman · Cornwall · Akwesasne · Morrisburg · Prescott · Brockville · Gananoque · Kingston 47 **ON** Kingston · Odessa · Napanee · Tyendinaga · Deseronto · Picton · Belleville · CFB/BFC Trenton · Trenton · Brighton · Colborne · Cobourg · Port Hope · Bailieboro · Peterborough **48 ON** Peterborough · Lakefield · Curve Lake · Bridgenorth · Omemee · Lindsay · Orono · Newcastle · Bowmanville · Courtice · Oshawa 49 **ON** Oshawa · Whitby · Ajax · Pickering · Whitchurch-Stouffville · Markham · Richmond Hill · Thornhill · Toronto **50 ON** Toronto · Aurora · Newmarket · Sharon · Keswick · Bradford · Nobleton · Bolton · Nashville · Kleinburg · Vaughan · Brampton **51 ON** Brampton · Norval · Georgetown · Acton · Milton · Toronto · Mississauga · Port Credit · Clarkson · Oakville · Burlington · Hamilton 52 **ON** Hamilton · Stoney Creek · Fruitland · Winona · Grimsby · Beamsville · Vineland · Jordan · St. Catharines · Thorold · Virgil · Niagara-on-the-Lake · Queenston · Niagara Falls **53 ON** Niagara Falls · Chippawa · Fort Erie · Port Colborne · Welland · Fonthill · Dunnville · Cayuga · Caledonia · Six Nations · Brantford **54 ON** Brantford · Paris · Scotland · Simcoe · Delhi · Courtland · Tillsonburg · Aylmer · St. Thomas · Oneida of the Thames · Chippewas of the Thames · Munsee-Delaware · Rodney · Ridgetown · Blenheim · Chatham 55 **ON** Chatham · North Buxton · Tilbury · Comber · Leamington · Point Pelee National Park · Kingsville · Essex · McGregor · Amherstburg · Lasalle · Windsor 56 **ON** Windsor · Tecumseh · Bkejwanong · Wallaceburg · Corunna · Aamjiwnaang · Sarnia · Forest · Strathroy · London 57 · Day off / Congé · **58** Day off / Congé **59 ON** London · Thamesford · Ingersoll · Woodstock · Tavistock · Stratford · Shakespeare · New Hamburg · New Dundee · Cambridge · Waterloo · Kitchener 60 **ON** Kitchener · Guelph · Erin · Alton · Orangeville · Shelburne · Mount Forest · Durham · Hanover · Walkerton · Kincardine · Tiverton · Port Elgin · Southampton · Saugeen · Owen Sound **61 ON** Owen Sound · Meaford · Thornbury · Blue Mountain · Collingwood · Wasaga Beach · Elmvale · Wyebridge · Penetanguishene · Midland · Creemore · Angus · CFB/BFC Borden · Alliston · Cookstown · Barrie **62 ON** Barrie · Orillia · Rama · Gravenhurst · Bracebridge · Huntsville · Wasauksing · Parry Sound · Sundridge · South River · Powassan · North Bay 63 **ON** Nipissing · Temagami · Latchford · Cobalt · Haileybury · Temiskaming Shores (New Liskeard) · **QC** Notre-Dame-du-Nord · Timiskaming · Évain · Rouyn-Noranda · Cadillac · Malartic · Val-d'Or 64 **QC** Val-d'Or · Pikogan · Amos · **ON** Virginiatown · Larder Lake · Kirkland Lake · Matheson · Iroquois Falls · South Porcupine · Timmins 65 **ON** Onaping · Dowling · Chelmsford · Sudbury · Espanola · Massey · Elliot Lake · Blind River · Mississauga (FN/PN) · Thessalon · Ketegaunseebee · Sault Ste. Marie **66 ON** Sault Ste. Marie · Wawa · White River · Marathon · Terrace Bay · Schreiber · Red Rock (FN/PN) · Nipigon · Thunder Bay **67 ON** Fort William · Thunder Bay · Kakabeka Falls · Upsala · Ignace · Dryden · Vermilion Bay · Wauzhushk Onigum · Kenora 68 **ON** Kenora · Keewatin · Iskatewizaagegan No. 39 · **MB** Falcon Lake · Richer · Ste. Anne · Steinbach · Dugald · Oakbank · Selkirk · Winnipeg **69 MB** Gimli · Peguis · St. Laurent · **70 MB** Winnipeg · Oak Bluff · Sanford · Brunkild · Carman · Roland · Winkler · Morden · Elm Creek · Oakville · Portage la Prairie 71 **MB** Dakota Tipi · Portage la Prairie · Long Plain · Gladstone · Neepawa · Minnedosa · Forrest Station · CFB/BFC Shilo · Brandon 72 **MB** Brandon · Sioux Valley Dakota · Virden · **SK** Moosomin · Yorkton · Melville · Fort Qu'appelle · Regina 73 **SK** Regina · CFB/BFC Moose Jaw · Moose Jaw · Caronport · Mortlach · Morse · Herbert · Swift Current **74 SK** Swift Current · Kyle · Elrose · Rosetown · Delisle · Vanscoy · Saskatoon · Wanuskewin Heritage Park · Warman · Osler · Hague · Rosthern · Duck Lake · Prince Albert **75 SK** Prince Albert · Shellbrook · Leask · Blaine Lake · Hafford · North Battleford · Battleford · Moosomin (FN/PN) · Saulteaux (FN/PN) · Cochin · Maidstone · Lashburn · Marshall · **AB/SK** Lloydminster 76 **AB/SK** Lloydminster · **AB** Kitscoty · Vermilion · St. Paul · Vegreville · Sherwood Park · Fort Saskatchewan · Namao · St. Albert · Edmonton **77** Day off / Congé **78 AB** Stony Plain · Spruce Grove · Enoch · Devon · Beaumont · Leduc · Camrose · Wetaskiwin · Hobbema · Ponoka · Lacombe · Sylvan Lake · Red Deer 79 **AB** Innisfail · Bowden · Olds · Torrington · Trochu · Three Hills · Drumheller · Rosedale · Hoodoos · Siksika · Gleichen · Brooks · Ralston · CFB/BFC Suffield · Redcliff · Medicine Hat **80 AB** Medicine Hat · Seven Persons · Bow Island · Burdett · Grassy Lake · Taber · Coaldale · Coalhurst · Lethbridge 81 **AB** Kainai · Fort MacLeod · Head-Smashed-In Buffalo Jump · Granum · Claresholm · Stavely · Nanton · High River · Okotoks · Calgary · **82 AB** Calgary · Chestermere · Strathmore · Irricana · Beiseker · Crossfield · Airdrie **83 AB** Calgary · Canada Olympic Park · Springbank · Cochrane · Stoney Nation · Nakiska · Exshaw · Canmore · Banff · 84 **AB** Banff · Lake Louise · **BC** Kicking Horse Pass · Field · Golden **85 BC** Golden · Nicholson · Parson · Edgewater · Kootenay National Park · Radium Hot Springs · Shuswap · Invermere · Windermere · Akisqnuk · Fairmont Hot Springs · Canal Flats · Kimberley · Marysville · Cranbrook **86 BC** Elkford · Sparwood · Fernie · Cranbrook · Moyie · Yahk · Kitchener · Erickson · Creston · Kootenay Pass · Salmo · Ymir · Nelson **87 BC** Nelson · Shoreacres · Tarrys · Robson · Castlegar · Genelle · Fruitvale · Beaver Falls · Montrose · Trail · Warfield · Rossland · Christina Lake · Grand Forks · Greenwood · Midway · Rock Creek · Osoyoos **88 BC** Osoyoos (FN/PN) · Osoyoos · Oliver · Okanagan Falls · Kaleden · Penticton · Penticton (FN/PN) · Summerland · Peachland · West Kelowna · Westbank (FN/PN) · Kelowna · 89 · Kelowna / Lake Country · Coldstream · Vernon · Spallumcheen · Armstrong · Enderby · Grindrod · Sicamous · Malakwa · Revelstoke **90 BC** Revelstoke · Craigellachie (Last Spike) · Canoe · Salmon Arm · Sexqeltqin · Tappen · Blind Bay · Sorrento · Chase · Pritchard · Kamloops **91 BC** Revelstoke · Craigellachie (Last Spike) · Canoe · Salmon Arm · Sexqeltqin · Tappen · Blind Bay · Sorrento · Chase · Pritchard · Kamloops · Tk'emlups · Kamloops · Barriere · Clearwater · Little Fort · Lone Butte · 100 Mile House · 108 Mile Ranch · Lac La Hache · 150 Mile House · T'exelc · Williams Lake · 92 · Williams Lake · Kersley · Lhtako · Quesnel · Hixon · Prince George · Valemount · McBride **93 BC** Mackenzie · Prince George · Fort St. James · Nak'azdli · Vanderhoof · Fort Fraser · Fraser Lake · Stellat'en · Burns Lake · Lake Babine · Topley · Houston · Telkwa · Smithers · Moricetown · New Hazelton **94 BC** Dawson Creek · Tumbler Ridge · Chetwynd · Saulteau · Hudson's Hope · Fort St. John · Hagwilget Village · Gitanmaax · Hazelton 95 **BC** Fort Nelson (FN/PN) · Fort Nelson · Haisla · Kitimat · Terrace · Kitsumkalum · New Aiyansh · Prince Rupert **96 BC** Bella Bella · Gwa'Sala-Nakwaxda'xw · Port Hardy 97 **BC** Kwakiutl · Port Hardy · Port McNeill · Sliammon · Powell River **98 BC** Powell River · Saltery Bay · Earls Cove · Pender Harbour · Madeira Park · Sechelt · Shíshálh · Roberts Creek · Gibsons · Hopkins Landing · Langdale · Lions Bay · Furry Creek · Britannia Beach · Stawamus · Squamish **99 BC** Squamish · Brackendale · Whistler Olympic Park · Whistler 100 **BC** Whistler · Pemberton · Lil'wat · Tsalalh · Sekw'el'was · Lillooet · Xaxli'p · Ts'kw'aylaxw · St'uxwtews · Cache Creek · Ashcroft · Logan Lake · Scw'exmx · Merritt **101 BC** Merritt · Princeton · Hope · Seabird Island · Harrison Hot Springs · Agassiz · Rosedale · Chilliwack · Abbotsford **102 BC** Mission · Maple Ridge · Pitt Meadows · Walnut Grove · Fort Langley · Aldergrove · Langley (Township) · Langley · Cloverdale · Surrey 103 **BC** Surrey · White Rock · Peace Arch · North Delta · New Westminster · Tsawwassen · Tsawwassen (FN/PN) · Ladner · Richmond **104 BC** Bowen Island · Horseshoe Bay · Squamish (Xwemelch'stn) · North Vancouver · Tsleil-Waututh (FN/PN) · North Vancouver (District) · West Vancouver 105 **BC** Belcarra · Anmore · Port Moody · Port Coquitlam · Coquitlam · Burnaby · Musqueam (FN/PN) · University of British Columbia · Vancouver **106 BC** Vancouver · BC Place

Torchbearers / *Porteurs de flambeau* **1** Julie Adams · Kristy Aikman · Rick Anderson · Dan Beddoes · Marcella Bernardo · Pierre-Philippe Bibeau · Annie Braiden · Connor Brown · Robert Brunet · Andrew Byrnes · David Calder · Cynthia Cameron · Brianne Camilleri · Mahisha Canagasuriam · Jieru Cen · Joseph Chan · Jamie Cheveldave · Rob Chiasson · Susie Clee · Murray David Collins · Mel Cooper · Walter Corey · Jillian Coutu · Kevin Crawford · Allie Delarge · Marie Denton · Alexandre Despatie · Emma Djilali · Iqbal Dodd · Nicholas Dronsfield · Clarice Durnerin · Shelley Eaves · Heike Eckert · Victoria Elliott · Jeneece Endroff · Diane Falconer · Allison Forsyth · Barbara Fosdick · Doug Foster · Chris Gailus · Jill Gardiner · Edward Robert George · Beatrice Gill · Joseph Gollner · Rich Gorman · Meghan Griffiths · Bryan Hall · Kyle Hamilton · Patricia Jeanne Hannah · Neil Harbun · Simon Harrington · Roxanne Harris · Aimee Hawker · Herbert Hopkins · Malcolm Howard · Shannon Huff · Bill Jones · Chris Kantowicz · Christine Katnich · Aun Kazmi · Makenzie Konwick · Dimitrios Koutougos · Adam Kreek · Kevin Kwasinski · Anthony Laporta · Silken Laumann · Catriona Le May Doan · Bonnie Leadbeater · Karen Leggett · Emily Lerhe · Sharlane Letwin · Kevin Light · Craig Logan · Cheryl Longo · Ed Low · Shauna Lukaitis · Ian MacDonald · Suzie Mack · Jason Mackay · Rebecca Mand · Brian Marshall · Gary Maclean Mason · Adele Matte · Joshua Maurer · Dave McGregor · Jon McKay · Benjamin Meek · Charlotte Mitchell · Ashley Molholm · Shelagh Morrison · Denise Myhre · Aaron Nakatsu · Geneva Nam · Siamak Namazee · Walter John Natynczyk · Alex Nelson · Graham Obee · Terrance Owen · Daphne Panter · Alicia Pawluk · Loring Phinney · Max Plaxton · Louis Poirier · Henry Polessky · Derek Porter · Carl Powell · Danielle Preyser · Brian Price · Pamela Pysyk · Rob Reid · Daniel Rhodes · Gregory Rickwood · Morgan Grace Roberts · Lloyd Robertson · Marc Saunders · Linda Schaumleffel · Dominic Seiterle · Ken Shields · Roger Skillings · Dave Small · Brigitte Soucy · Mike Spracklen · Katie St.John · Janet Sutherland-Hansen · Gregory Swift · Moogly T. Hamel · Alysha Taylor · Chad Tenney · Sally Tian · Morgan Tierney · Lucie Tremblay · Lee Turner · Aalbert Van Schothorst · Wayne Verch · Josianne Vlitos · Dean Walker · Jennifer Wesleyson · Jake Wetzel · Simon Whitfield · Sean Wiggins · Racheal Wilkie · Erinne Willock · Kimberly Winiski · Douglas Woodward · Les Yard · Melody Zaleschuk **2** Hadi Abassi · Stephen Aikman · Lindsaye Akhurst · Tammy Amber · Luke Antrim · Karen Armstrong · Jane Arnold · Pat Battie · Thomas Benson · Fred Blue · Patricia Brady · Tanner Brady-Springer · Rick Brant · Heather Brekke · Jack Broodo · Blaire Brown · Michael Burgess · Erin Burrett · Barb Byrne · Ji Ye Cao · Val Carver · Patricia Cheung · Daniele Chiesa · Dean Christie · Dawn Coe-Jones · Wendy Cracknell · Steven Cross · Maureen Cuddy · Michael Cunliffe · Michelle Cuthbert · Raffi Daghlian · Tiffany Darian · Ninon Daubigeon · Anton Dharmaseelan · Patricia Domingo · Lydia Dorman · Jeffrey Dubney · Riley Dunlop · Laurie Dyck · Christine Elliott · Richard Ellis · Tom English · Archie Erigaktuk · Annie Ewart · Evan Fagan · Micheline Fedorko · Toby Fender · Erica Finnsson · Ursula Fisher · Vincent Fong · Donnalyn Forbes · Laney Galloway · Nancy Gerein · Drew Gervais · Owen Green · Richer Guinto · Nicole Hall · Antony Harris · Carolyn Harty · Dale Harvey · Philip Haseldine · Ron Hinkelman · James Ho · Jeff Hollands · Mila Huebsch · Christopher Iverson · Gina Jung · Susan Kelsey · Jennifer Kennedy · Bob Khalil · Melanie Knight · Jennifer Kroeker-Hall · Albert Lee · Ryan Lock · Tanya Logan · Lindsay MacAskill · Graham MacLachlan · Jennifer Marr · Shelley Marshall · James Mather · Darian Maxwell · Pooja McArthur · Patty McCann · Gary McCollum · Seamus McGrath · Shelagh McGrogan · Eileen McMurchy · Deb Melnyk · Corbin Miller · Lani Mino · Laura Mongeau · Derral Moriyama · Sky Mundell · Roger Mundell · Carolyn Murray · John Nightingale · Donald Elmer Nykiforuk · Tina Obrien · Beau Olmstead · Michael O'Rielly · Miles Ostler · Sandra Owens · Selena Owsienko · Chris Pagan · Arielle Past · Dylan Paul-Seward · Livia Pellegrino · Richard Peter · Gordon Planes · Wayne Procter · Jim Reed · Sarah Renowden · Darcy Rezac · Carole Robertson · Gary Rodwell · Stephen Ross-Recalma · Laura Sampson · Susan Sanderson · Inci Sarp · Elise Schoeller · Dan Scott · Richard Scott · Paul Seaman · Nicole Seeley · Donald Senft · Jacqueline Shan · Audrey Shaw · Harold Sheck · Marian Sieradzan · Trish Smiley · Vince Smith · Bruce Sprague · Michelle Stilwell · Molly Summerhayes · Jared Szabo · Lawrence Tang · Derek Tangedal · Janelle Timmins · Hailey Toriglia · Neil Tracey · Linda Tremblay · Tom Turnbull · Matthew Varey · Susanne Ventura · Francis Viscount · Mary Wallace · Melissa Weder · Jessica White · Jordan Wilson · Kodiak Woods · Ben Yip · Kirsten Yu · Grant Zink **3** Keri Adams · Christian Arbez · Jacobus Arentsen · Joe Audette · Wendy Avis · Claire Beckstead · Janet Beedle · Rebecca Bianchini · Ivan Bilenki · Darren Bodner · Michele Boivin · Zita Botelho · Paul Brandl · Shivauna Brown · Raphael Bruhwiler · Lindsay Brumwell · Andy Buchan · Stephen Burton · Curtis Carmen · Glen Carter · Anne Chalmers · Leo Chan · Carol-Anne Chemko · Carol Christie · Lee Kyung Chun · Rob Clements · Aleisha Cline · Angus Cook · Melissa Coon · Michelle Cooper · Travis Cross · Mark Cunningham · Donald Currie · Gord Cutler · Mario da Silva · Kya Dalton · Bailey Dalton · Elizabeth Davidson · Lee Davis · Lisa Denton · Peter Devries · Terry Dewispelaere · Kate Dunford · Jennifer Erickson · David Facey · Laura Fauth · Joanne Flasch · Ian Fraser · Shane Fraser · Sharon Froud · James Gallic Sr · Charles Garrett · Eleanor Garrett · Glen Garrick · Benny George · Robert Goguillot · David Grace · Janice Greenwood-Fraser · Al Greir · Christopher Hakes · Juliann Hamilton · Donna Hansey · Gerold Haukenfrers · Lesley Hazeldine · Bruce Hoggard · Mark Holliday · Natalie Holloway · Aaron How · Amy Hung · Rusty Hunt · Anthony Irwin · Sean Jamieson · Jennifer Janssens · David Johnson · Janice Karasiuk · Ayisha Karim · Warren Keller · Shane Kerwin · Mohsen Kheari · Brian Kossey · Angela Koulyras · Steven Krakowka · Kristina Krieck · Adam Laird · Sarah Larose · Cory Lee · Adam Long · Brendan Lundy-Sam · Tu Ly · Alex Mainella · Alon Marcovici · Angus McAllister · Bruce McBride · Samantha McBride · Roger McDonell · Bruce McHardy · John McInnes · Leeland McNabb · Jason Minter · Riley Monnet · Virginia Mulhall · Leslie Murray · Derek Niziol · Bryon Noble · Kelly Nordman · Dan Norman · Tammie O'Rourke · Jeff Osgarby · Gord Pace · Derek Page · Austen Perry · Amanda Pitre-Hayes · Caren Porter · Andrea Price · Scott Rae-Arthur · Peter Raptis · Marlo Raynolds · Bryan Read · Oscar Reeves · Cliff Reynolds · Paul Richardson · Serge Roy · Tim Rundle · Ruth Sadler · Lisa Saffarek · Jason Salisbury · Tim Scott · Leeann Signorotti · Richard Stasuik · Jason Stevenson · Joanne Stone-Campbell · Brian Sugiyama · Susan Takashiba · Stephen Tam · Dave Tanchak · Camela Tang · Denise Taschereau · Isaiah Taylor · Scott Thomas · Donna Marie Thompson · Kelsey Thorne · Kyla Todesco · John Tom Sr. · Geoffrey Tourond · Emily Tranfield · Heather Tremain · Carmen Turner · Yvonne Visser · Bonnie Warren · Suzanne Watson · Hughie Michael Clint Watts Jr. · Michelle Weldon · Eliot White-Hill · Alan Whittall · Kathleen Wlodarczak · Elaine Wong · Daniel Hanwei Wu · John Zaplatynsky **4** Eric Alexandre · Emily Armstrong · Lauren Baldwin · Janet Bauer · Patricia Beaudin · Richard Black · James Blake · Isabelle Boisvert · John Bonell · Steve Boultbee · Barbara Boyling · Matthijs Bruining · Michael Burke · Terry Burns · Beth Burt · Rodger Burton · Jerry Byca · Lorenz Cagna · Courtney Cameron · Brian Cant · Michael Casagrande · Barb Cassidy · Shaelyn Chase · Darren Comeau · Charlene Conn · Heather Corra · Debbie Coulson · Laurel Crosby · Susan Cumberland · Anne Davey · Donald Davis · Gordon Delaval · Katherine Deschutter · Cody Despins · Dirk Driedger · Robert Dumonceau · Carrie Dusterhoft · Diane Eccles · Gary Egli · Chloe Elston · John Elzinga · Sally Feast · Arlene Forbes · Chris Forbes · Steve Ford · Donna Fraser · Jordan Fraser · Chris Gadsby · Vaughan Garrett · Stacy Gorman · Valerie Gould · Judy Grattan · Jim Greenwood · Stephen Grundy · Maya Gunawan · Brenda Gunn · Cameron Haight · Peter Haley · Dana Hall · Helen Hall · Daniel Hanton · Bent Harder · Richard Hardy · Mandeep Hayer · Dave Hederson · Elizabeth Heinz · Darrell Hillier · Meaghan Hock · Daniel Hogarth · Elaine Holoshka · James Hopkins · Grace Howard · Bobbi Howard-Muir · Janet Jenkins · Christine Jochimski · Rachel Johns · Ramona Johnson · Virginia Johnston · Robert Joncas · Peter Judge · Raj Kalsi · Mark Kelsey · Catalina Kennedy-Burgoyne · Deborah Kitchener · Karen Koppel · Wayne Krawchuk · Michel Lalumiere · Jo-Anne Landine · John Lapp · Rosamund Latvala · Haley Lauten · Serena Leblond · Daryl Michael Lecompte · Nathan Lee · Tony Lee · Cassandra Lee · Tom Lennox · Dave Lineker · Sharon Lingenfelter · Mark Lovick · John MacKenzie · Rachel Madera · Alexander Malekyazdi · Nader Malekyazdi · Shahram Malekyazdi · Lynda Malkoske · Stevan Mandy · Eric Mansueti · Daniel Marshall · Tracy McMicking · Steve McNamee · Bob McNary · Bryan Mills · Tony Mok · Robert Mondeville · Linda Moore · Steve Nagle · Drew Natland · Shannon Nering-Moody · William Ng · Kevin O'Neill · Ray Owens · Tina Pace · Joanne Parkes · Michelle Petherbridge · Leslie Phillips · Cindy Phillips · Joanne Phillips · Angela Plamondon · Robert Podhrasky · Carol Pomeroy · Meagan Prokopanko · Al Pullin · Cora Pullin · Tej Rasoda · Jessie Recalma · Graham Reid · Kyle Rennie · Lana Riva-Crerar · David Roach · Blaze Roberts · MacKenzie Roth · Flynn Saunderson · Ken Schley · Elaine Shymko · Tom Slater · Shawna Smythe · Kevin Spicer · Andrea Stapff · Jeff Stipec · Michaela Strain · Gil Stuart · Tara Stump · Terry Thomas · Bonaventure Thorburn · Shawn Tomczyk · Robert Trainor · George Tsonis · Brian Turnham · Stephen Unser · Joanne Van Egmond · Lauren VanSickle · Carmen Vonpetzinger · Russ Wagg · Janet Weikum · Chris White · Ed Widenmaier · Shirley Wong · Milton Wong · Sarah Louise Champion Wuntke · Kevin Young · Patrick Young · Joe Zemp · Amber Zirnhelt **5** Cheryl Alexander · Cassandra Andrew · Montana Bailie · Stacity Bailie · Gary Bailie · Pamela Bangart · Maureen Benoit · Michel Bernier · Chelsea Bien · Colby Blair · Skyler Boulton-Brown · Fay Branigan · Tabitha Brown · Sara Burke-Forsyth · William Callaghan · Billy Callahan · Julianna Campbell · Autumn Carlick · Charquinta Carlick · Deana Carlick · Brett Chandler · Jamie Clinch · Micah Copland · Jenelle Cousins · Andrew Crist · Rodney D'Abramo · Bill Dallas · Nathan Dawson · Nadia Eddy · Tom Fairman · Ramesh Ferris · Aurora Gowler · Joseph Graham · Sharon Greer · Red Grossinger · Justin Halowaty · Jami Harris · Lorri Hume · Jocelyn Janzen · Samuel Johnston · Hal Jordan · Lynsey Keaton · Calvin Laveck · Britanee Laverdure · David Laxton · Kara Lepine · Tanya Lucci · Carol-Lynne Luelo · Tippy Mah · Thoa Mai · Kim McMullen · James Mills · Alan Moore · Owen Munroe · Kiana Palamar · Maya Poirier · Jessica Pruden · Courtney Quinn · Wilhemina Robert · Chad Scully · Sean Sheardown · Brandi Smith · Sean Smith · Brenda Spicer · Jamie Tetlichi · Mike Thorpe · Steve Tippett · Charissa Tizya · Stewart Tizya · Christopher Vance · Brandon Webb · Percy Williams · Willard Wilson · Mark Wykes · Dallas Yeulett · Kat Zrum **6** Rebecca Baxter · Martha Benjamin · Allan Benjamin · Alisa Camplin · Trey Charlie · Fred Church · Nellie Cournoyea · Suzanne Crocker · Sharon Firth · Lance Gray · Joan Groothuysen · Micalah Hanthorn · Annah Hanthorn · Sarah Hanthorn · Joel Hanthorn · Elizabeth Illasiak · Margie Kormendy · Joseph Lirette · Lorraine Lokos · Kevin Mendelsohn · Peter Menzies · Mark Lee Orbell · Anita Pettersen · Matthew Skinner · Abel Tingmiak · Erika Tizya-Tramm · Annika Trimble **7** Gavin Ayalik · Jordon Balanuik · Kris Ballard · Julie Belliveau · Cara Benoit · Helena Bolt · Kelly Ann Boucher · Marty Bouvier · Terence Brace · Ryan Charlo · Pooja Chugh · Chris Cochrane · Harley Crowe · Darlene Dahl · Jason Daniel · Conan Donahue · Dianne Dul · Marry Enerio · Boris Eyakfwo · Alain Flamand · Ritchie Football · Jeff Gardiner · David Gilday · Shauna Goulet · Edward Hunt · Mark Huntley · Regan Jeremick'ca · Colin Jerome Judas · Terry Kuliktana · Jimmy Laboline · Steven Lafferty · David Lafferty · Thomas Lafferty · Donna Latremouille · Dori-Ann Lefoin · Terrance Liske · Nelson Mantla · Rusty Mantla · Laura Mcbride · Douglas McCannan · Dave Monroe · Conrad Nabess · Crystal Navratil · Sarah Nesbitt · Dolphus Nitsiza · Albert Jr Nitsiza · George Nitsiza · Leon Nitsiza · Molly O'Callaghan · Kate Pierce · Geela Qaqqasiq · Elton Rabesca · Aaron Reid · Victor Rentura · Joy Roberts · Trudy Schlosser · Megan Shaben · Darren Sharko · Larry Sterns · William Stirling · Kathleen Sullivan · Jerry Sweet · Shaun Thagard · Gordon Thompson · Eleanor Tolentino · Kim Truter · Benjamin Veldman · Adam Wixted · Mike Yakabuski · Jeanne Yurris **8** Eric Anderson · Erin Anderson · Lindy Beauchamp-Chester · Tanya Bond · Gilles Brine · Laura Brophy · Carol Costello · Annemarie Diachinsky · Marie-Eve Doucet · Kaibree Drake · Marie-Sonia Dubreuil · Michelle Elliott · Murray Gauthier · Paul Gemmiti · Leigh Goldie · Garth Grubisich · Maureen Hall · Christopher Adam Horch · Steven Jani · Carrie Jazwinski · Chandrashekhar Jere · Audrey Jordan · Sammy Kenol · Kevin Kleininger · Daniel Labonte · Daryl McIntyre · Megan McKenny · Emma McMahon · Gerard Messier · Pierce Mimura · Meghan Monette · Shannon O'Halloran · Jacques Plante · Karen Poirier · Cory Robertson · Joe Rodier · Gary Sandeman-Allen · Jason Sarrazin · David Scharf · Francene Scott · Douglas Shannon · Kelly Sutherland · Mark Terstappen · Keith Thibault · Barbara Ann Totti · Brian Michael Walsh · Brian Wareham · Franz Ludwig Wiesmann · Patricia Zofia Wrobel · Elsie Yanik · Josephine Enid Yearley · Mikaela York **9** Eric Anderson · Erin Anderson · Lindy Beauchamp-Chester · Tanya Bond · Gilles Brine · Laura Brophy · Carol Costello · Annemarie Diachinsky · Marie-Eve Doucet · Kaibree Drake · Marie-Sonia Dubreuil · Michelle Elliott · Sean Daniel Finnegan · Murray Gauthier · Paul Gemmiti · Leigh Goldie · Garth Grubisich · Maureen Hall · Christopher Adam Horch · Steven Jani · Carrie Jazwinski · Chandrashekhar Jere · Audrey Jordan · Sammy Kenol · Kevin Kleininger · Daniel Labonte · Daryl McIntyre · Megan McKenny · Emma McMahon · Gerard Messier · Pierce Mimura · Meghan Monette · Shannon O'Halloran · Jacques Plante · Karen Poirier · Cory Robertson · Joe Rodier · Gary Sandeman-Allen · Jason Sarrazin · David Scharf · Francene Scott · Douglas Shannon · Kelly Sutherland · Mark Terstappen · Keith Thibault · Barbara Ann Totti · Brian Michael Walsh · Brian Wareham · Franz Ludwig Wiesmann · Patricia Zofia Wrobel · Elsie Yanik · Josephine Enid Yearley · Mikaela York **10** Deborah Bowker · Dylan Burton · Suzanne Charest · Darryl Foster · Terry Gibbons · Sylvain Giguère · Muhtar Kent · Krzysztof (Kris) Kumor · Louise Lawrie · Roxanne Lodge · Jason Macaulay · Inootiq Manik · Ron Mechefske · Daniel Mikkonen · Mark Overby · Roel Pacheco · Graham Pope · Joe Pope · Carter Roberts · John Ryan · Daniel Smith · Karl Spital · William Stafford · George Stewart · Joanne Stover · Gilbert Tremblay · Geétan Tremblay · Morgan Wilson **11** Brent Aitken · Michel Albert · Maxine Angoo · Rae-Lynne Aramburo · Chad Aramburo · Moses Aronsen · Karen Ball · Sarah Brown · Mary Carillo · Carol Anne Chiasson · Cindy Cowan · Celine Devlin · Jessica Dewar · Sead Dizdarevic · Darrell Dunn · Brenda Eckalook · Larry Fawcett · Marc Gabriel · Sammie Gary · Attima Hadlari · Victoria Hann · Sidney Horlick · Beth Idlout-Kheraj · David Iou · Elisapee Ipeelie · Johnny Issaluk · Akeeagok Jayko · Paul Kaludjak · Corey Kanzig · Earle Kielly · Ailsa Lapp · Clifford Laurin · Jamie LeBlanc · Tim Letemplier · Thomas Levi · Caleb Little · Jessie Lloyd · Robert Long · Katie MacDonald · Duncan MacKay · Janna MacLachlan · John Maurice · Patrick McClarty · Eva Michael · Jesse Mike · Sharla Mulley · Chantelle Noble · Steven Nungaq · Susie Pearce · Rudy Santos · Kyle St. Laurent · Alex Stult · Joe Tikivik · Crystal Tobin · Simon Tookoome · Svetlana Tumilty · Dwayne Twerdin · Natar Ungalaq · Kristine Watsko · Sherri Young · Daniel Young **12** Anthony Arreak · Serge Belanger · Gaston Bernier · Normand Bouchard · Gilles Briand · Mathew Cabot · Kevin Caouette · Claudine Duke · Jacques Frigon · Clemence Gagnon · Raymond Gallant · Donald Gonthier · Lise Grace · Marie Grenier · Camille Huard · Cindy Koneak · Manon LaBillois · Marie Labrie · Michel Lachance · Leonard Landry · Jean-Pierre Lantelgne · Debra Laurie · Guillaume LeBlanc · Andre Lessard · Camil Mckinnon · Margot Methot · Janie Paquet · Yves Perron · Chantal Pitt · Serge Roy · Bernice Savoie · Evelyne St-Onge · Brad St-Onge · Lukasi Tukkiapik · Roger Vachon · Yvon Valliere **13** Andrew Battcock · Krista Blizzard · Brian Bowerman · Jennifer Davis · Keith Dort · Sue Goguen · Rachel Gordon · Joe Goudie · Sarah Hanna · Joan Harvey · Dotty Kelland · Aimee Lavallee · Jody Lawrence · Joshua Lawrence · John Lorimer · Ann Massie · Raegan Meadows · Catherine Maria Murphy · Jamie Nui · Karen Oldford · Alf Parsons · Betty Parsons · Norman Peddle · Max Peddle · Nickshantess Penashue · Sterling Peyton · Fay Pittman · Larry Pittman · Troy Randell · Jeremy Reid · Annie Thibodeau · Ross Tourout · Mary Tourout · Jonathan Tourout · Tim Tuttle · Dean Vey · Teena Vivian · David White · Dave Winters **14** Gabrielle Allingham · Willie Allingham · Callie Applin · Nancy Baines Toope · Kylie Beals · Chelsea Caines · Robert Cecil Cole · Sarah Coombs · Stacie Coombs · Sidney Coombs · Brady Cunard · Devon Doyle · Lisa Doyle · Miguel Dredge · Alex Gibbons · Jasmin Gibbons · Frank Humber · Amanda Kean · Bradley Mahar · Boas Mitsuk · Michael Mitsuk · Margaret Myers · Wade Richards · Brittany Scanlon · Brandon Sinnicks · Bernice Smith · Colton Tatchell · Daniel Windeler · Grant Young **15** Mike Adam · Bonnie Andrews · Laurie Andrews · Alexa Bailey · Richel Abigail Balatbat · Alison Ball · Jillian (O'Donel) Balsom · Gary Beck · John Bennion · Jill Benoit · Rick Bidgood · Derm Bishop · Pauline Bohnec · Ron Brennan · Nadia Brenton · Chad Brinson · Sharon Brophy · Deanne Burton Snow · Albert Butler · Paul Campbell · Christophe Caron · Stephen Clark · Albert Clarke · Mary Cook · Curtis Coon · Lyne Cormier · Adam Courage · G. Andy Crewe · Ross Crocker · Elly Culligan · Tony Cumby · Darryl Day · Brittany Dean · Paula Delaney · Stacie Devereaux · Katie Dicker · Michael Dinn · Mark Dobbin · April Drake · Guy Dredge · Danielle Drover · Catherine Ducey · Sheila Ereaut · Jerry Evans · George Faulkner · Coral Field · Brent Foote · Ellen Ford · Scott Giannou · Adam Gilbert · Joylan Gonsalves · Kelsey Guy · Brian Haines · Ashley Hammond · Jim Harris · Gerard Hayes · Ed Hedderson · Lesley Herridge · Kristine Hibbs · Bert Hickey · Jonathan Hicks · Jeff Holmes · Colin Howse · Gordon Ingram · Andrew Ivey · Brad Jacobs · Sharon Jacques · Terry Jeremie · Rod Jerrett · Eileen Joe · Victoria Kaminski · Melva Kelland · David King · Darinka Kolenko · Gillian Lambert · Matthew Lehman · Maureen Lethbridge · Nicole Lewis · Don Ludlow · Jason MacDonald · Roy Donald MacGregor · Joshua Marshall · Karen Martin · Diane Martin · Kevin Martin · Chris Martin · Gary Martin · Bud Mercer · Karen Miller · Trevor Murphy · Nicole O'Brien · Maggie O'Dea · Donna O'Grady · Susan Onalik · Seamus O'Regan · Dan Owens · Pat Parfrey · Marguerite Parsons · Krista Parsons Butler · Jon Pawson · David Penner · Shawn Peters · Rick Piercey · Melanie Pinsent · Daniel Pottle · Lucas Power · Robin Purcell · Daiwantie Ramphal · Rebecca Raymond · Janet Reddy · Emma Reelis · Tatiana Revenco · Timothy Rider · Jordan Ridgeley · Lorie Robbins · Lesley Robertson · Nikki Rose · Katarina Roxon · Susan Ryan Goldsworthy · Jacqueline Selma · Solomon Semigak · Rebecca Sharr · Christopher Sheppard · Bambie Sherwin · Mina Fatemeh Shirvani · Tina Slunt · Terri-Lynne Smith · Scott Smith · Kyle Smook · Erika Sottile · Paul Sparkes · Lynn Sparkes · Marcia Spence · Brenda Spurrell · Mark Stanford · Terence Stone · Gerry Taylor · Sean Tobin · Andrew Troy · David (O'Donel) Tucker · Chris Turnbull · Ryan Valleriani · Patty Valleriani · Karen Wakeham · Lynn Walker · Adele Walsh · Egbert Walters · Andrea Ward · Angela Wareham · Tiffany Warren · Phyllis Weir · Sherry White · Madonna Whitten · Jeremy Whittle · Toni-Marie Wiseman · Polly Wong · Peter Woodward · Lynn Young **16** Don Bartlett · Monisha Bedi · Cameron Bennett · Garry Best · Seamus Boyd-Porter · Ryan Bradbury · Allison Bragg · Noelle Breen · Michael Burke · Kayla Cantwell · Diana Carroll · Linda Chao · Sandy Chiasson · Roy Chiu · Tracy Coish · Mark Colbourne · Corvin Colbourne · Michelle Connors · Jean Corbett · Edward Davis · John Dawson · Maria Delahunty-O'Brien · Paula Devereaux · Michelle Duke · Jason Fancey · Kieron Fardy · Jordan Fewer · Anthony Flannigan · Allan Frecker · Darryl George · Gary Gordon · Arthur Gorham · Dale Green · Corey Gregory · Jordan Hannam · Jodie Hawco · Jeremy Hickey · Walter Higdon · Vanessa Howlett · Kim Howson · Emily Ingram · Laura Jenkins · Michelle Kennedy · Amber Kennedy · Tony Kyritsis · Danielle Lewis · Ta Loeffler · Samantha Marsh · Jillian Mason · Shane Morgan · Teri-Lynn Myers · Claudia Navarro · Harry O'Gay · Hannah O'Leary · Janie O'Leary · Brady O'Leary · Frances O'Neill · Lana Quinn · Rodney Ralph · Victoria Ralph · Kelly Roche · Dawn Rogowski · Rosalie Russell · Sonya Sheaves Simms · Sandra Shute · Chris Tremblett · Sharon Vere-Holloway · Niranjan Vivekanandan · Miranda Walsh · Craig Wicks · Brenda Woodman **17** Juan Acosta · Jose Luis Aguilera · Heather Alexander · Sheila Allen · Dwight Ball · Jackie Barrett · Loretta Berkshire · Taylor Best · Ashley Bishop · Stephen Brunt · Ivan Cassell · Raymond Cole · Derek Covington · Rev. Douglas Crosby · Asher Cutting · Dwayne Decker · Dave Dooley · Benjamin Dornan · Morene Eddison · Bill Evans · Joel Goodyear · Jim Hawco · Taryn Hearn · Ruth Hillier · Jamey Jennings · Michael Johnson · Daniel Kelloway · Darryl Kelly · Dr. Brendan Lewis · Glenn Littlejohn · Helen MacDonald · Ryan Manuel · Hon. Tom Marshall · Helen McCarthy · Caleb McNiven · H.P. Menne · Shirley Merrigan-Buckle · David Mock · Jane Moran · Jennifer Mullett · Sarah Mulrooney · Mark Murdoch · Kelvin Parsons · Jade Parsons · Keith Pelley · Sarah Pieroway · Jodi Pinsent · Robert Poirier · Brenda Power · Jamie Preston · Jennifer Randell · Leslie Reid · Paul Rogers · Jane Rumball · Stacie Ryan · David Sampson · Debra Simms · Gail Simms · Carol Ann Smith · Rhonda Terry · Dr. Brent Thistle · Mark Thompson · Zachary Thorne · Geoffrey Tucker · Tanya Tuff · Jose Luis Ulloa · Geraldine Wall · Frank Walsh · Cathleen Wayson · Carla Wells · Hope Wiseman · Matthew Young · Jerry Young **18** Mary Lou Andrea · Marcel Aucoin · Carly Avery · Ryan Avery · Daniel Avery · Lauchie Beaton · Patsy Blais · Dorris Boriel · Jason Boudrot · Jeanne Bourgeois · Margaret Boyd · Valerie Boyer · Amanda Brooks · Gordon Broussard · Jim Brown · Frank Bruleigh · Larry Burke · Kelly Campbell · Shawn Campbell · John Charlton · Emily Chisholm · Holly Chisholm · Dakota Nathaniel Christmas · Angus Cockburn · Lyndon Connolly · Marybeth Connolly · Kelly Connors · Megan Cook · John Cremo · Shawn Curran · Holly Denny · Louis Deveau · Breagh Shaelynn Devereaux · Nicholas Dort · Trina Doucette · Craig Eveson · Christina Flemming · Zack Fraser · Marie Frosst · Amy-Leigh George · Mike Gibbon · Peter Giles · James Gillis · Hannah Gillis · Karla Googoo · Jarvis Googoo · Edward Hanifen · Robert Hanley · H. John Harker · Michael Hatt · Olivia Hendsbee · Mary Hines · Jasmine Hochman · Jessie Jawanda · Eleanor Jost · Clinton Keay · David Keefe · Cindy Lefebvre · Clint Lettice · Teagan Lombardo · Ruth MacInnes · Allison Macaskill · Jessica MacDonald · Justin MacDonald · Ed MacDonald · Wayne MacDonald · Denise MacDonald · Neil MacEachern · Coline MacEachern · Anna Lee MacEachern · Marina MacEachern · Taylor MacInnis · Neil MacInnis · David MacIsaac · Duncan MacKeigan · Lana Maclean · Tracy MacLellan · Katherine MacLeod · Cody Shawn Macleod · Brian MacLeod · Taylor MacMillan · David MacNeil · David MacNeil · Geroge Tex Marshall · Dave Martin · Wendy Martin · Denver Mason · Laurie McFarlane · Brittney Melnick · Nick Morris · Brenda Morrison · Taylor Murray · Savannah Newton · Troy Nixon · Lisa O'Brien · Shantel O'Neil · Lisa Parsons · Stefano Pasian · Zacchary Paul · Colynda Pelley · Katherine Perro · Renee Pertus · Teresa Petrazzuoli · Jessi Pothier · Jennifer Purvis · Mitchell Pye · Christian Reid · Julia Rivard · Mason Rudderham · Lynette Sampson · Steve Sarty · Conor Scallion · Jenna Shea · Justin Shelley · Kim Simon · Adam Simon · Dorothy Slaney · Christine Smith · Matthew Smith · Sheila Snow · Tracey St Germain · Gina Stevens · Ria Van Der Linden · Nicholas Vince · Melanie Wagar · Gordon Warnica · Roberta Watts · Jonathan White · Cathy Wilton **19** Don Adams · Irveen Anand · Lisa Baird · Ralph Bastarache · Bryan Bell · Gabriel Belliveau · Kelly Belliveau · Joe Bondy · Kerry Brown · Kent Brown · Judy Brown · Leah Butler · Richard Chipman · Lisa Clancy · Carmelle Cleary · Jessica Colson · Margaret Corio · Percy Crosby · Paulette Cullins · Tina Daid · George David Delaney · Karey-Beth Delorey · Paula Delorey · Mary Delorey · Rachel Dennis · Jayna Doshi · Jensyn Doyle · Helena Fiore · Darren Flemming · Suzanne Fougere · Stuart Fraser · Graham Gallant · Leanne Gallant · Matt Geddes · Eric Gillis · John Grace · Rhea Hamlin · Sally Hancock · Paul Harrington · Leroy A. Hodder · Dorian Hudec · Jeff Irving · Terry Isenor · Nicole Johnston · Miriam Kaiser · David Knockwood · Wendy Kraglund-Gauthier · Scott Lancaster · Veronica Landry · Dannielle LaPierre · Donna Larade · Wayne Latimer · Doug Logan · Gordon Lott · Reginald Loughead · Judy MacDonald · Gary MacDonald · Daniel MacDonell · Colleen MacDougall · Cecilia MacEachen · Kaitlin MacIsaac · Megan MacKay · Harris MacLean · Mark Malowski · Frank McAuley · Wanda McDonald · Heather McLane · Rilla McLean · Joseph McNeil · Jeff Miller · Craig Miller · Cindy Miller · Keith Miller · Lucy B. Miller · Stephen Mills · Cathy Mock · Kevin Morash · Terry Morris · Zacheriah Muise · Sean Murray · Brad O'Brien · Brock O'Brien · Kate Page · Kerry Parsons · Diane Paul · Darren Peach · Bob Piers · Stephen Pottie · Will Richardson · Julie Rolph · Al Simpson · Edward Smook · Monique Sobey · Rob Sobey · Beverly Stevens · Robert Mark Stroud · Randi Sullivan · Mike Tate · Danielle Taylor · Ikue Teshigawara · Brian Thompson · Jill Trinacty · Larry Urquhart · Crystal Valcourt · Lynn Violette · Vernon Walsh · Shelley Wendell · Judy Wentworth · Natasha White · Todd Williams · Wayne Wismer · James Wooder · Robert Yuill **20** Laura Allen · Donna Alteen · Lee Anne Amaral · David Anderson · Rhonda Baxter · Stuart Beaver · Kirk Boudreau · Janine Boutilier · Shawn Brennan · Sarah Bryson · Davis Butler · Julie Caissie · Scott Campbell · Bill Cantelo · Robert Cervelli · Calvin Cholock · Madeleine Clare · Jesse Clarke · Vanessa Jane Clements · Jimmy Collicutt · Mike Condy · Sarah Conrad · Allison Cook · Irene Cooper · Larry Corbin · Mike Cormier · Sidney Crosby · Valerie Crossman · Ginette Currie · Norma Jean Decoste · Pierre Demontigny · Brian Dickson · Robert Edgett · John Ells · David Fallows · Barbara Fickes · Natasha Louise Fillmore · Alana Fisher · Farida Gabbani · Elaine Giffen · Steve Giles · Amber Gillespie · Joan Glode · Katya Gorlova · Ryan Lengyel Gouthro · Greg Grice · Ron Griffis · Rachel Gullage · Tracy Hackett · Thomas Haight · Mitchell Hamilton · Jennifer Hart · Mina Hashish · Frank Hayden · Rodney Helpard · Dave Hendren · Evan Hickey · Kristen Hiltz · Liz Hooper · Donald Horne · Bev Hoyt · Tom Hudson · Andrew Aaron Hunt · Leigh Alexander Hunt · Wanda Maureen Hunt · Matthew Leigh Hunt · Jocelyn Huot · Paul Jewer · James Johnson · Sharon Joyce · Sanjin Karabegovic · Nikki Keating · Kevin Kennedy · Shawn Kennedy · Anita Kent · Michel Khoury · Tim Lauterbach · Bryann LeBlanc · Jamie LeBlanc · Keile Legge · Blair Lewis · Derek Linders · Wayne Lloyd · Lynn Longendyke · Tamara Lorincz · Pete Luckett · David Lune · Scott Lynch · Richard Macaulay · Bernie MacDonald · Mickey MacDonald · Randy MacDonald · Donna MacKay · Evan MacLean · Joe Macleod · Doug MacNeil · Donna MacNeil · Mieke Manley · Lorraine Manthorne · John Marshall · Neal Martinelli · Jillian Mason · Jevens Franklyn Matheson · Jason Jevens Matheson · Mary Effie Matheson · Jennifer Matheson · Kelly Marie McArel · Barry McCallum · Lori McCauley · Elizabeth Coleen McCormick · Glenda Mary McCormick · Ian Frank McCormick · Colin Roderick McCormick · Roderick Joseph McCormick · Kenneth Anthony McCormick · Roderick Shawn McCormick · William Murray McKay · Kevin McNamara · Danny McNamara · Wendy McNamara · William Moore · Lynn P. Morrison · Susan Mosher · Karlheinz Muhr · Elizabeth Munn · Cara Murray · Denroy Myers · Trevor Negus · Richard Niedermayer · Michael O'Connor · Kolby Olsen · Fiona Orr · Roberta Ouellette · Owen Parker · Lawrence Paul · Greg Peet · Ian Penny · Ambrose Pierce · Candice Porter · Matthew Rhodes · Brian Richard · Christine Riley · Sandie Rinaldo · Muslim Rizvi · Collette Robert · Colin Robertson · Denise Robson · Kris Rofe · John Rogers · Michael Ross · Debra Ross · Brenda Rowe · Andrew Russell · Caleb Sager · Tamara Scheme · George Searle · Sylvain Simard · Dan Simpson · Stephen Slauenwhite · Glen Slauenwhite · Rustum Southwell · Debbie Spackman · Jim Spatz · Nicole Spidle · Gregor Stabenow · Tatianna Stabenow · Brittany Stephens · Shaifuddin Suman · Thomas Swinkels · Tim Tabor · Bryden Tate · Bruce Turner · Cia Tweel · Ben Welsh · Daren White · Katelyn White · Elizabeth Wile · Deborah Wiles · Mark Wilkinson · Robert Wilson · Dan Woods · Jason Young · Sarah Young-MacDonald **21** Brenton Bergeron · Judy McEwan · Carew Meuse · Heather Morse · Nelson Mullen · Berton Murphy · Rosalind C. Penfound · Nathan Walsh **22** Murray Aalders · Lynn-Marie Amiro · Janel Anthony · Janica Arsenault · Jessica Avery · Patricia Baker · Stephen Bates · Angelique Beals · Wendy Bedingfield · Andre Bergeron · Erika Best · Jane Beveridge · O'neal Blackman · Rick Blouin · Francine Boucher · Andrea Bowie · Bradwell Brewer · Savannah Buckley · Alison Buckley · Barbara Burns · Angelina Cain · Ken Caldwell · Myriska Caulier · Max Clarke · Wade Cogswell · Caroline Couture · Mathieu Crepin · Mark Croft · Cindy Croft-Schofield · Karen Dean · Henry Demone · Chris Dewolfe · Lorie Dickie · Michael Dymond · Jim Eisenhauer · Mike English · Moya Farrell · Joyce Felker · Joel Florecki · Megan Fraser · Charlee Fry · Jonathon Gatehouse · Fred George · Laura Gillham · Beth Gillis · Robert Glibbery · Jacob Goulden · Justine Graham · Doug Graham · Steve Graham · Adam Hack · Sam Hall · Rubina Havlin · James Hickey · Edward Hillier · Gary Hollett · Jacqueline Howatt · Roman Husiuk · Derek Hutchison · Marci Ien · Mireille Imbleau · Mike Ivey · Jim Jardine · Kirsten Johansen-Slaunwhite · Shelley Johnson · Frank Johnston · Allison Jollimore · Colleen Jones · David E. Kerr · Crystal Kikuchi · Ruth Lamb · Sarah Leahy · Travis Livingston · Josh Lowery · Sarah MacLeod · Shawna MacPherson · Malcolm Madden · Courtney Masey · Lena Masters · Rebecca Mayo · Sean McCarthy · Conner McCrae · Bonnie Lynn McNeil · Brent McNeil · Court Milley · Chris Morrissey · Kym Muller · Allan Murnaghan · Dalise Nelligan · Audrey Nelson · Samantha Nielsen · Carolyn Nobes · Patrick O'Neil · Elaine Oulton · Eric Plante · Tiffany Polson · Steve Rice · Hugh Richards · Peter Richardson · Sherry Ritcey · Kirk Robar · Ian Roberts · Elizabeth Ross · Charbel Rouhana · Judy Rozee · Mallory Sanford · Bill Seymour · Dana Shaw · Brittany Smith · Marie Soehl · April Spinney · Paul Stewart · Krista Stockman · Rose Sveinson · Patsy Sweet · Linda Tanner · Wendy Taylor · Grzegorz Terepka · Joel Thomas · Ian Thompson · Alma Tower · Ted Vaughan · Dianne Vickers · Brenda Virtue-Ellis · Sherri Walkinshaw · Jack Waller · Allister Walsh · Sean Warner · Ken Whitehead · Terry Whynot · Shirley Wile · Katie Willoughby · Andrew Wilson · Caroline Winters · Rebecca Wolff · Mike Wong · Claudia Wunder **23** Ben Adams · Amy Atkinson · Jeremy Avery · Lisa Baldwin · Sherry-Anne Bedminster · Sandy Bishop · Mathew Boswell · Matt Bruce · Abbey Burgess · Alex Burlatschenko · Allan Callard · Harris Campbell · Betty-Jean Carter-Thompson · Matthew Caseley · Tim Clayton · Lori Collins · Bobby Cooper · Tara Costello-Ledwell · Tanya Craig · Chrissy Crane · Andrew Cross · Anna Cudmore · John Daly · Wendy Dick · Jennifer Dignan · Sonia Doiron · Waheeda Dundee · Jillian Durant · Ashley Ellis · Nicholas Falt · Sally Fleming · Debbie Fraser · Gisele Gallant · Brett Gallant · David Gallant · Bob Gibson · Samanjot Gill · Matthew Gillespie · Olimpia Gilmour · Gio Greco · Sandra Hayes Hickey · Keith Higgins · Lonsdale Holland · Jim Honsberger · Keith Hotchkiss · Julie Huh · Stephanie LeBlanc · Michael MacDonald · Erinn MacDougall · Emma MacEachern · Shaylagh MacKay · Kevin B. MacLean · Peter MacPhail · Krista McDow · Mike McKenna · Patrick McKenna · Marie-Belle McKinnon · Bill McKinnon · Michael Moors · Jason Murphy · Taylor Nicholson · Matt Penny · Colleen Petrie · Bruce Riggs · Kaileb Salsman · Joel Spriet · Joanne Steeves · Jennifer Thomson · Barry Tomalin · Trish Vardy · Chansey Veinotte · Daniel Viau · Jen White · Matthew Whynacht · Patrick Wilmot · Sam Wood · Marion Yorke · Danielle Yuzik · Greg Zwicker **24** Paul Alan · Shane Arbing · Dale Armstrong · Shelby-Lynn Arsenault · Alex Bain · Jason Belliveau Wood · Josh Bowman · Amy Bowman · John Bowser · Julia Brothers · Marlene Bryenton · Kyle Bryenton · Robbie Burt · Bill Butler · Patricia Butler · Bearnard Butler · Ben Cameron · Susan Campbell · Cassie Campbell-Pascall · Teresa Chan · Elaine Chessman · Linda Clements · Mitchell Colp · Rachel Creamer · Negin Dahya · Drew Dalziel · Allie Devries · Terry Doney · Nicolle Dunphy · Warren Ellis · Jeff Ellsworth · Trever Ferguson · Peter Figura · Jamie Fox · Vanessa French · Alana Gallant · Meghan Gallant · Karen Gallant · Douglas Gillespie · Heather Gillis · Cheryl Gotell · Bailey Green · Diane Greening · Kitty Gundaker · Debbie Hall · Nancy Hamill · Scott Harper · Wensel Harris · Alanna Hawthorne · Adella Henderson · Donna Herlihy · Kaci Holmes · Bill Hooper · Henry Hsiao · Emily Jasper · Taylor Johnston · Anthony Kamphuis · Gerald Kamphuis · Linda Keane · Fred Kikkert · Denis Kim · Willie Koughan · Karla Koughan · Marcus Koughan · Anne Koughan · David Kozak · Josephine Lam · Brian Lau · Sheilagh Lavandier-Annear · Don Leary · Ken Leclair · Bernie LeFort · Mike L'Heureux · Maiqi Maggie Li · Shelley Lilly · Rachael Loggie · Gladys Longaphie · Malcolm MacDonald · Sean MacDonald · Adam MacKinnon · Bobbi MacLennan · Shelley MacLeod · Justin MacPhee · Heather Mandoli-Alschuler · Holly Martin · Jamie Matheson · Ryan McCarron · Mike McKee · Daniel McKeown · Barb McNeill · Tera Mitchell ·

Benoit Morin · Keith Morrell · Megan Morrison · Jonathan Moser · Heather Moyse · Danny Murphy · Kathleen Murphy · Mairead Murphy · Eric Mutch · Anisha Nayar · Mark Newcombe · Darlene O'Rourke · Gurjeet Panesar · Julia Phillips · Justin Pinksen · Derek Profit · Sophia Qureshi · Jordan Ramsay · Trent Ranahan · Erin Redmond · Danielle Reid · Clayton Reid · Breton Reid · Yvette Reid · Yolande Richard · Ryan Richardson · Andrew Richardson · Anna Rogers · Kate Rundle · Joanne Sallay · Contessa Scott · Kayo Shinomiya · Graham Smith · Marie Stevens · Donna Stewart · Glenn Suart · Pam Sweetapple · Eugene Tanase · Alexis Thibeault · David Thompson · Harriet Thornhill · Trish Thorpe · Jennifer Tory · Adrian Trainor · Joseph Tuplin · Robert Upshall · Taylor Veinotte · Julien Verdier · Jonathan Vos · Valerie Vuillemot · Lisa Wallace · Cathy Williams · Tricia Wilson · Mark Wilton · Yang Yang · Rose Yen · Samantha Yeo · Jeffrey Zidichouski **25** Mark Allaby · Patty Amirault · Emma-Lee Arsenault · Mélanie Arseneau · Matthew Aucoin · Stephane Audet · Pat Aylward · Marco Bandiera · Christian Belanger · Brenda Benson · Whitney Bittern · Yves Boudreau · Michelle Boudreau · Jessie Bourque · Allain Bourque · Chris Briggs · Karyn Brown · Marc Brunelle · Albert Burke · Sara Caissie · Brian Carlton · Amanda Carson · Adnan Cekic · Qiupeng Chen · Remi Christianson · Esther Collicutt · Debbie Crowther · Jaime Cruickshank · Barbara Curry · Rodney Cyr · Chris Darrach · Saro Der Haroutiunian · David Dickson · Marc Diotte · Monique Durepos · Kelsey Eatmon · Keegan Eatmon · Elizabeth Edwards · Robert Forbes · Samantha Foster · Jason Freeman · Odette Frigault · Lisa Fury-Allen · George Gallant · Paul Goobie · Scott Gregory · Joanna Gyurkovics · Peter Hachey · Monica Hay · Luc Hebert · Brenda Henry · Monica Hitchcock · Russ Howard · Bianca Hunter · Brent Jacob · Kristine Johnston · Darryl Johnstone · Brianne Kinden · Kim Kirkpatrick · Ashley Knockwood · Jon Kreplin · Bruno Lainey · Jordan Landry · Giancarlo Lanzetta · Marc-Andre LeBlanc · Nick LeBlanc · Alfred LeBlanc · Maurice LeBlanc · Normand LeBlanc · Pierrette LeBlanc-Robichaud · David MacCormack · Ashley MacDonald · Gerry Alexander MacDonald · Denise MacDonald-Vail · Julie Maillet · Lucie Masse-Jutras · Ryan Maye · J. Frank McCallum · Ben McCarron · Taylor McIntyre · Peggy McLean · Albert McRobb · Daniel Mellon · Shelby Merrithew · Nancy Morrison · Scott Myers · Adrian Nauss · Elleas Nicholas · Christine Nisbet · Doreen Nowlan · Alexandra Ouellette · Zach Pavlovic · Paul Phillips · Suzanne Poitras · Nicole Power · Kelly Proudfoot · Michael Putulik · Josh Pye · Gilles Ratte · Norma Reid · Candice Rempel · Alvin Richard · Stephane Richard · Krista Richard · Emilie Roy · Stephanie Roy · Jesel Ryan · Bill Schurman · Virginie Segard · Jean-Pascal Servant · Marie Shannon · Anna Sheridan-Jonah · Matthew Sides · Tony Smith · Donna Smith · Jaleh Sobhanifar · Elaine Stanley · Jamie Steele · Ceire Storey · Margaret Streatch · Francis Theriault · Andre Touchburn · James Tucker · Taylor Tweedie · Lana Ward · Heather Wasson · Mark Whiteway **26** Andrea Addison · Anabela Almeida · Kevin Anthony · Gabriel Arsenault · Brittany Arsenault · Gracia Arseneau · Gary Arthurs · Gaston Aubé · Fabio Avella · Megan Baisley · Cindi Baisley · Mary Jane Banks · Jordan Bedard · Mark Bellefleur · Lise Bellefleur-Jonah · Brandon Bennett · Andre Bouchard · Sophie Boudreau · Kevin Braun · Rick Briggs-Jude · James D. Carroll · Mark Carter · Randolph Chau · Erica Chestnut · Mike Christie · César Cielo · Antoine Clark · Gary Clark · Kris Clarke · Debbie Cooper · Bryan Copeland · Bridget Coughlan · Simon Cracknell · Heather Craig · Scott Darling · Mary Dever · Cheryl Lee Devereaux · Sean Dewinter · Malcolm Dixon · Carol Dixon · Derek Doiron · Nathalie Doiron · Sherry Doiron · Lucienne Donelle Easton · Cynthia Dukes · Stephanie Dupuis · Dave Evans · Jordan Ferguson · Jennifer Fernandez · Marilia Figueiredo · Jennifer Forbes · Ryan Foster · Gordon Friars · Danielle Gallan · Callaghan Gillis · Jeannine Gould · Vincent Gregg · Cameron Grout · Patricia Guitard · Jamie Haggarty · Pat Harasymew · Jodie Henry · Andrew Hunt · Emily Jamieson · Jordan Jamison · Rachel Jefferson · Luke Jefferson · Len Jillard · Heath Johnson · Azor Johnson · Katelyn Johnson · Sara Kalbouneh · Adam Keirstead · Michael Kennedy · Charlene King · Kelsey Knowles · Nidhi Laroiya · William Law · Justin Lawson · Larry Laznovsky · Lori Laznovsky · Monique M. LeBlanc · Guy LeBlanc · Dean Leland · Brittany Livingston · Casey Losier · Taylor Losier · Tim Lowery · Morgan Lucas · Megan Lucas · Christian Mackin · Robert Magee · John Maisey · Philippe Mallet · Kim Mason · Lisa Mattison · Deborah McAllister · William McBeath · Thomas McCauley · Winnie McKee · Molly McLaughlin · Megan McNulty · Annie Michaud · Kandy Mitton · Ben Monahan · Lori Montpetit · Rebecca Moore · Mark Morgan · Drew Morgan · Hrishikesh Muzumdar · Alice Ness · Dan Newman · Carolyn Novick · Andrew O'Dell · Daniel Oliver · Jeffrey Osei-Bonsu · Jason Peters · Betty Phillips · Michelle Pittman · Todd Pye · Julija Rans · Ben Rans · Jesse Reid · Jason Rempel · Samuel Richard · Elizabeth Rigney · Murray Rogers · Dale Ronalds · Ronald Roper · Brenda Ross · Cara Rossiter · Gisele Saindon · Brandi Schaump · Clint Schile · Mike Schulze · Kristen Scott · Bob Sherrard · Barry Short · Carolyn Simon · Dan Sinclair · Pierrette Sloan · Keith Steeves · Rick Stephen · David Strickland · Gabrielle Surette · Lynn Symington · Budrow Tozer · Liza Tsui · Alan Turner · Pritti Vagadia · Jack Vandenbroek · Donald Violette · Matthew Ward · Mark Webb **27** Mark Allaby · Patty Amirault · Emma-Lee Arsenault · Mélanie Arseneau · Matthew Aucoin · Stephane Audet · Pat Aylward · Marco Bandiera · Christian Belanger · Brenda Benson · Whitney Bittern · Yves Boudreau · Michelle Boudreau · Jessie Bourque · Allain Bourque · Chris Briggs · Karyn Brown · Marc Brunelle · Albert Burke · Sara Caissie · Brian Carlton · Amanda Carson · Adnan Cekic · Qiupeng Chen · Remi Christianson · Esther Collicutt · Debbie Crowther · Jaime Cruickshank · Barbara Curry · Rodney Cyr · Chris Darrach · Saro Der Haroutiunian · David Dickson · Marc Diotte · Monique Durepos · Kelsey Eatmon · Keegan Eatmon · Elizabeth Edwards · Robert Forbes · Samantha Foster · Jason Freeman · Odette Frigault · Lisa Fury-Allen · George Gallant · Paul Goobie · Scott Gregory · Joanna Gyurkovics · Peter Hachey · Monica Hay · Luc Hebert · Brenda Henry · Monica Hitchcock · Russ Howard · Bianca Hunter · Brent Jacob · Kristine Johnston · Darryl Johnstone · Brianne Kinden · Kim Kirkpatrick · Ashley Knockwood · Jon Kreplin · Bruno Lainey · Jordan Landry · Giancarlo Lanzetta · Marc-Andre LeBlanc · Nick LeBlanc · Alfred LeBlanc · Maurice LeBlanc · Normand LeBlanc · Pierrette LeBlanc-Robichaud · David MacCormack · Ashley MacDonald · Gerry Alexander MacDonald · Denise MacDonald-Vail · Julie Maillet · Lucie Masse-Jutras · Ryan Maye · J. Frank McCallum · Ben McCarron · Taylor McIntyre · Peggy McLean · Albert McRobb · Daniel Mellon · Shelby Merrithew · Nancy Morrison · Scott Myers · Adrian Nauss · Elleas Nicholas · Christine Nisbet · Doreen Nowlan · Alexandra Ouellette · Zach Pavlovic · Paul Phillips · Suzanne Poitras · Nicole Power · Kelly Proudfoot · Michael Putulik · Josh Pye · Gilles Ratte · Norma Reid · Candice Rempel · Alvin Richard · Stephane Richard · Krista Richard · Emilie Roy · Stephanie Roy · Jesel Ryan · Bill Schurman · Virginie Segard · Jean-Pascal Servant · Marie Shannon · Anna Sheridan-Jonah · Matthew Sides · Tony Smith · Donna Smith · Jaleh Sobhanifar · Elaine Stanley · Jamie Steele · Ceire Storey · Margaret Streatch · Francis Theriault · Andre Touchburn · James Tucker · Taylor Tweedie · Lana Ward · Heather Wasson · Mark Whiteway **28** Day off / *Congé* **29** Amy Anderson · Stephanie Anglehart · Amy Appleby · Jason Arsenault · Melanie Barry · Josh Barry · Chris Bird · Fred Blaney · Mark Bordage · Doug Borthwick · Suzanne Boucher · Mario Boudreau · Donna Brake · Norman Brown · Bruce Burdock · Laura Bursey · Maxine Caissie · Meredith Caissie · Sara Chow · Greg Corcoran · Julia Cormier · Guy Cormier · David Davies · Cody Doyle · Joelle Drolet-Ferguson · Barbara Dugas · Donna Durelle · Chris Edgett · Hassan Emran · Gary Foley · Gail Francis · Adrian Francis · Renee Frenette · Patrick Frigault · Mitchell Furlotte · Chris Gallop · Shawn Gauthier · Delores Ginnish · Jean Goodfellow · Anne Gorges · Kathleen Groves · Gaetan Fl Haché · Carl Harper · Clarissa Harris · Peter Hartley · Brad Henderson · Sue Hetherington · Bill Hickey · E. Nadine Holmes · Mary Lynn Jardine · Nicola Jardine · Benjamin Johnson · Karen Johnston · Adam Joyce · Cassie Kervin · Ray Kokkonen · Patrick Lanteigne · Melanie Lavigne · Delaney LeBlanc · Zoé LeBlanc · Bernard LeBlanc · Stephen LeBreton · Jason Logelin · Darlene MacDonald · Kim Mackenzie · Aldo Mallet · Karen Matchett · Jessica McCallum · Judy McCarty · Kathy McCormack · Lucy McCray · Brad McLellan · Laurie Meaney-Tobin · Erin Metcalf · Annie Mae Morrison · Melissa Near · Giang Nguyen · Sandie Nicholson · Mark Noel · Jacqueline Noseworthy · Ginette Pellerin · Donald Peters · Robert Powell · Ethan Pyke · Patricia Quek · Erin Redshaw · Jeremie Richard · Tanya Rideout · Fabiola Robichaud · Malcolm Rogers · Jacques Roussel · Barbara Russell · Sonia Sabourin · Laila Saleh · Jeremy Savoie · Charlene Smith · Nadine Stewart · Matthew Sullivan · Lisa Taylor · Jim Thorburn · Adam Thornton · Michelle Tobin-Forgrave · Marilyn Underhill · Martinus Van Rijn · Travis Webb · Natalie Weir · Tony Whalen · Elizabeth White · Jeremy White · Shelby Wilson **30** Daniel Ackerson · Pascal Adams · Reta Alexander · Bernadette Arpin · Guy Arseneault · Melinda Audette · Frances Baltzan · Anne-Marie Beaulieu · Don Belanger · Claude Benoit · Karine Bernier · Eric Bijeau · Amélie Blanchard · Amber Brewer · Rene Chamberlain · Wilson Chau · Réjeanne Chouinard · Tyson Collier · Michel Coté · David Couturier · Claire Dennie · Gerald Desjardins · Marc-Andre Desjardins · Daniel Doucet · Adam Douthwright · Amelie Dube · Marc Dube · Patricia Duffy · Dawn Dunham · Stephane Durepos · Katherine Eglington · Mary Farrell · Gail Fellows-DeGrace · Brenda Firlotte · Reynald Fortier · Denise Fournier · Jonathan Fraser · Kevin Gallant · Farrah-May Gendron · Linda Gillespie · Cathy Godbout · Hermel Godbout · Rodney Harquail · Garry Hogan · Jedd Jamieson · Hafeez Kassam · Barry Kyle · Caroline Lagace · Pat Lajeunesse · Stephen Lawson · Reginald LeBlanc · Nathalie Lemoy St-Onge · John LePage · George Levesque · Rita Levesque · Gabrielle Levesque · Rino Long · Beatrice Long · Rory MacDonald · Derrick MacDougall · Lynda MacDougall · Jaclyn Macmillan · Christian Madore · Rina Martin · Katie Martin · Luc Martin · Kourtney Martin · Richard Mckillop · Yves Michaud · Gilles Michaud · Keshia Moffat · Natasha Moreau · Julie-Christine Morin · Pierre-Olivier Morin · Pierre-Olivier Nadeau · Chuck Nearing · Robin Nichol · Alaina Noel · Michael O'Toole · Daniel Ouellette · Caroline Pagé · Karla Perez · Gordon Pitre · Jean-Guy Poitras · Dawn Preston · Christina Robichaud · Howard Ross · Bona Roussel · Carmelle Marie Roy · Joan Rutherford · Caroline Sauve · Rejean Savoie · Jason Silva · Linda Simard · Luc Sirois · Jeffrey Soucy · Andrew St-François · Joey Tardif · Ari Taub · Chantal Theriault · Flavien Theriault · Milaine Theriault · Celine Theriault · Jean Theriault · Michel Theriault · Danielle Theriault · Scott Toner · Rita Toner · Guy Toner · Mark Toner · Francois Violette · Lyne Walker · Tammy Jane Waye · Teresa Yerxa **31** Brad Akerley · Gaston Allard · Herve Arseneau · Annie Arseneau · Alex Baron · Frédéric Barriault · Guillaume Bastille · Andreanne Bastille · Phil Beaudry · David Bedard · Michel Belanger · Shane Bennett · Pierre Bergeron · Myra Bérubé · Mélinda Bérubé · François Bérubé · Vincent Bissonnette · David Blouin · Christian Bolduc · Barbara Bouchard · Gabriel Bourgoin · Rob Braknis · Olivier Brissette · Shana Brown · Eldred Bucci · Lourice Capili · Margel Cauvier · Camille Cimon · Claudia Ciorei · Eric Cloutier · Linda Cloutier · Danielle Cook · Xavier Côté-Talbot · Jessica E. Daigle · Nancy Daigneault · Mario Darsigny · James Day · Jean-François Desgagne · Martin Desrosiers · Mario Dionne · Marc-Emile Dionne · Glorianne Doucette · Mario Dube · Raynald Dufour · Marco Dumais · Johanne Dussureault · Marc-André Farmer · Francis Fillion · Martin Fleury · Leopold Fontaine · Felix-Antoine Fortin · Olivier Fortin · Rene Fortin · Claudie Fournier · Annie Fournier · Sebastien Fournier · Rio Francoeur · Robert-Charles Gagné · Nathalie Gagnon · Bastien Garon · Kelly Gauthier · Yoan Gauthier · Josee Gingras · Simon Girard · Gabriel Goulet · Catherine Goulet · Yvon Grondin · Lise Guignard · Hermann Guy · Pierre Harvey · Valérie Hudon · Rachel Isabelle · Paul Iza · Michel Jalbert · Luc Labrecque · Vanessa Lachance · François Lagacé · Jessica Lapalme · Danyka Leclair · Alexandra LeGresley · Joanie Levesque · Real Malenfant · Melanie Marin · Michel Martin · Nadine Martin · Chantal Michaud · Domenico Micheletti · Steve Mitchell · Gerrit Moleman · Marie-Pierre Nadeau · Daniel Ng · Roland Noel · Daniel Ouellet · Jean-François Packwood · Claudette Paradis · Monica Patry · Erick Pelletier · Martin Pelletier · Clement Pelletier · Jordan Pomerleau · Jonathan Proulx · Isabelle Provost · Pierre-Paul René · Claudie Robert-Robitaille · Gilles Rousseau · Katia Roussel · Carole-Anne Roussel · Mathieu Roy · Louis Roy · Frederic Savage · Axel Schulz · Christiane Sirois · Denyse Soucy · Maude St-Pierre · Katherine Stuy · Denis Talbot · Benoit Theriault · Marie-Claude Theriault · Pierre Theriault · Richard Theriault · Alexandra Valentin · Madison Vine · Daniel Violette **32** Martine Albert · Mario Arsenault · Camille Arsenault · Severine Arseneau · Etienne Beauclair · Rosaire Beaupré · Benoit Bedard · Alain Junior Béland · Pauline Belliveau · Daniel Berube · Alexandre Berube · Sabrina Bérubé · Carol Bouchard · Léonie Boucher · Lucie Boudreau · Jean-Pierre Bouffard · Etienne Bouffard-Cloutier · Gabriel Bourque · Jean-François Canuel · Dean Carbonneau · Rose Cardinal · David Carruthers · Jerry Castonguay · Alexandre Charest · Viateur Charest · Maude Charron · Tony Ciorra · Johanne Cloutier · Dany Corriveau · Laurence Côté · Matthew Day · Eve Dechamplain · Alex Denis · Roland Desterres · Frédéric Dionne · Paul-Olivier Dubé · Jani Dubé-Roy · Daniel Dufresne · Marie-Eve Dumais · Patrick Dupont · Dave Durette · Jean-Pierre Fournier · Lyse Fournier · Christina Froud · Mathieu Furlong-Landry · Jasmin Gagné · Marie-Pier Gagnier · Jerome Gagnon · Maude Gagnon · Élora Goudreault · David Haag · Sylvie Harrison · Rita Harrisson · Éric Imbeault · Sandra Kirby · Clément Labrie · Anders Lafon · Julie Lagacé · Ghislaine Langelier · Réald Langlais · Antoine Langlais-Riou · Maxime Langlois · Valérie Langlois · Berangere B. Lauzier · Martine Lavoie · Berthe Lebel · Michel LeBlanc · Laura Leblond · Céline Leclerc · Ferdinand Leclerc · Louise Lefebvre · Nicole Lessard Vachon · Jacqueline Levesque · Bobby Marmen · Sergio Marrone · Louise Martineau · Raymond Menard · Jacques Morissette · Ben Mulroney · Marc Munger · Claude Murray · Nicolas Murray · Joan Muzzey · Christian Nadeau · Marc Otis · Samuel Otis-Chapados · Frédéric Otis-Chapados · Chloé Ouellet · Fabrice Paquet · Guillaume Paradis · Andrée-Ève Pelletier · Amélie Pettigrew · Carrye Proulx · Carl Richard · John Richardson · Karine Richer · Francis Ross · André Rouleau · François Rouleau-Fournier · Jean-Charles Rousseau · Carol Roy · Kimberley Sears · Louis-Patrick St-Pierre · Abdul Syed · Dominique Tremblay · Catherine Vaillancourt · Patrick Vignola · Sydney Williams **33** Tony Allaire · Carla Anderson · William Archambault · William Archibald · Martin Beaulieu · Simon-Michel Bélisle · Eric Bergeron · Sylvain Bergeron · Paul-Henri Bergeron · Audrey Bherer · Barbara Boivin · Pierrot Bouchard · Laurence Boucher · Joel Brough · Steeve Brown · Veronique Canuel · Marie-Pier B. Claveau · Bruce Colby · François Collard · Philippe Cote · Marie-Claire Cote · Marie Michèle Côté · Lisanne Côté · Nadine Côté · Andre Coulombe · Sylvie Coulombe · Martin D'Astous · Luc Denis · Eric Desbiens · Anaïs Deschênes · Charles Dionne · Sylvain Dionne · Christine Doré · Alain Doré · Joël Drapeau · Phillip Dufour · Hirlse Dufour · Benoit Farcy · Roupina Farra · Desiree Gabriel · Steve Gagne · Rémi Gagnon · Nadine Gagnon · Marc Gagnon · Koraly Gagnon · Alain Garant · Karine Gaudreault · Carole Gaudreault · Guy Grondin · Karen Harvey · Linda Heathcott · Selynn Kanape · Lucie Laflamme · Thomas Landry · Gabrielle LapointE · Linda Lapointe · Maurice Laurencelle · Vincent LeBlanc · Gilles LeBlanc · James Leduc-Mondrzejewski · Sylvain Lenden · Pierre-Luc Letourneau · Marie-Josee Longpre · Alexandre Lord · Patrick Marcil · Jean-Philippe Marcoux · Sabrina Martel · Claude Martin · Gilles McNeil · Katia Montminy · Marc Morissette · Frederic Munger · Andy Nasr · Elizabeth Noel · Mathieu Noel · Cali Odorizzi · Katherine Ouellet · Charles Page · Karl Pagé · Louis Picard · Rapahaël Picard · Sarah-Kim Pilote-Fortin · Francois Poulin · Pierre Racine · Gary Rehel · Michael Reid · Isabelle Rodgers · Daniel Rondeau · Stéphanie Ross · Alain Roy · Mario Ruel · Denis Servais · Roger Siegner · Julie Stevens · Mario Tardif · Luc Toupin · Pierre Tremblay · Bernard Tremblay · Patrick Tremblay · Nelly Tremblay · Nicolas Turcotte · Pierre Villeneuve · Sylvain Vinet · Anne Voyer · Karen Wallace **34** Rejean Asselin · Nicolas Aubut · William Barthe · Martin Bellavance · Dean Bergeron · Claude Berube · Marc Blais · Jérémy Bonneau · Caroline Bouchard · Carol Boucher · Maud Boucher · Keven Boutet · Serge Brassard · Alex Bussieres · Pierre Caplette · Aurora Casale · Chantal Chartrand · Jean-Pierre Claveau · Martin Cloutier · Marie-Marthe Cote · Mélanie Courtois · Cynthia Cousineau · Eric Couture · Josee Crane · Nadia Cyr · Sophie Dallaire · Bianka Dallaire · Jacques Dion · Dave Doucet · Caroline Duchesne · Joe Dufour · Sonya Fiset · Catherine Fleury · Monia Fleury · Sara Fournier · Pierre Gagne · Chantal Gagne · Philippe Gagnon · Fernand Gaudreault · Raymond Gauthier · Paule Gauthier · Benoit Gauvin · Eli Gladstone · Alain Gobeil · Charles Gravel · Brendan Hollands · Jeanne-D'arc Houde · Maxime Huot · Denys Huot · Christian Kardos · Guylaine Keable · Pierre Lachance · Lynn Lachance · Louis Laflamme · Sylvie Lamontagne · Anne-Marie Lavigne · Richard Lavoie · Ginette Lavoie · Julie Lavoie · Cathy Lavoie · Gabriel Lemieux · Roland Lortie · Jean-François Maltais · Dominique Marceau · Mathieu Marquis · Mélanie Mayrand · Perry McKenna · Keven Mercier · Jean-Luc Meunier · Helene Monette · Manon Morin · Michel Ouellet · Jean Page · Éric Pelletier · Francisco Javier Perlaza Tofino · Michel Perrier · Francine-Alice Perron · Philippe Perron · Beatrice Pineau · Mathieu Proulx · Josee Roy · Charles Samson · Sylvie Sanscartier · Marie-Claude Savard-Gagnon · Jacqueline Sicluna · Frédéric Simard · Ginette Sirois · Eric Thibault · Stéphane Thinel · Diana Tremblay · Jonny Tremblay · Brigitte Tremblay · Harold Tremblay · Isabelle Tremblay · Mélanie Turgeon · Paul Van OtterDijk · Jean-Pierre Verreault · Sarah-Maude Vezina **35** Cynthia Aleman · Antonio-Guy Aleman · Sylvain Archetto · Marcel Aubut · Mario Audet · Daniel Beaulieu · Julie Beaulieu · Guy Bélanger · Myriam Bélanger · Benoît Bergeron · Patrick Bernier · Charles Boily · Gaston Boisvert · Hughes Boisvert-Simard · Jocelyn Bordeleau · Eddy Bouchard · Renald Bouchard · Gaétan Boucher · Conrad Boucher · Alain Boudreau · Isabelle Bourque · Eric Bradette · Pierre Brindamour · Olivier Caron · Alex Carter-Labbe · Francois Charest · Reena Chawla · André Côté · Yanick Côté · Luc Daigle · Tan Nhan Trung Dang · Jean-Marie De Koninck · David Debilly · Nicolas Deguire · Sylvain Dion · Mathieu Drouin · Christopher Duchesneau · Jonathan Elster · Joannie Ferland · Félix-Antoine Ferland · Earle Fisher · Frédéric Fortin · Maxime Fortin · Eric Fraser · Lise Fréchette · Julie Fréchette · Marie Josee Gagne · Louis Garneau · Ross Gaudreault · Chantale Gaudreault · Philippe Gauthier · Helene Gauvin · Andre Gelinas · Gilles Gilbert · Linda Girard · Hercule Gosselin · Sophie Gosselin · Marie-Pier Grenier · Yves Groleau · Gabriel Guay · Marc Guerard · Valerie Hamel · Waneek Horn-Miller · Étienne Huot · Sébastien Huppé · François Imbeau · Dominique Jean · Marcel Jobin · Vassily Kiselev · Andre Laberge · Caroline Labrie · Mériane Labrie · Kim Lacasse-Aubin · Louis-Martin Lachance · Stéphanie Lacourse · Jasmin Laferriere · Gilles Lafond · Pascal Laganieve · Leandre Lajeunesse Beriault · Samuel Lanouette · Benoit Lapan · Sandrine Larchet · Coppelia LaRoche-Francoeur · Line Lavoie · Pierre-Christian Le Noble · Suzanne Leclerc · Martin Leclerc · Camil Leclerc · Harold Leduc · Denis Leduc · Anne-Marie Lefrancois · David Lehoux · Jean-Jacques Lemaire-Martin · Marylin Lemay · Kellie Lemieux · Dany Lemieux · Francine Lemieux · Daniel Leroux · Ben Lo · Rocco Lofano · Carl Loubert · Chantal Machabée · Claude Mailhot · Anne Mainguy · David Malenfant · Élise Marcotte · Stephane Martel · Francois Martin · Eric Masson · Luc Metayer · Aimé Michaud · Charles MiLliard · Anik Montpetit · Denis Morissette · Myriam Nadeau · Richard Naud · Philippe Nobert · Marie-Christine Noel · Pascal Ouellet · Robert Paquette · Myriam Paquette · Véronique Paradis · Helene Pedneault · Stephane Pelchat · Gilles Pelletier · Christopher Perron · Jean-Francois Picard · Ghislain Picard · Jean-Sébastien Porlier · Josianne Proulx · Raymond Proulx · Dominic Quintal · Marc Racine · Reginald Raju · John Reilly · Julien Rémillard · Martin Richard · Kalyna Roberge · Ginette Robert · Stephane Robitaille · Myriam Robitaille · Marc Rochon · Mathieu Rodrigue · Justin Rodrigue · Martin Rose · Sara Rousseau · Maryse Roy · Anne Ruel · Louis Sansfaçon · Sonia Sansoucy · Steve Sauvé Jr. · Peter Schlickenrieder · Maria Soler · Luc Soucy · Solange Talbot · Carl Tardif · Robert Tellier · Jean-Sébastien Thériault · Brett Thompson · Mauricio Tortello · Frédéric Toulouse · Terri Toyota · Odette Tremblay · Guy Tremblay · Claudia Turgeon · Frederic Villeneuve **36** Francine Amyot · Sonia Anctil · Thomas Audet · Alex B. Perron · Jean Baron · Georges Barrette · Paméla Beaudoin · Alexandre Beaudoin · Marc-Andre Beaulieu · Francoise Beaulieu · Charles Bellegarde · Frédérique Bernard · Justine Bernatchez · Sylvie Bernier · Pierre Bernier · Mathieu Bérubé Beaumont · Vanessa Bilodeau · Richard Bisson · Diane Denise Bisson B · Amélie Blais · Guy Blanchette · Karine Boivin · Jean-Philippe Bolduc · Nicolas Bordeleau · Alain Bouchard · Nicolas Boulianne-Verschelden · Pierre Bourassa · Pierre Boutet · Nicholas Boutin · Jurgen Braun · Alexandre Breton · Jonathan Breton-Robert · Vincent Breton-Robert · Pierre Brisebois · Gilles Brouillette · Mireille Brousseau · Brigitte Busque · Geneviève Campeau · Rebecca Carnduff · Louis-Philippe Caron · Denis Casavant · Jean Cauchy · Stéphane Chevarie · Patric Clavet · Nicole Corbin · Annie-Claude Couture · Jean-Claude Crevier · Bruno Croteau-Labouly · Charles Dallaire · Michel De Lair · Denise De-Landreville · Nicole Delfour · Surendrakumar Desai · Jennifer Dibblee · Isabelle Dionne · Matei Dragutescu · Éric Dubuc · Martine Dugrenier · Guillaume Dumas · Pier Dutil · Marie-Philippe Duval · Roxanne Faucher · Denis Fortin · Michel Fournier · Marie-Claude Fournier · Roger Fradette · Myriam Gagné · Sophie Gagnon · Martine Gaillard · Jacques Gauthier · Kevin Giroux · Pualine Giroux · Philippe Gobeil · Nathalie Gosselin · Nicolas Gosselin · Roger Goulet · Nancy Goulet · Marylise Goyette · Pierre Grenier · Alexandra-Maude Grenier · Rosalie Grenier · Johanne Grenier · Justine Groleau · Elisabeth Higgins · Amélie Jacques · Mathieu Jerome · Bènyi Johnson · Laurie Johnson · Perry Kandyba · Panayiota Karapanos · Sabrina Laberge Gauthier · David Labrecque · Sylvain Lacasse · Geneviève Lacasse · Jean-Francois Lachance · Ariane Lafrance · Pierre-Olivier Lajeunesse · Nathalie Lamarche · Renee Lamy · Chantal Leboeuf · Nancy Leclair · Guylaine Lecours · Johanne Lemelin · Marie-Eve Lemieux · Luc Lessard · Ariane Loignon · Dave Loiselle · Isabelle Loubier · Martine Magnan · Jean-Philippe Maranda · Chantal Marleau · Charles Marois · Jennifer Marois · Robert Marois · Jean-Paul Marquis · Yves Mathieu · Steeven Mathieu · Maxime Mathieu · Joelle Mercier · Michel Métivier · Andre Montambault · Alain Morency · Louis Morin · Josee Morin · Pierrette Morin · Elsa Morin-Vallières · Helene Nadeau · Annie O'Connor · Francis Ouellet · Micheline Paquet · Pierrette Paradis · Yanick Parent · Frank Pelletier · Nicky Petiquay · Jacques Piuze · Kary-Anne Poirier · Jérôme Poisson · Johanne Pomerleau · Olivier Provencal · Pauline Quirion · Olivier T. Raymond · Philippe Reitz · Marie-Pier Roberge · Nadine Rolland · Francois Routhier · Marie-Noëlle Roy · Francis Roy · Karine Royer · Jean-Francois Samuel · Dominique Savard · Marco Seguin · Martin Simard · Pascale St-Louis · Louise Taillefer · Colomb Talbot · Sorin Tanasie · Esther Thibault · Francois Tremblay · Sophie Tremblay · Laurence Vachon · Robert Vachon · Sylvain Van Gele · James Veilleux · Claire Vignola · Anne-Marie Villeneuve · Simon Willeme · Brendan Young **37** Jacynthe Angers · Pierre Arsenault · Christine Barcelo · Kelly Batten · Samuel Beaudoin · Cynthia Beaulieu · Berhier Bédard · René Béliveau · Francois Bernatchez · Megane Birote · Sebastien Blanchard · Pierre Bouchard · Claude Boucher · Bernard Bourgault · Marie-Josée Bousquet · Marc Breton · Jacques Brouillette · Maryline Brousseau · Martin Brûlé · Karine Charron · Asmara Ciampa · Steve Clavet · Olivier Cloutier · Martin Colgan · Sam Coppa · Sylvain Cote · Denis Dalzill · Jean-Pierre Dargis · Patrick David · Louise Davignon · Shane De Wit · Marie-Claude Demers · Lise Denman · Renee Desautels · Richard Doyon · Francois Drapeau · Dominic Ducharme · Cindy Fluet · Marc André Fortier · Julien Fortin · Gaetan Gagnon · Louise Gagnon · Sandrine Gamache · Claude Gauthier · Annick Gazaille · Richard Germain · Marie-Luce Giguere · Sylvain Gilbert · Charles-Olivier Gilbert · Maxime Girard · Tina Marie Girimonte · William Girouard · Maryse Gosselin · Nathalie Gouin · Chantal Goupil · Zach Groom · Carl-Éric Guérard · Charles Hamel · Genevieve Hardy · Eryn Hessian · Carol Hsieh · Samuel Johnston-Morin · Andre Jutras · Robert Karam · Lynn King · Jean-Pierre Labbe · Jean-Francois Lajoie · Valérie Lambert · Pascale Landry · Caroline Lapointe · Pierre-Luc Lauziere · Cathy Lebarbé · Carl Lebel · Winona Lefebvre Castillo · Nancy L'Étoile · Ian MacDonald · Paul Mailhot · Marcel Mallette · Sarah-Eve Martin · Jocelyn Mathieu · Eliot Mathieu-Proteau · Jean-Francois Matte · Richard Mckibbin · Elizabeth Menard · Alexandre Moreau · Christophe MourEau · Jean-Louis Parr · Sebastien Pepin · Jean Perrault · Christine Pinet · Amélie Plante · Jean-François Poirier · Charles-Etienne Poirier · Sylvain Porlier · Chantal Poulin · Marie-Michèle Quirion · Michelle Reddick · Josee Ricard · Yvon Rioux · Jean François Rioux · Nicolas Rivard · Marie-Josée Roy · Louis-Ghislain Roy · Clement Ruel · Eric Samson · Yanick Sansoucy · Heidi Schmid · Elisabeth Ste-Marie · Pierre St-Hilaire · Stéphanie St-Pierre · Éric Tanguay · Michael Thibeault · Nicolas Tremblay · Karen Turcotte · Mathieu Turcotte · Sylvain Turcotte · France Turgeon · Guy Valois · J-P Vanloo · Francis Veilleux · André Veilleux · Madeleine Villeneuve · Martin Villeneuve · Terry Warner · Josee Yergeau · Ned Young **38** André Allard · Robert Auger · Nancy Ballabey · Hervey Beaubien · Pascal Beauchemin · Lynn Beebe · Pierre Bellefeuille · Barry Bellware · Yann Benoit · Ginette Bernard · Marie-Andrée Bilodeau · Stephane Blais · Jean-Claude Bourassa · Philippe Bourassa · Pier-Jean Bourassa · Eve-Marie Bourque · Jean Bouthillette · Richard Brochu · Marc-Antoine Brodeur · Geneviève Brouillard · Manon Caouette · Marcelo Cardoso · Julie Champigny · Patrick Chauvette · Julien Cossette · André Courchesne · Melanie Cutting · Roland Amakoe d'Almeida · Isabelle Descoteaux · Mario Deslauriers · Michel Doyon · Jonathan Doyon · Bernard Drainville · Lyne Drapeau · Nancy Drolet · Marie-Eve Drouin · Daniel Duchemin · Chantal Duchesne · Daniel Dudemaine · Francine Dulude · Carlos Figueiredo · Michel Flageol · Veronique Fournier · Fortunato Francella · Elizabeth Gagnon · Luc Gagnon · Nicholas Gavin-Rocheleau · Roxane Gendron · Michel Godin · Susan Godwin · Danielle Goyette · Steve Groleau · Nancy Groleau · Pierre Guerette · Gabriel Guy-Hénault · Yasmine Hazen · Laura Heathfield-Capaldi · Jacques Hudon · Jean Huot · Marie-Pier Imhof · Louis Jourdain · Marie-Josée Jubinville · Darlene Kerr · Thomas Kingston · Michael Kowal · Eve La Riviere · Marie-Josee Labelle · Melissa Laberge · Gaston Lacroix · Richard Lacroix · Alain Lafrance · Sylvio Lajoie · Lyne Lamarre · Marc Lambert · Louise Lamothe · Éric Lampron-Goulet · Francois Lamy · Penelope Landry · Frederique Landry · Christian Laporte · Mathieu Larivière · Eric Lavoie · Audrey LeBlanc · Andrée LeBlanc · Marcel LeBlanc · Marie-Thé LeBlanc · Genevieve LeBlanc · Manon LeBlanc · Andréanne LeBlanc · Daniel LeBlanc · Francis Lecomte · Nick Lesey · Aline Levi · Martin Levreault · Roch Loignon · Pascal Lussier · Daniel Maher · Michael Malone · Johanne Marotte · Francois Martin · Marilyn Marzitelli · Caroline Massicotte · Denise Massicotte · Yann Mathieu · Lucas McCartney · Alannah McGruer · Nicole McKinnell · Marie-Claude Mercier · Richard Morin · Daniel Morin · Shelby Munro · Lyne Nadeau · Joanie Noel · Jocelyne Normandin · Hussain Obaid · Michael Ohayon · Tomy Parent · Julien Premont · Stephane Quintal · Roxanne Rheault · Chantal Roy · Alain Ruest · Silvio Russo · Jason Sangster · Ryan Segal · Daniel Sicard · Jérôme Sicard · Charlène Sicard · Josélie Sicard · Louis-Pier Sicard · Emilie Simard · Olivier Taillon · Richard Tellier · Michel Tellier · Marie-Eve Tétreault · Janie Thelemaque · Dave Whittom · Stephen Zatylny **39** Arie Alter · David Anctil · Sophie Arpin · Monique Bachand · Ryan Barber · Jean-François Baril · Jean-Marie Baron · Pauline Beaulieu · Jean Bedard · Jean Berthiaume · Guillaume Berube · Michel Bienvenu · Luc Blanchard · Manon Boisvert · Guylaine Boutin · Richard Braniff · Isabelle Brasseur · Melodie Brault · Therese Brisson · Benoit Bussieres · Thomas John Cappelli · Francois Caron · Louis Castonguay · Simon Champagne · Benoite Chamussy · Pascal Chayer · Eve Christian · Yvan Cloutier · Philippe Collette · Robert Collin · Raymond Côté · Louis Coutu · Nancy Daviault · Evelyne Delisle · Jerome Demers · Gordon Denison · Simon Deslauriers · Jocelyne Desnoyers · Audrey Desormeaux · Katherine Dooling · Joelle Dube · Réjean Dubord · Pierre Dufresne · Daniel Dupuis · Robert Fleury · Jean-Philippe Fortier · Benoit Fournier-Pelletier · Daniel Gagnon · Daniel Gamache · Martin C. Gaudet · Pierre-Luc Gauthier · Mario Gélinas · Olivier Gervais · Lyne Gervais · J.C. Gonzalez-Mendez · Jean Gosselin · Marjolaine Goulet · Raymond Goulet · Sylvie Gravel · Olivier Gravel-Racine · Suzanne Guay · Jean-Sebastien Hannigan · Sue Holloway · Carole Huculiak · Benoît Huot · Pascal Jetté · Martin Junior · Marc Labrecque · Jérémie Lacerte · Bruno Lambert · Michel Lapierre · Luc Larocque · Jean-Sébastien Lavigne · Angie Lebessis · Julien L'ecuyer · Martin Lefebvre · Sylvie Lemay · Etienne Lemay · Jullen Lemay Hardy · Marc Letendre · Gilles Létourneau · Patrice Liautaud · Anne-Marie Linteau · Steve MacLean · Chantal Mailhot · Robert James Manovich · Michel Marinelli · Johanne Marino · Isabelle Martel · Charline Mathieu · Melanie Mathieu · Annie Menard · France Mercier · Christian Michaud · Mario Millette · Alain Mimeault · Diane Mondou · Julie Morin · Eric Nadeau · Claude Nadeau · Vivano Nget · Mai-Anh Ngo · Anne No Delaide · Denis Oakes · Richard O'Bomsawin · Francisco Olano · Bill Olshefsky · Jean-Guy Ouellette · Richard Payette · Patrick Perreault · Evelyne Perron · Laurianne Plante · Matthieu Proulx · Genevieve Renaud-Bouchard · Matthieu Robitaille · Carol Ross · Nathalie Seguin · Walter Sieber · Charles Stojc · Matthew Svorcsek · Brigitte Trudeau · Sylvie Vachon · Daniel Valiquette · Luc Vigneault · Bernard Voyer · Alexander Watson · Michael Webber · Trevor Wieskopf · Marieve Wilson · Nathan Wong · Carmen Woo **40** Tommy Adamopoulos · Katherine Adams · Hilary Adams · Debra Arbec · Carmen Archambault · François Armand · Pierre Arpin · Antoine Aylwin · Evert Bastet · Janelle Beauchemin · Carl Beauchesne · Dominique Beaudet · Sebastien Beaupre · Jean-Francois Beauregard · Laun Bell · Nicholas Belliveau · Michael Bennett · Michel Bernard · Chad Birk · Karine Bissonette · Annie Blanchette · Patrice Boily-Martineau · Sarah Boissé-Habel · Olivier Bonvoulour · Yanick Bouchard · John Boudreau · Myriam Bouffard · Michel Boulos · Louis-Olivier Brassard · Jean-Luc Brassard · Yoan Breton · Alain Brisebois · Burtsel Carrigan · Cassandra Castillo-Lamarche · Eliane Cayouette · Frédéric Chagnon · Catherine Charron-Delage · Craig Cheek · Caroline Chochol · Marie-Helene Claveau · Yannick Cloutier-Désy · Antonio Colasurdo · Michel Courtemanche · Fabien Cuisinier Raynal · Dagmar Daghofer · Edouard Darche · Martine Daval · Anthony De Vincentis · Laura De Wael · Haigo Derian · Marie-Soleil Deschenes · Andre Desmarais · Valerie Dewald · Tanya Di Bennardo · Salimata Diarra · Alan Dizdarevic · Lara Augusta Dizdarevic · Sophie Dubuc · Jean Durocher · Benoit Ethier · Joelle Ethier · Monique Ethier · Marc Ethier · Santo Fata · Ellen Filippelli · Lucia Formenton · Emilie Fournel · Jean-Marc Fournier · Amelie Fournier · Denis Fragias · Gerry Frappier · Maurice Gagné · Marie-Pierre Gagné · Benoit Gagnon · Sophie Gagnon · Sébastien Galarneau · Paul Gallagher · Wendy Galley · Raymond Garneau · Pierre Gauthier · Jean-François Gauthier · Jean Marc Genereux · Caroline Genest · Camille Gignac · Nathalie Giguere · Martin Gilbert · Diane Girard · Simon Godin · Luc Grenier · Natasha Groves · Henry Hering · Pablo Hernandorena · Lawrence Herscovici · Carolyne Hudson · Martin Isabelle · Margaret Jackson · Cosmin Jelea · Alexandre Kaidbey · Robert Kelly · Dan Kratochvil · Jeffrey Kroll · Yves Labarre · Nadia Labonte · Josée Laflamme · Jocelyn Lafond · Angela Lambrow · Maxime Lariviere · Christine Lavallée · Andre Lavoie · Emmanuelle Lebeau-Guertin · Robert Lebel · Annabelle Lefebvre · Philippe Lemay-Hardy · Pascal Lemieux · Simone Pierre Lessard · Sauvé Lise · Wendy Loucks · Ecaterina Lungutescu Marin · Tamara Lynch · Xin Miao Ma · Jason Magder · Julie Mahoney · Cheryl Anne Makinson · Frederick Mallette · Marie-Eve Marleau · Mariline Martel · Beatrice Martin · Stéphane Massicotte · Daniel Ménard · Brett Michalak · Paul J. Mirshak · Lyse-Andrée Mondou · Maxime Monnet · Alwyn Morris · Benjamin Mumme · Jo-Ann Munro · Carolyn Oliver · Alan Orton · Michael Pagano · Melanie Palumbo · Panikos Panagi · Marco Pasteris · Bernard Pepin · Elizabeth Proulx · Jonathan Provencher · Frederik Provencher · Peter Ramadeen · Isabelle Rayle-Doiron · Bertrand Raymond ·

Lise Remy · Richard Renaud · Lise Richard · Catherine Riendeau · Nancy Rivard · Jonathan Rivard-Cloutier · Julie Roch · Olivier Roy · Kristiana Salmon · Adam Samson · Samuel Samson · Michel Saucier · Jacques Sauve · Claude Sauve · Chadd Sessenwein ·Nanci Ship · Meagan Sledge · Mark Smith · Aurélie Tabarah · Gilles Tessier · Christian Thu-Thon · Caroline Tison · Anne-Josee Trepanier · Shannon Valliant · AmanDa Willey · Cathy Wright · Francis Young **41** Day off / *Congé* **42** Alan Abrahamson · Amos Alter · Stephane Ashby · Joseph Assalian · Jenna Baker · Paul Balthazard · Shawn Bardell · Sarah Barron · Samuel Beauchesne · Pierre Beaudoin · Jeff Beauger · Johanne Beaulieu · Luc Bellemare · Travis Benoche · Alain Bergeron · Guylaine Bernier · Louis-Philippe Bernier · Issam Bidi · Dan Bigras · Claude Boivin · James Bolvari · Allison Boothroyd · Genevieve Borne · Eric Bouchard · Marc-Andre Boucher · Paul Bravi · Samuel Bruneau · Valérie Brunet · François Bucci · Doreen Canatonquin · David Cape · Guy Carignan · Pierre Chamberland · Yick Shun Eason Chan · Kristopher Chapman · Pierre Charron · Shawnee Chartrand · Sarah Chartrand · Andre Chatelain · Sylvie Chénier · Kingsley Cheung · Josée Chouinard · France Chretien-Desmarais · Marcia Cintra · Sarah Cook · Josée Corbeil · Richard Corbeil · Bryan Crisalli · Angela Cutrone · Sylvie Daigle · Zachary Daunoravicius · Shauna Dawson · Caroline Deitcher · Colette Delaney · Cynthia Dellsle · Alain Demers · Michel Dépatie · Dean Di Maulo · Melody Drapeau · Gilles Drapeau · Jesse Druxerman · Jean-René Dufort · Jacques Dumont · Jean Dupre · Sandra East · Daniel Etcovitch · Bob Eyton-Jones · Gordon Farrell · Herb Finkelberg · Brent Flowers · Danny Foisy · Stéphanie Fontaine · Demetrios Jimmy Frantzeskos · Guylaine Gagné · Daniel Gagnier · France Gagnon · Benoit Gagnon · Connie Gelber · Mireille Gendron · Lucie Genereux · Michael Gilbert · Martin Giroux · Rachel Giulione · Peter Goodin · Kelsey Gossen · Payal Grover · Jean-Marc Guay · Roland Guillon · Marie-Erika Gutt · Thomas Hall · Marina Hartl · Alexandra Hartnell-Godin · Alexandra Herrington · Justin Hunt · Marc Hunter · Elena Isinbaeva · Brent Jackle · Lindsay Jacques-Antoine · Dominique Jamet · Martine Jasmin · Joey Kasz · Masudul Hai Kazi · Anna Kolakowski · Alexander Korneev · Hugo Lachambre · Charles Laflamme · Michael Lafleur · Nathalie Lambert · Yves Lamontagne · Josee Lariviere · Robbie Laxer · Bernie Lebovits · Michel Lefrancois · Richard Legare · Maxime Leroux-Gagnon · Mario Letourneau · Michel Levasseur · Annie Levesque · John Lewicki · Yan Liu · Jean-Christophe Lortie · Enza Lucifero · Kelsey Madejchuk · Peter Mammas · Francine Marcotte · Eric Martineau · Jordan Daniel McAran Bourque · Andrew McMillin · Sebastien Melo · Lucie Mirandette · Geoff Molson · Allen Mon · Lisa Mon · Bhavnik Kaur Nanda · Frederick Newman · Marc Normandeau · Alexandre Oakes-Camara · Mathieu Ouellet · Carmela Palermo · Toso Pankovski · Marcel Patenaude · France Patenaude · Michael Patone · Michel Patry · Michel Paul · Ryan Anthony Payne · Jean-Luc Peloquin · Natalie Pepiot · Marc Plamondon · Alexandra Plante · Van Be Quach · Pierre Remillard · Maxime Rémillard · Serge Renaud · James Timothy Richards · Salvatore Rivera · Julie Robert · Larry Rossy · Julie Rouette · Eric Routhier · Charles Roy · Lisa Rubin · Kendra Ryan · Jacques E. Samson · Danistan Saverimuthu · Mike Sciscente · Ken Scott · Kevin Shaw · Olivia Sheehy-Gennarelli · Greg Shulkin · Mark Simonson · Michael Sinclair · David Smocot · Robert Soly · Robert St. Germain · Sonia Stergar · Peter Sterling · André St-Jean · Zeshan Syed · Maryse Taillefer · Rebecca Taylor · Ben Temple · Ida Teoli · Robert Tremblay · Pierre Trépanier · Jason Upton · Jean Vachon · Kevin Vallely · Todd Van Der Heyden · Guillaume Vanasse · Michelle Vanderzon · Jacques Villeneuve · Marc Walder · Maria Walliser Anesini · Lynette Whiley · Patrick Wilson · Nomiki Zografakis · Pirmin Zurbriggen **43** Robert Alain · Graham Allan · Zora Ammarguellat · Ginette Auclair · Bob Baggs · Rene Belanger · Francois Belle-Isle · Frédéric Bergeron · Marc-Andre Bertrand · Luc Boivin · Ruchama Borno · Olga Botygina · Alain Bouchard · Jessica Bouchard · Keith Braye · Jeff Broughton · Silvia Cademartori · Serge Charbonneau · Roxanne Charette · Alain Charette · Louise Chevrette · Laura-Alexie Chevrolat · Maude Cigna · Alexandre Cigna · Jim Cooke · Daniel Cousineau · Donald H. Creppin · David Dryden · Mélanie Dubé · Pierre Ducharme · Sylvie Dussault · James Eadie · James Erskine · Sameh Fahmy · Claude Falardeau · Rodrigo Fernandez · Mike Fisher · Richard Fitzbay · Ellen Fraser · Danny Gagne · Bernard Gay · Annyck Gervais · Louis Giguère · Sonia Girard · Jacques Gravel · Gérard Gravelle · Christian Groleau · Jacques Groulx · Dan Groulx · Louise Groulx · Kathleen Grzyb · Amanda Hamilton · Paul Harrison · Simon Hawkins · Peter Heilmann · Paul Hines · Judy Howard · Ali Jaber · Denise Joanette · Ed Kane · Bruce Kidd · Tom King · Derek Kopke · Anna Kozlovskaya · Philippe Labelle · Sylvain Labelle · Jean Labonté · Marcel Lacroix · Marie-Pier Lafortune · Manon Lafortune · Yanic Lanthier · Gary Large · Julie Lavallée · Sylvain Leduc · Benjamin (Yoong-Il) Lee · Jean Pierre Léger · Amélie Léger · Yanik Lussier · Paul MacInnis · Philippe Marion · Joey Mc Guirk · Andrew McClelland · Sue McLennan · Simon McMullen · Gary Meador · Jean Moreau · Denis Normand · Cory O'Neill · Karen Ouellette · Lana Paxton · Marc Pelosse · Josée Pépin · Pierre Piche · Sylvie Pilon · GuylainE Plante · Réal Plourde · Raymond Poulin · Marc Poulin · Robert Presland · Amy Qi · Steve Requin · Mariela Alejandra Rivera · Gilles Rochette · Thomas Roussy · Marie-Christine Roy · Joe Rubino · Clarence Ruddy · Wayne Russell · Luc Sabourin · Joey Saputo · Elena Savilova · Francois Seigneur · Andre Serero · Sergey Shivrin · Larry Smith · Don Stewart · Pierre St-Jean · Bruny Surin · Katherine Symonds · Patrice Tellier · Kevin Tressler · Marie-Claude Viau · Nathalie Vinette · Alex Vit · Marisa Volpe · Helen Walsh · Peter Werthner · George Wilkinson · Graham Young **44** Luc Adam · Christine Aquino · Bernie Ashe · Amber Asp-Chief · Caroline Assalian · Jonathan Ball · Anya Barrett · Michel Beauchesne · Jean Beaudoin · Audrey Beauséjour · Tara Beitel · Karl Belanger · Philippe Bergeron · David Bernatchez · Jenny Beyer · Lija Bickis · Emma Bischof · Lise Blanchard · Heidi Bonnell · Antoine Boulet · Neil Bouwer · Kait Bowser · Jeff Boyd · Gilles Brisebois · Alain Brisson · Michael Brossard · Betty Brown · Melissa Pauline Brunet · Janet Burnside · Celina Cada-Matasawagon · Guylaine Cadoret · Patrick Cammaert · Michael Chambers · David Charette · Cheyanne Charley · Shannel Charley · Crystal Charley · Al Charron · Paul Chauvin · Charline Clement · Mike Coates · Jessica Contant · Joanie Cooper · Jeff Costello · Rita Cote · Nancy Cotnoir · Ron Currie · Roméo Dallaire · Cecile Dalpe · Mike Dash · Zach Desousa · Carl Dessureault · Gavin Deutscher · Jennifer Dorr · Claude Dubuc · Annie Durand-Brunet · James Duthie · Veronica Engelberts · Keegan Eshkawkogan · Tim Fagan · Laurel S. Fallon · Frederic Filion · Rebecca Fleming · Robert Fleury · Eric Foget · Timothy Foisy · Mark Gall · Karen Gaumond · Lesley Gay · Anne Nila George-Alfred · Lorraine Gouin · Shady Hafez · Kevin Haime · Stephen Hale · James Hall · Joanne Hanlon · Brittany Hanna · Gail Haskins · Patrick Haussler · Shelby Hayter · Christopher Henderson · Elaine Huisman · Randy Huyck · Lori Ierullo · Lloyd Jamieson · Joé Juneau · Alexandra Kangok · Tom Kawasaki · Karol Kincek · Brenda Kinsella · Kathleen Knezevic · Marc Lacelle · Brigitte Lanois · Andre Leclerc · Kathryn Lefebvre · Dominique Lefebvre · John Leslie · Steven Lively · Jonathan MacDonald · Matthew MacDonald · Vimal Maheshwari · Robert Marland · Jean Marmoreo · Peter Masson · Guy Matte · Patrick Maynard · Charles McCabe · Donna McCrady · Airlie McGhee · Jane McLaren · Carol Anne Meehan · Dion Metcalfe · Heather Michel · Telisa Miller · Erin Moore · Marina Moraitis · Karl Morel · David Morrow · Elaine Murphy · Mike Murray · Bryan Murray · Kelly Murumets · Molly Mutiisa · John Kevin Newman · Tiffany Noddin · Johanne Norman · Claude Ottawa · Dipa Patel · Bhavini Patel · Mike Patterson · Harvey Patterson · James Peltier · Miguel Perez · Alex Perrier · James Peters · Trinh Phan · Gilles Picard · Kris Picard · Dany Plante · Natalie Poirier · Anica Praught · Kingue Quan · Emilie Rabeau · Robert Ramsay · Robert Reid · Greg Richards · Campbell Rodgers · Yves Rolland · Calin Rovinescu · Denise Saeki · Conrad Sauve · Joseph Sayer · Ben Scheffel · Nate Schipper · Mark Brian Shuffler · Cathy Smith · Derek Spencer · Denise St. Louis · John Stackhouse · Robert St-Amour · Henry Starzynski · Christian St-Jacques · Beverley Sunday · Christiane Talbot-Horne · Marilyn Tan · Michael Thompson · Caitlin Tolley · Chau Tran · Mark Tremblay · Lina Tsakiris · Tony Tulugak · Dean Utting · Fotis Vassilyadi · Wendy Verbaan · Jasmine Viau · Tony Viner · Carolyn Waldo · Ed Walker · Allison Wawryn · Debbie Weinstein · Jodi White · Josee Young **45** Stephanie Ashton · Erinn Baptiste · Brad Bennett · Murray Braddock · Derek Burney · Rob Buwalda · Maxine Cammock · Annel Carballo · Brian Carty · Mauro Catana · Don Churchill · Daniel Connor · David Cote · Russell Coughlin · Bill Courchaine · Olivia Crack · Cora Lynn Craig · Barb Danford · Geoffrey Dean · Marilyn Delarge · Brian Dinwoodie · Elizabeth (Liz) Dobrovich · Robyn Edge · Mubarek Faris · Dorothy Ficuciello · Luc Fleurant · Adrian Frei · Dean Frohwerk · Michelle Galipeau · Brian Gear · Graham Gleddie · Nicholas Glennon · Tracy Gorman · Aundre Grant · Mike Grue · Jade Guilbert · Dianne Hinds · Laura Hodson · Mike Hoftyzer · Brenda Hoople · Dwight Hounsell · Rodney Hudgin · Dennene Huntley · Zeeshan Hussain · John James · Robert Janes · Tatiana Jean-Venne · Carol Jefferies · David John · Simon Johnson · Andrew Jones · Allison Jones · Howard Kack · Angela Kirk · Alexander Lang · Mark Lau · M. George Lewis · Vadim Lichnev · Kelly Lopes · Michael Lordon · Douglas MacDonald · Jean MacLean · Wayne Majaralie · Elizabeth Manley · Tam Matthews · Tara McCrory · Mark McDonnell · Jessica Meneray · Jody Mitic · Mark Mooder · Danielle Morrison · Julie Noel · Ted Paluch · Christopher Parker · Mary Parson · Sophie Pellicano · Robert Perry · Sabiha Rahman · Stewart Ray · Dariusz Rempel · Sylvie Richard · Morgan Ring · Lisanne Roy · Martin Ruddy · Mark Sabad · Barbara Ann Scott-King · Deborah Shaman · Bob Shropshire · David Shulist · Kathleen Smiley · Allison Smith · Willard Smith · Bruno Solby · Roxane Stevens · Karine Tawagi · Charmaine Tedford · Trevor Thompson · Andrew Townsend · Michael Trauner · Peter Trus · Cynthia Urquhart · Eda Van Der Linden · Tony Van Muyden · Sharon Vanier · Katryne Villeneuve · Darlene Walker · Connie Walsh · William Watt · Laura Welsh · Natalie Westrup · Nancy Worsfold · Richard Yeo · Mickey Yuen · Alexander Zolotoochin **46** Josee Adam · Ewan Affleck · Neda Amani · Andrea Austen · Angie Balian · Gerry Barnes · Alan Thomas Bates · Mike Benedict, Jr. · Christiane Besner · Andrea E. Bolger · Andrew Brewin · James Brown · Barry Bruce · Dave Buckingham · Edward Bush · Beverley Cameron · Kevin Chapman · Susan Charlebois · Betty Clarke · Marjorie Coakwell · Colleen Cotter · Anna Cutland · Brita Danielson · Keivan Daryushnejad · Luisa De Amicis · Anne Doig · Kevin Dunseath · Morgan Duval · Bill Eggertson · Louis-Michel Elie · Chris Fehr · Alison Fowler · Sean Fry · Tina Fusano · Shiri Gabriel · Bruno Gagnon · Nicholas Giacomantonio · Darlene Gillard · Alexandra Glover · Trina Gorr-Alllson · Moya Greene · Sean Groves · Edwin Haas · Peter Higgins · Shung Hay Ho · Yvonne Holland · Ian Holstead · Kathryn Jackson · Anne Jardin Alexander · Sam Jawad · Peter Jechel · Van Johnston · Traci Jorgenson · Greg Joy · Dawn Juneau · Vicki Keith · Vicki Kenney · Susan Matilda King · Lauree Knight · Alexander Kolodziej · Kathy Lamont · Joanne Langlois · Jacques Laplante · Jeff Lay · Cyril Leeder · Michel Leger · James Logan · Sara MacLeod · Katherine Eileen McNally · Jeanne McNeill · Maryanne Morin · Edward Murphy · Gavin Nash · Amy Nickerson · Kenneth Noakes · Rosemary O'Brien · Carlene Paquette · John Partridge · Katie Pelley · Kerry Piccinetti · Mario Pinard · Tobey-Ann Pinder · Todd Piquette · Camille Poirier · Mark Potter · Sophie Pyne · Jean Margaret Rawling · Alan Richards · Chantale Robertson · Andre Robichaud · Danielle Rourke · Rik Saaltink · Stephen Samis · Kevin Saunders · Ken Scott · Kim Sebrango · Donna Seguin · Erin Seymour · Brent Shaw · Alissa Simpson · Catherine Sinnott · Jeffrey Solatchki-Quiroz · Clay Spero · Lisa Stubbings · Adam Summers · Stephanie Teal · Donna Thomlinson · Ed Timson · Christine Trudeau · Pierre Vanderhout · Steven Vandevisch · Kathy Varty · Todd Watkins · Cindy Wendler · Kristi Whaley · Desmond White · Ashly Wind · Michele Wright · Gordon Vernon Young · Philippe-Jacques Zaor · Narciso Zorzi **47** Daniel Abramowitz · Jason Aguirre · Scott Allison · Noah Aychental · James Barnes · Taylor Barr · Josh Bart · Ann Barton · Rachael Boyd · Dan Braund · Yvan Breton · John Briscoe · Todd Brown · Mario Brum · Trevor Bumstead · Lee Burgess · Sarah Cadman · Arlene Campbell · Nathan Card · Richard Carrier · Renée-Claude Carrière · Cheryl Carrière · Roger Chernuck · Greg Christian · Cecily Clarke · Jeremy Coughler · Jessica Currie · Silvana da Silva · Marny Dalglish · Celeste Denesuik · Jason Derbyshire · Josh Eikens · Julie Elkie · Terry Fitzgerald · Bruce Forrester · Maris Fraser · Bob Gainey · Chris Gallagher · Adam Gilbert · Connor Godin · Chloée Godin-Jacques · Peter Goodman · Bridget Graham · Sarah Graham · Dominic Grandmaison · Danny Gray · Jeff Guthrie · Martin Gysbers · Sharon Hall · Robert Hampson · Joy Haveman · Larry Hilborn · Kevin Hill · Carol Holme-Killingbeck · Tom Hoppe · Janice Hung · Louis Hurteau · Nicole Irvine · Tim Irwin · Susan Jikeli · Amy Johnson · Matthew Kennedy · Shauna Kennedy · Siavash Khallaghi · Cathy King · Dave Kirkland · Andrew Kollo · Jennifer Kroschel · Daniel Lauzon · Joey Lavender · Stephanie Le Camp · Ben LeBlanc · Robert Lemelin · Marie Lemelin · Melody MacPherson · Camelia Maracle · Deborah Maycock · Barry McCamus · Nicole McFarland · Jo-Anne McGarvey · Gord McGregor · Lori McLeod · Colin McLeod · Alexander McNaught · Audrey Ménard · Rebecca Micallef · Karen Michelsen · Linda Middleton · Madeline Mills · Gerry Moore · Lynnette Moore · Connor Mulders · Sheila Munro · Susan Nelson · Janet Nickason · Francis Parkinson · Matthew Peca · Paul Peters · Gregory Pigeon · Mélanie Plante · Brittany Provost · Gerald Putman · Chengbo Qian · Alexandra RainVille-Barzey · Linda Ready · Peter Reid · Rocco Ribuffo · Mark Rickards · Barry Robinson · Daniel Rose · Al Rose · Bonnie-Lee Ross · Patricia Russell · Lisa Sansom · Robert Savage · Tammy-Lise Schroeder · Wayne Scott · Douglas Seeley · Duncan Seston · Travis Sharpe · Dean Shepard · Nicole Shepherd · Cameron Sherratt · Michael Skinner · Roger St.Jean · Bevin Stephenson · Scott Strickland · Raven Tabobandung · Kailey Taplin · Bev Thomson · Gregory Thuemen · Nancy Tighe · Vishal Tulsi · Jeff Van Duynhoven · Darren Vance · Bhavana Varma · Laurie Walker · Graeme Watson · David Weir · Steve Weller · James Whalen · Lewis Craig White · Garry Whorpole · Tina Williams **48** Ben Adair · Amy Addison · Ryan Albright · Laurindo Alves · Cathy Andrew · Paul Appleman · Hadley Archer · Alana Ashley · Marie Asuncion · Robert Daniel Aziz · Debbie Bailie · Leslie Joanne Barrow · Sadie Bartoli · Gerry Beelen · Ryan Biggar · Emma Blackwood · Eva Blevins · Sandy Bolan · Mark Bonokoski · Kaitlyn Bosy · Charles Brown · Julianne Bruce · John Burgess · Rachel Butler · Paul Butler · Glenn Butler · Ronald Cameron · Dan Carter · Tony Carvalho · Laura Churchman · Brent Clemens · Dani Cohen · Paula Collick · Vincenzo Colucci · Tanya Connolly · Alexandrea Cullen · J.C. Cunningham · Heather Dart · Phillipe Dass · Gail Dawson · Michael de la Roche · Laura DeGeer · Georgia Derrick · Amanda Doris · D'Arcy Dykeman · Liana Eftaxias · Arturo Elias · Jessica Enman · Darren Joel Fife · Dennis Fletcher · Chris Fraser · Tanya Fusco · Joseph Pierre Andre Gagne · David Garard · Barry Gardner · Mike Garvey · Lawson Gay · Cody George · Sukhdeep Gill · Azzy Golshani · Tim Gordon · Trevor Gregory · Eric Guenette · Ilka Guttler · Blair Halchuk · Harvey Hall · Alex Hallink · Mary-Jean Harris · Eli Hawman · Jeff Hayes · Michael Heffernan · George Henderson · Valerie Henry · Brandy Hewitt · Peter Higley · Brian Hodgson · Diane Howarth · Roger Hunter · Christine Jaros · Ntina Karakitsos · Dick Kauling · Rebecca Keegans · Cheryl Kelly · Sarah Kelly · Sydney Kidd · Stephen Kim · Sandra King · Lyn Krattiger · Andreas Labrakos · Juan Lahmann · Aman Lally · Jamie Lees · Cindy Legare · Marie-Claude Leroux · James Lingard · James Locke · Heather Lowe · Sue Lupton · Gwen Ma · Jason Ma · Garry Maclean · Anthony Manna · John Maraston · Barry Marr · Anne Marshall · Tabitha Marshall · W. Kenneth McCarter · Grant McKenzie · Jody McKinnon · Kevin McReelis · Monica McVeigh · Anique Mercier · Robert Messervey · Nora Mickee · Jacques Mignault · Jack Miller · Karen Moloney · Maurice Mondou · Greg Murphy · Todd Murray · James Nava · Bruce Ogilvie · Geoff Owen · Britt Packer · Catherine Pappas · Julie Parent · Ian Perry · Daniel Pichie · Andrew Pilkington · George Pineau · Steve Poulson · Jennifer Powles · Domenic Primucci · Jack Prins · Sharon Quizon · Carly Ramsay · Katlyn Reed · Marc Renaud · Mike Rennie · Chelsea Ripley · Richard Rivera · Faye Roberts · Jack Robinson · Bridget Rusk · Rachel Ryan · Danielle Ryan · Linda Sargent · Rod Schaaf · Kristina Schaefer · Liana Schepanow · William Schlitt · Robert Seguin · Sandra Shatilla · Barrie Shepley · Mike Sherwin · Jenny Smith · John Srebrnjak · Katie Stevenson · Kate Stock · Sarah Suarez · Angela Suh · David Swaine · Susan Tantalo · Phillip Terry · Mike Theobald · Stephanie Thomson · Joanne Thomson · Chris Tymofichuk · Casey Warren · Jim Watson · Jim Watson · Christina Westcott · Alyssa Wilcox · Laura Williams · Chris Williamson · Craig Wilson · Tim Wilson · Shannon Winlove-Smith · Albert Wintjes · Dimitrios Zarikos **49** Lorena Abitrante · Pauline Albert · Rami Altaher · Sean Amato-Gauci · Ramya Amuthan · Lina Antezam · Elio Antunes · Adam Antunes · Sarah Armstrong · Kyle Balkos · Christina Bardes · Meg Barham · Thomas Barlow · Stephen Beatty · Sandra Beck · Leslie Beck · Doug Beeforth · Stephanie Belanger · Sarah Ben · Gavin Bennett · Christine Bentley · Bernie Bertrand · Landra Berwick · Yoel Berznoger · David Bester · Roberta Bondar · Dennis Bonney · Sunni Boot · Shannon Brant · Matt Brook · Megan Brown · Danielle Brown · Lance Brown · Domenic Calce · Michael Cameron · Krista Camick · Evelyn Carleton · Christine Carter · Tiffany Carver · Kevin Chambers · James Chiu · Tina Chreppas · Dan Cimoroni · Kelly Cooper · Noel Coward · John Craig · Paul Craig · Phillip Crawley · Bill Crothers · Catherine Crozier · Judy Crute · Steve Curry · Corey Dalton · Joe daSilva · Madeleine Davidson · Shannon de Leon · Jan de Vries · Harmond DeJuan · Adam Desjardins · Nerysa Devon · Jordan Di Nardo · Steven Dimitropoulos · Ben Donnelly · Murray Dowey · Owen Duckman · Melissa Duff · Paul Ellis · Chinyere Eni · David Evans · Desmond Fan · Glenn Farber · Carol Farrenkopf · Chris Faulds · Courtenay Ferguson · Robert Finlay · Nicole Forrester · Maria Fortier · Grant Froese · Marien Gehrels · Ellie Geronikolos · Tony Gerosa · Kimberly Glasgow · Lynn Goad · Sue Good · David Grant · Melissa Grelo · Ashy Habib · Kareen Hague · Sam Haines · Paul Halayko · Eric Hammell · Robert Hampson · Tara Hanley · Curt Harnett · Don Harris · Jason Harrow · Jason Hatch · Paul Henderson · Neil Hetherington · Cody Hodgson · Tiffany Hubbard · Craig Hutchison · Kazi Imad Iqbal · Andrew Isaacson · Ferdinand Ismael · Anita Jackson · Hussain Jasim · Dyane Jean Francois · Mark Jones · Janet Jones · Karen Kain · Aneeta Kang · Darren Karasiuk · Tommy Karjalainen · Winston Kassim · Steven Keith · Jane Kelly · Jason Keown · Craig Kielburger · Marc Kielburger · Marek Kloda · Cameron Knox · Brittany Kolenberg · Akshay Kumar · Arthur Kwok · Bernard Kyte · Micheal Lai · Joel Lalla · Marc-Olivier Landry · Magnus Larsson · Dale Lastman · Graydon Lau · Tom Laurie · Daniel Le Blanc · Young Lee · Lindsay Leo · Bellamy Leung · Rick Lewchuk · Graham Lindsay · Edward Lisinski · Tammi Lisson · Barry Lockwood · Tim Logan · Frank Lopes · Jon Love · Tim Lute · John Macfarlane · Craig Machel · Matt Maclean · Shelagh Mair · Nick Majtenyi · Hasaan Malik · Mohamed Manji · Kulbinder Mann · Bryan Marjoram · James Mastorkis · Anne Maxwell · Glen McArthur · Marnie McBean · Lillian Anne McGregor · Erin McLean · Deepa Mehta · Jessica Miller · Leah Miller · Deb Moore · John Moore · Rob Moore · Cole Moro · Caroline Moul · Carolyn Mountjoy · Dave Murray · Mary Murudumbay · Nick Nickolau · Gordon Nixon · Megan Oates · Thomas O'Neill · Brian Orser · Sarah Palmeter · Stephanie Parigoris · Sarah Patel · Runa Patel · Patricia Pearce · Richard Peddie · Marion Penny · Elly Pierre · Jim Pitblado · George Quarcoo · Kelsey Quesnelle · Heather Radford · Lou Ragagnin · Bilaal Rajan · Donna Ramnath · Nicholas Rastasulozas · Jason Reitman · Ivan Reitman · Salvatore Rende · Brian Richardson · Christopher Rigney · Austin Roberts · Alain Robichaud · Sandy Robinson · John P. Roddey · Ann Rohmer · Joseph Rotman · Sandra Rotman · Carrie Russell · Luis Santiago · Cathy Sattelberger · Elfi Schlegel · Robin Sciascia · Catherine Scott · John Scott · Ken Shaw · Evelyn Shelton · Phill Snel · Sheila Solby · Kai Elmer Sotto · David Spear · Joanne St. Bernard · John Stanton · Brian Stemmle · Melanie Stewart · Robin Stewart · Joseph Stokes · Jordan Stone · Stephen Streich · Anna Sturino · Vicky Sunohara · Maha Tam · Jim Telfer · Jayme Teplin · Sritharson Thillanather · Pierre Tomiczek · Robert James Torrance · Mary Jane Torrie · Jay Triano · Lianne Trout · Ben Van der Bloom · Mike Venton · Hilda Vlasic · Owen von Richter · Giorge Voutsas · Paul White · Sheila Whitmore · Harry Willmot · Kris Wong · Norman Wong · Dominic Wong · James Worrall · Peter Wright · William Young · Douglas Youngson · Nicole Zaharopoulos · Ruth Zelding · Jessica Zhu **50** Peter Aceto · Kemal Ahmed · Jack Ammendolia · Harvey Anderson · Christian Andonoff · Katherine Armstrong · Ryan Babcock · Ayoub Bahri · Brad Baker · Robert Balk · Sandra Banks · Shaquille Baptiste · Ryan Bennett · Tim Bethune · Arthur Biyarslanov · Jamiyla Bodkyn-Bryce · Doug Bolger · Wayne Bossert · Zack Boyd · Wesley Brown · Zeljko Bulovic · David Burkholder · Gerald Butts · Janet Caverly · Sarita Chaim · Brian Chandler · Avianna Chao · Paul Chapman · Nina Chen · Johanne Choiniere · Allan Cooney · Cody Cornale · Kayla Cornale · Erin Corrado · Jeremy Cruz · Patricia Davenport · Wanda Day · Christina de la Cruz · Ella Den Elzen · Marilyn Denis · Manjeet Dhuga · Nick Di Nizio · James Dowhaniuk · Dillon Elliotson · Paul Epton · Alyssa Fenuta · Joe Ferraro · Julia Filinski · Wayne Finch · Stephen Finch · Jennifer Finnigan · May Lynne Fong · Frank Fortino · Steve Fox · Sherron Fraser · Nancy Garard · Tony Genco · Olivia Genovese · Steven Gonsalves · Nitin Goomber · Peter Grater · Richard S. Graves · Diane Grunwell · David Harris · Yvonne Hayes · George Heller · Isaiah Henry · Damien Higgins · Sandra Hinojosa · Jamie Hodgson · David Hopkinson · Farhan Hossain · Alexandra Howe · Atif Hussain · Jessie Isberg · Ellis Jacob · Michael Jantzi · Karen Jardim · Mike Joslin · Yana Kabirova · Joan Kahrs · Amekala Kanapathippillai · Lorie Kane · Mara Keaveney · Gillian Kendall · Sheldon Kennedy · John Kimmel · George Kioussis · Mitch Klinger · Nikos Koumettis · Clare Kowaltschuk · Tim Lalach · Frances Lankin · Michael Latimer · Allan Lee · Tina Lee · Michelle Leong · Adina Levy · Richard Lewin · Frank Li · Lei Li · David Lin · James Little · Anne Lockie · Anthony Longo · Laura Longstreet · Ted Lyon · Michael Macmillan · Morteza Mahjour · Margaret Maillet · Mithuran Manogaran · Lindsay Marshall · Alastair Mccluskey · Calvin McDonald · Dave McKay · Matthew McKay · Jim Miller · Laura Miller · Kailey Miller · Cheryl Miller · Bria Mitchell · Cody Mulhern · Laith Nakash · Azad Nassar · Catherine Newman · Laurel Olson · William Onuwa · Kaila Orr · Hasini Palihapitiya · Michael Parise · Ross Parker · Peter Patterson · Donna Peters-Imbrogno · Dushan Petrovich · Judy Piccioni · Mathew Piccioni · Marcus Pidek · Leeanne Pires · Shantee Plummer · Tinisha Powell · Vivienne Poy · Robert Pulkys · George Raios · Madeline Regent · Shawn Reid · Melissa Reinders · Cy Richards Samuels · Joel Richardson · Dwight Robinson · John Rothschild · Terry Rowe · Louise Russo · J. Ken Rutherford · K. Rai Sahi · James Sammut · Robert Santos · Sebastian Sardegna · Donna Sas · Stephen Satchel · Eddie Savaia · Poonam Sethi · Hari Sihvo · Charlie Sims · Laveda Sobieraj · Mike Sorley · Nicholas Sottosanti · Rohan Sovig · Greg Stremlaw · Steven Sugar · Mårten Swahn · Nina Tablon · Paula Tablon · Fernand Taillefer · Emily Tenwesteneind · Adam Terlecki · Mark Thomas · Barbara Thompson · Rod Thompson · William Thompson · Cara Thorne · Vincent Timpano · Youdon Tsamotshang · Sandy Vassiadis · Hank Verbaan · Lisa Virgini · Matthew Vitale · Julia Hon Ngai Wan · Yongjun Wang · John Warren · Bruce White · Kodee Williams · John Willson · Gary Winkworth · Lily Yee · Carli Yim · Raymond Young · Baylee Young · Maggie Zhao **51** Juanita Aden · Tania Alarcon · Stephanie Allard · Paul Allen · Ignatios Antoniadis · Sonia Baldassarre · Lucie Barbera · Jay Barker · Ron Baugh · Noel Bautista · David Bedford · Mary Blake · Regan Blakesly · Nicole Bleiwas · Rolf Bodmer · Carrie Boschman · Sylvie Boucher · Royal Boult · Roger Bourbonnais · Devin Bourbonnais · Sukhdeep Brar · Tom Brown · Phil Brown · Gavin Browne · Kurt Browning · Jessica Bryce · Nick Burgel · Brian Burke · Claire Byrne · Dolly Calderon · Barbara Calderone · Leslie Camm · Susan Campbell · Bill Campbell · Anita Carlyle · Doug Carmichael · Barry Carroll · Beverly Carroll · Rani Chatoorgoon · Steven Cherwenka · Carolyn Chomolok · Sherry Chow · Jesuchrista Chowdhury · Tim Coleman · Stephen Covic · Erika Cowen · Brenley Crawford · Kendall Cripps · Jane Currie · Elaine Dang · Alysia DaSilva · Gianvito De Micheli · Dolly Dhaliwal · Riyaad Dinath · Ken Dinshaw · Mark Dockeray · Nada Drozd · Grazyna Dudar · Matt Dunigan · Brandon Elliott · Mike Elwood · Eric Elwood · Bradley Fay · Larry Figas · Pasquale Finelli · Timothy Fischer · Ron Foxcroft · Janice Fukakusa · Liban Gaashaan · Laura Gage · Neil Gao · Paul Gardiner · Matt Giffen · Beena Goldenberg · Antonio Gomes · Calvin Gomes · Vaishakhi Gopal · Laura Greer · Jan Gregor · Ehin Gukhool · Andy Hale · Jacob Hale · Chris Hamilton · Mark Hardy · John Harrison · Chris Hilborn · Richard Holloway · MIke Hone · Paul Hutchinson · Paul Iamundo · Ken Jackson · Pamela Johnson · Pam Jolliffe · Rod Jones · Brian Karn · Moez Kassam · April Kellie · Brian Kellie · Kathy Khong · Yu-Na Kim · Andrew Kisby · Kelli Knatchbull · Katarina Kovac · John Kozolanka · Lucas Krist · Kathy Kulina · Gary Lafee · Jessica Rae Langelaan · Georges Lariviere · Amy Laski · Peter Lau · Darrell Leadbetter · Avery Lee · Robert Lee · Brian Lee · Natali Leko · Joanna Leung · Vanessa Lewis · Gail Lilley · Scott Lindsay · Jane Luck · Irma Lushi · Kristen MacEachern · Peter MacKinnon · Fawzi Mahmoud · Danijel Margetic · Andrew Markow · Shauna Mathers · Hazel McCallion · Daniel McCartney · Elizabeth McCready · Connie McCulloch · Dympna McCully · Daniel McGrath · Andrew Melito · Andrew Mellegers · Kevin Mellegers · Paul Methot · Mark Meyer · Wendy Milne · Chris Miron · David Miskus · Hannah Moffitt · Lageishon Mohanadas · Rebecca Moran · Connie Morton · Lucas Motyka · Ann Mulvale · Kaitlin Murphy · Brenda Murray · Adeena Niazi · Paul Nieuwland · Moyan Olejko · Vicky Pasqualini · Salim Patel · Jeff Pattison · Robin Pawlak · John E. Peller · Monica Perdomo · Andrew Perkins · Greg Petrie · Dalton Philips · Vanessa Pick · Matthew Porter · Derrick Porter · Cheryl Pounder · Fabio Pozzobon · Min Qi · Michael Quaglia · Crystal Quast · Kiersten Rasmussen · Pareekshit Ravi · Fiona Renzi-Fantin · Cathy Robbins · Deana Rokowski · Andrea Rozzi · Mark Rutledge · Holly Sarvari · Stephanie Scherle · Justin Schlupp · Toni Schofield · Joyce Scott · Tina Scott · Shireen Shaath · Arya Shanab · Iqra Sheikh · Jessica Ashley Shepley · Justin Sherwood · Shantel Singh · Anthony Skrinjar · David Slade · Michael Solby · Julie Sommerfreund · Murray Speers · Cathy Sprague · Jordan Stanford · Scott Stewart · Shawn Stillman · Luke Stockden · Brian Sutton · Abbas Syed · Kirk Synyard · Reka Szabo · Landon Tamas · Susannah Teney · Doug Thompson · Alan Thomson · Lorrie Tomlinson · Garry Tsaconas · Kami Valkova · Adam van Koeverden · Richard Vernon · Jake Verrips · Dennis Villalta · Glen Walter · Kevin Warren · Michael Watson · Murray Webb · Mike West · James Westlake · Greg Westlake · Larry White · Jim Wickware · Kelly Winkiewicz · Aaron Wolkoff · John Wood · Trevor Wrobel · Rhoda Wurtele Eaves · Rhona Wurtele Gillis · Yuan Xue **52** Mike Abbas · Danish Abdali · Mike Accursi · Collette Acres · Clifton Agard · Hughie Ahearn · Taylor Amos · Sandy Annunziata · John Arnold · Isac Arruda · Rick Atkinson · Christopher Balz · Mark Bancroft · Paul Barchiesi · Richard Beaubien · Brian Berry · Nilesh Bhavsar · Cynthia Black · Taylor Black · Robin Black · Cody Black · Shawna Blancher · Twane Boettinger · Nick Bontis · Jim Book · Ashley Bowen · Patti Brien · Jane Broderick · Nathan Butterworth · Edward Cajucom · Tracey Chappell · Kelvin Chen · Belinda Ching · Patricia Chioua · Natalie Chu · Sandra Clement · Tony Collini · Kathy Corbett · Celeste Corless · Phillip Cox · David Craig Mccausland · Sharon Creelman · Denzil Croning · Daniel Cross · Richard Currie · Andrew Czajkowski · Verna Dalgleish · Mike Dekok · Matthew Di Leo · Claire Diffey · Sarah Doherty · Colleen Doppelhofer · Paresh Rajendralal Doshi · Bryant Douglas · Neil Earl · Wade Ellis · Joseph Fegan · Michael Feldbloom · Dawn Fell · Patrick Festing-Smith · Mario Franciosa · Celine Frerotte · Julia Friesen · Leah Furtney · Bo Fusek · Ngonidzashe Francis Garwe · Heather Gerrits · Gregg Gleason · Jacqueline Glenney · Marlin Gold · Jason Goldberg · Don Gordon · Alison Gorham · Craig Green · Jessie Guardsman · Nels Guloien · Sara Hagerman · Michelle Harkness · Melissa Hill · Tom Hipsz · Arnold Huffman · Robert R. Hunter · Katya Hvostova · Kathy Inman · Robert Jacques · Inderpaul Jassal · Paul Je · Colin Jenkins · Valerie Johnson · Gilbert Jones · Bernard Jones · Rachel Jones · Susan Jones · Larry Jones · Mathew Jones · Cathy Jones · Rick Jones · Robert Jones · Charles Juravinski · Archie Katzman · Pat Kearse · Bev Keogh · Jayden Kerr · Gord Kerr · Robert Kirby · Laurie Kirk · Tim Knechtel · Robert Korver · Alexan Kory · Nathalie Krauss · Henry Krauss · Kayla Kuyvenhoven · Michael Lambert · Jack Langelaan · Jo-Ann Lefko-Johnston · Noelle Leslie · Dave Lewis · Max Lightstone · Clark Lishman · Sean Littler · Anna Lydall · Mark Lynch · Karen MacDonald Carey · Marg MacVinnie · Cait Mancuso · Evan Mann · Greg Marchetti · Peter Marlow · Grant Martin · Jeanne McGlenister · Timothy McGrath · Kim McLean · Dale Mcleod · Carol McPherson · Christine Medland · Andrea Middaugh · Mark Middleton · Meaghan Mielke · Joshua Miller · Tom Minard · Alexander Morrison · Les Myers · Bill Nagy · Alexandra O'Brien · Susan Palmer-Komar · Nick Perpick · Devi Persaud · Joshua Peters · Susan Phillips · Angela Pollock · Rob Proctor · Kim Puryear · John Raftery · Ashif Ratanshi · Brady Reardon · Percy Rescorl · Aislynn Reynolds · Kimberley Ribble-Orr · Maureen Roberts · Tamara Roberts · Colin Roberts · Craig Robinson · Trisha Romance · Sonya Romanowski · Mitchell Rudman · Maryam Saleemi · Paul Saltzman · Don Sardinha · Kelly Sargent · Mitchell Sawatzky · Julie Scott · Gordon Shand · Henry Silva · Gordon Singleton · Zev Skolnik · Ken Smith · Kristen Steiner · Lorelei Stolpmann · Suliman Sulimankhil · Carina Tiozzo · Josh Trinder · Lynn Truckle · Daniel Unger · Ted Van Geest · Max Van Valkenburg · Mark Varey · Maria Vidotto · Ajay Virmani · Colleen Walker · Martha Westgate · Carolyn Whelan · Mary Williams · Brian Wiser · Robert J. Wismer · Matthew Wyatt · Donald Yeomans **53** Brad Adams · Brent Aitchison · Alexandra Albert · Lydia Allaire · Leanne Ambis · Arunas Antanaitis · Sam Baio · Mary Ann Barnes · Melissa Barzanjah · Sharon Beaudet · Bev Beaver · Clark Bernat · Stephen Bewcyk · Phyllis Bomberry · Brenda Bookbinder · Dr. Risa Bordman · William Borgmann · Pete Borsellino · Dr. Rob Boulay · Lesley Bracken Coyne · Dr. Sandy Buchman · Karen Burka · Thomas Burke · Caytlen Burning · Fern Burning · Christopher Byl · Sarah Calder · Dr. Ian Casson · Kate Caughey · Hugh Caughey · Guy Celli · Mike Chalupka · Linda Cheung · Bianca Ciccarelli · Joseph Coneybeare · Michael Cooper · Naoml Cowan · Shawlena Curley · Domenic Della Penna · Lorene Dick · Harold Dion · Kathy Doherty-Masters · James Dol · Philip Dulude · Keith Eliuk · Edwin Evans · Mike Foderick · Laura A. Gainey · Lauren Gallaccio · Andrea Garvie · Craig Gay · Brian Geerts · Francie Govan · Andrew Greenaway · Daniel Grincevicius · Benoit Guay · Stacey Guest · Dr. Cal Gutkin · Anissa Hamel · Jennifer Hedger · Robert Henry · Brittany Hicks · Warren Hill · Scott Hill · Marty Hill · Joanne Hill · John Hobbs · Chris Hoekstra · Dr. Clarissa Holding · Alastair Hood · Lesia Hucal · Fizan Jaffar · Randall Jegins · Jason Johnson · John Johnstone · Stan Jonathan · Grace Kelly · Evelyn Kelly · Dr. Jonathan Kerr · Catherine Kiley · Melanie Kok · Adam Koscielak · Teri Kramer · Dr. Sarah Kredentser · Harry Laforme · Sharlene Langan · Audrey Lanigan · Paula Lederman · Joline Lee · Dr. Michael Lee-Poy · Dr. Francine Lemire · Greg Longboat · Lourdes Lopes · Iain Lowe · Mary Lumsden · Crystal MacDonald · Robert Mackay · Dr. Cathy Maclean · Katie MacLeod · Megan Maharaj · Ashley Malek · Dr. Bernard Marlow · Karen Martin · Chezney Martin · Yvonne Martin-Cowhig · Dr. Frank Martino · Darryl McDonald · Maria McKinnon · Michel Menard · Eric Miller · Sandra (Sam) Miller · Joe Montour · Nadine Moroziuk · Stephanie Murtland · Dave Muzyczuk · Dr. Ieva Neimanis · Joel Noden · Dr. Kendall Noel · Alix Nori · Maria Nowak · Anna Olson · Dylen Pake · Adrian Palencar · Derek Palmer · Sabrina Parrotta · Tracy Phelps · Olivia Piluso · Dr. Nick Pimlott · Craig Point · JeNnifer Poppe · Chantal Primeau · Bradley Quinn · Dr. Val Rachlis · Lori Rayner · Heather Renzella · Robert Reynolds · Robert Ribaric · Cheryl Rowe · Amanda Rowley · Sivarajah Saiyanthan · Joseph Sawicki · Janie Schirrmacher · John Sharpe · Rebecca Sillers · Scott Simmons · Terry Smith · Sid Smith · Stan Socha · Kristina Strojin · Barbara Stymiest · Kevin Sullivan · Leah Taggart · Jen Tarnowski · Linda Thom · Jerrica Thomas Hill · Natasha Thombs ·

Matt Thompson · Michelle Tobias · Lorenzo Tomei · Richard Tupholme · Jason Vaillant · Nick Veloce · Michael S. Ventresca · Tonya Verbeek · Gerry Vitiello · Janae Vlaar-Philbrick · Barb Wadden · Janet Wallace · Dr. Allyn Walsh · Michael Walthius · Shayne Ward · Sharon Wickham · Alexis Williams · Duff Williamson · Ruth Wilson · Thomas Wilson · Laurel Yama · Robert Yamich · Kenneth Yik · Adam Zimmermann **54** Laura Almeida · Gregory Angrish · Mary Antone · Richard Austin · Arieanna Balbar · Heather Barker · Christopher Beausoleil · Cathy Bechard · Jim Bexis · Sue Birtch · Shaun Bisson · Sara Boccanfuso · Dennis Boileau · Catherine Bond · Lindsay Boyd · David Boyko · Bonnie Brady · Dean Braund · Kenneth Burke · Thomas Butler · Krystyna Buxton · Kelsey Cabral · Dan Campana · Dana Cathcart · Sarah Chinnick · Alexander Ciccocelli · Mike Clark · Doug Consiglio · Elizabeth Czenczek · Blair Davies · Wayne Day · Darin Dees · Shannon C. Denny · Remi Desjardins · Alexis Devos · Steven Donker · Jennifer Dorland · Lindsay Doxtator · Crispin Duenas · Wayne Durst · Diane Easton · Cam Erwin · Mahan Farshidfar · Wade Feere · A.J. Fordham · Madison Furlan · Mirjana Garcia · Brent Gordon · Tracey Graham · Darren Grant · Haylee Groot · Richard Haddow · Christine Harrop · Mike Hodgkinson · John Hondzel · Anne Huggins · Sally Jacquart · Chase Jacques · Katrina Joosse · Dimple Joshi · Sonny Kreitzer · Bryan Labadie · Kelly Lanthier · Barbara Lavery · George Ledressay · Jane Ledressay · Peter Lee · Douglas Lee · Tyler Legrand · John Lettieri · William Lew · Glenn Lickers · Jason Limberg · Jamie Lockington · Chris Lori · Paul Lovelock · Brock MacKenzie · Robert Martin · Laurel Martin · Tania Mask · Lincoln McCardle · William McComb · Monty II McGahey · Amy McGee · Steve Michalopoulos · Jillian Miller · Tara Miller · Hugh Mitchell · Shayna Moor · Drake Mugridge · Chris Munro · Stuart Owen · Leslie Parking · Gregory Parnell · Kyle Pearce · James Penner · Zelia Pereira · Amanda Perini · Frank Peruzzi · Cory Petznick · Keegan Pittuck · Richard Plaquet · Andrea Pountney · Debbie Pratt · David Purdy · Joshua Reaume · John Redfern · Joe Richards · April Rietdyk · Barbara Roberts · Helen Robertson · Brian Rose · Lari Sabbe · Dale Scott · Nancy Sherritt · Cam Sinnesael · William P. Smith · Richard Stewart · Allan Taverner · Angela Taylor · Jan Tebbutt · Michael Therrien · Sharon Thorpe · Ashley Toscani · Donnamarie Traina · Eric Ursic · Brandon Van Wyk · Brad Vandehogen · Henry Vehovec · Susan Veltri · Monica VonOppeln · Jodie-Lynn Waddilove-Corbiere · Jim Waite · Meg Welch · Jacob Wicks · Wilson Zhang · Brandon Zoldy **55** Bill Abbott · Tom Adams · Anna Adragna · Rose Agg · Connie Allcock · Matthew Andrews · Magen Annis · Taylor Balkwill · Sarah Baxter · Jessica Benacquista · Chris Bene · Marc Beneteau · Denise Benning-Reid · Lance Berrisford · Tara Berze · Laura Bezaire · David Bird · Mary Birkner · Jordan Bitove · Kevin Black · Christopher (Mark) Bogle · Paul Bolohan · Jason Bond · Brent Boundy · Stuart Bowden · Gail Bridgett · Jason Brown · Shelley Brown · Ryan Brownlee · Haydn Burdett · Scott Butler · Jennifer Button · Laura Callery · Julie Campbell · Emily Campbell · Dennis Carlini · Matthew Charbonneau · Cameron Charlton · John Chausse · Walt Cherneski · Jason Chiasson · Robert Ciccarelli · Anna Ciesielski · Emily Clancy · Stubby Clapp · Michael L. "Pinball" Clemons · Marina Clyde · Rob Comber · Jabari Cooper · Jeannie Couture · Craig Crosby · Christina DelMedico · Joseph Demarce · Mike DiFazio · Monica Donaldson · Kari Dufour · Grace Enns · Glenn Ethridge · Cory Evans · Jeff Fitch · Gerald Freed · Chris Fuerth · Sondra Gallina · Casey Garno · Mary Ellen Gibbons · Anthony Giglio · Kate Gillis · Gerald Girard · Gary Glass · Geoff Hammond · Jenna Hampshire · Kerry Harrington · Noah Hawkeswood · Jamie Hedges · Richard Helmer · Aram Hermiz · Marc Hillier · Joshua Holland · Andrew Holmes · Nikiea Hope · Valerie Hopkins · Dave Hornby · Monica Howard · Gordie Howe · Ted Isard · Elizabeth Jappy · Paul Jnaikowski · Riley Johnson · Nic Keller · Mackenzie Kilbride · Nicholas Kilngbile · Rob Kinnear · Glen Knott · Maiya Konanur Cox · Mary Jo Kovacs · Melissa Krausse · Stacey Laliberty · Cynthia Lane · Jan Lawrence · Marylyn Liovas · Sean Lloyd · Masoud Malakoti-Negad · Gabriella Marano · Sue Markham · Carla Masterson · Steven Matteis · Rick McCleary · Anne McIntosh · Brittany Lynn Antoinnette McKeon · Helen McLaren · Meaghan McMahon · George McMahon · Chris Molyneaux · Bruce Moncur · Tracey Moore · Stan Mrnik · Lacey Munday · Erik Nielsen · Justin Oddy · Andrew Oleynik · Brian Petts · Natalie Phillips · Drew Plociennik · Julie Podesta · Melissa Power · Michael Puglia · Jake Pullen · Keith Punnett · Daniel Racicot · Matt Raffoul · Charlene Reaume · Kevin Reid · Victor Reid · Samantha Ricci · Cheryl Richardson · Taylor Robinson · Lester Rodrigues · Eddy Rota · Steve Salmons · Ronald Scarfone · Mike Schlater · George Schoebe · Clay Schroeder · Claire Schulthies · Christopher Schulthies · Lonnie Scott · Aziz Shariff · Sharon Shipstone · Cameron Shortt · Roger Sinasac · Andrew Sinclair · C.J. Smith-White · Kaaren Smyth · Patrick Soulliere · Randy Steinman · Justin Stevenson · Dan Stewart · Dr. John Strasser · Matthew Sutton · Melanie Sutton · Dave Taylor · Andrew Nathan Tepperman · Noah Tepperman · Scott Teron · Brad Tuckwell · Jessica Ulmer · Catherine Valle · Pauline van Beek · Wes Vickers · Diane Villalobos · Ashlee Vincent · Lucy Vollick · Tyler Vynckier · Samantha Westlake · Mike Wheeler · Addie White · Ching-Nam Wong · Crissie Wright · Elisa Wright · Alessia Zonta **56** Barbara Anderson · Kathy Arcuri-Arnott · Sara Bergami · Sarah Bilagot · Mitchell Blondin · Brian Burdett · David Calibaba · Leslie Darren Carey · Chris Cheong · Colby Clatworthy · Anna-Marie Cooney · Norma Cox · Natalie Crljenica · Ian Dantzer · Eamon Davey · John Davidson · Kimberley Davis · Sante Michael Deciantis · David Delchiaro · Nick Di Menna · Steve Down · Cathy Dufort-Gibbs · Dave Dufton · Gale Fanelli · Michelle Fernandes · Tom Fleming · Paul Foreman · Chris Fountain · Steven Gaboury · Linda J. Garon · Jon "Paul" Gibbs · Dante Giglio · Heather Giorgi · Carol-Lee Halcovitch · Terri Hiscox · Derek Hornbostel · Babak Hosseini · Chris Innes · Morgan Jean · Deb Jones Chambers · Tony Jovcevski · Nicole Kamarlingos · Natalie Klinard · Jon Lambert · Erinn Lee · Terry Lee · Kellie Leitch · Rebecca Lerner · Brittany Lewis · Gerald MacAlpine · Gavin Maddock · Elizabeth Manley · Idelma Marcon · Linda Martin · Craig Mason · Michael McCracken · Josh McFadden · Susan McNeil · Paul McQueen · Dorothy Morris · Alison Morrison · Ken Nguyen · David Patchell-Evans · Gordon Peterson · Corry Poaps · Katherine Potvin · Frank Pozzuoli · Dave Randorf · Andrew Reid · Chelsea Robinson · Bill Salter · Jade Scognamillo · Cheryl Scollard · Stuart Silcox · Craig Silverthorn · Agostino Sita · David Smith · Scott Snelgrove · Shawnie Snell · Amy Spadafora · James Szpak · Mckenzie Turner · Craig Turner · Eric Vandenbroucke · Nadeem Velani · Jennifer Verwey · Donald Vezina · Britt Walling · Willard Williams · Andrea Wilson · David Wolfe · Candice Worsfold **57** Day off / *Congé* **58** Day off / *Congé* **59** Mary Anne Afable · Jared Agar · Marcela Alexander · Molly Allgood · Jesse Anderson · Jeff Armour · Chris Askey · David Bajar · Jim Balsillie · Debbie Baverstock · Sharon Betker · Keith Bishop · Ian Bistany · Jane Black · Craig Bondy · Martin Brodigan · Sarah Bryson · Gary Byrne · Terry Caddo · Rachelle Cadman · Karen Campana · Andrew Capling · Patrick Capper · Kirstie Carter · Ryan Chang · Richard Chartrand · Rosie Chong · Kyle Christie · Pandora Chung · Charlotte Coates · Gary Corcoran · Anne Coulter · Dustine Crowley · Rob De Loe · Martha Deacon · Shelley Decaire · Rita Dhami · Jade Dhingra · Harry Dick · Denna Diehl · Brenda Dilling · Pat Doherty · Fab Dolan · Jacqueline Dunsmoor · Cathy Dyson · Trent Eickmeyer · Zona Endres · Kate Esztelecky · Kevin Fancey · Mike Fast · Venesa Finnie · Scott Fitzgerald · Ken Fitzpatrick · Peter Fonti · John Fryer · Mauro Galli · Tiziana Giovinazzo · Don Gosen · Dylan Gould · Dean Gresdal · Ruth Harland · John Hayman · Erin Hessey · Taima Hewitt · Adam Hill · Bill Hiltz · Christine Hitchen · Christine Hogan · Kelly Horne · Mike Hrycak · Alyssa Hugill · Peter Hyde · Pamela James · Tameka Jenner · Andrew Kates · Aaron Kochalittawut · Tyler Kohli · Rick Krause · Lisa Laflamme · Matthew Larke · Deanne Larsen · Glenn Laverty · Aaron Law · Alison LeNeve · Bryant Lewis · Mary Loggan · Wendy Madden · Peter Mansbridge · Linda Mantia · Lynn Martin · Dan Mathieson · Mimma McAndrew · Gray McCarty · Dave McEwen · Charlene McGlaughlin · Jane McKay · Kristin McKellar · Dave McLean · George Milla · Thomas Milroy · Sharlene Mohlman · Sharon Murphy · Sandra Nesbitt · Gary Neumann · Janice Newton · Mark Nichols · Evelyn Pai · Lee Parisani · Jeff Paulley · Ron Payne · Yves Pelletier · Kurt Penner · Allie Piatkowski · Michael Pinkney · Brian Pressman · Kyle Reid · James Rice · Connie Romano · Lorent Rose · Lee Roth · Kris Sangers · Adam Savage · Nancy Schwab · Matt Scott · Erica Smith · Matthew Smith · Cassidy Sneddon · Alexander Somers · Marissa Sorrell · Cindy Spence · Camille Taylor · Luke Turnbull · Sarah Van Allen · Derek Van Den Tempel · Jessica VandenBussche · Wilma VanHouwelingen · Krystal Viney · Tiffany Waque · Wyatt Weppler · Dwight Ross Wesenger · Bill Wettlaufer · Melody Whitehead · Emma Whitley · Jeanette Wielinga · Julia Wilkinson · Carol Wilkinson · Dan Wolczuk · Heidi Wright · Heidi Zehr · Rick Zeni **60** Rohit Aggarwal · Lisa Aitken · Christof Altorfer · Francis Alvero · Daniele Anderson · Alexander Araujo · Susitharan Aruliah · Stanley Bagg · Laurie Baker · Kata Barariu · Mary Bonevelle · John W. Braby · Maureen Bretz · Tania Breznik · Isabelle Brulotte · Jordan Brunet · Tony Burt · Gregory Buzbuzian · Cathryn Candusso · Peter Cashin · Joseph Cassidy · Linda Chaves · Dana Chivers · Peter Cino · Bill Clyne · Michael Cocev · Barbara Connolly · Francis Coral-Mellon · Babara Corbett · Corey Cormier · David Cormier · Jason Crone · Natasha Dang · Warren Darling · Anna Davenport · Ben DeJonge · Anna Maria Di Minno · Michael Doyle · Lee Elkas · Georgina Elliott · Crystal Estrada Munoz · Heath Everett · Mark Ferris · Michael Filion · Mark Fisher · David Frier · Thomas Frittenburg · Sonya Gabbana · Jacqueline Gagnier · Grant Gingrich · Susan Given · Julian Glowacki · Vithya Gnanakumar · Kristen Haisman · Dustin Hammond · Cortney Hansen · Justin Harris · Angie Hastings · Marilyn Haywood · Thomas Heintzman · Jason Helm · Melissa Hyde · Marilyn Ivanovick · Toby Jenkins · Carol Jerome · Jeff Jones · David Josephson · Henry Jeffery Kaluzny · Jesse Kancir · Jeff Karges · Adam KaufmAn · Rich Kawamoto · Gerry Keay · Pete Kelly · James Khan · Aisha Khatib · Mark Kinnin · Jordan Lavin · Christine Lebel · Priscilla Lopes-Schliep · Greg MacDonald · Carolyn MacGregor · Bryon Mackie · Margaret MacPherson · Erik Maier · Nathan Majury · James Malliaros · Asim Masood · John Mastroianni · Erick Matthiesen · Cynthia McGeoch · Dave McGregor · Janine McKay · Jeff McKinnon · Julie McNeil · Ron McRae · Teena Millette · Stephen Milone · Logan Naftel · Chase Nelson · Sharon Nelson · Robin-Lee Norris · Jill Oliver-Weeden · Thomas Ostapchuk · Kimberley Parrish · Robert Piggott · Rachelle Pilon · Kerry Pratt · Shannon Puma · Bonnie Rees · Mary Beth Reynolds · Frank Ridder · Peter Risteen · Jason Robson · Blane Roote · Maria Roth · Steven Roth · Stewart Saunderson · Richard Schlupp · Carolyn Scott · Sherry Scott · Raymond James Seto · Sanjeev Sharma · Allan Smith · Steven W. Smith · Rebecca Stap · David Stenning · Suzanne Strasberg · Patrick Sullivan · Dan Sullivan · Christian Thomson · Janice Anne Tijssen · Tin Thinh Vu · Lindsay Ward · Janice Weber · Colin Wells · Hannah Weppler · Gavin White · Paul Wightman · Brian Williams · Brent Williams · David Witherspoon · Candace Wormsbecker · Kimberly Zinger **61** Richard Adams · Mackenzie Allan · Penelope Baker · Rick Ball · Kristine Bannerman · Sergio Barbosa · Jessica Baumhour · Dylan Beaudry · Sarah Belanger · Callei Bellamy · Robyn Bishop · Nancy Boulton · Jackie Braden · Laura Brown · Callem Brown · Craig Busch · James Callaghan · Susan Carter · Chris Chessell · Nicholas Clements · David Coles · Gloria Connolly · Todd Cunningham · Giordano Debiasi · Ashley Desjardins · Terrel Dressel · Colleen Esch · Paul Fitzpatrick · Hilary Fletcher · Jack Ford · Stephanie Frucci · Jenn Gallagher · Brian Garriock · Doug Geffros · Lindsay Gibson · Dennis Glenn · Gertrude Louise Gowan · Chelsey Gregorini · Harry Hall · William Hamilton · Tom Hammond · Jason Harris · Zach Hayes · Scott Herfindahl · Mark Hickmott · Alison Hird · Tanya House · Michelle Elizabeth Houser · Hollle Jacobs · Jerry Janda · Mason Jeddore · Claudia Johnston · Brenda Jordan · Nicole Kalte · Coralea Kappel · Robert Kazmirchuk · Sharlene Kopec · Jason Kucherawy · Jasmine Lafreniere · Sabrina-Ayesha Lakhani · Martin Lapointe · Lauren Larocque · Jennifer Lee · Michelle Leigh · Linda Leuschner · William W. Linton · Kevin Luff · Faye Luppe · Mike MacInnes · Robert MacNaughton · Ranita Manocha · Jeffrey Mansbridge · Leah Markham · Brad Martin · Shane Martin · Caroline Martin · Sarina Mawji · Wendy McConnell · Jim McCreary · Kyle McLellan · Cindi Meyer · Bob Middlemiss · Georgette Mink · Tanya Monfils · Graeme Montgomery · Megan Moore · David Moore · Kevin Myketyn · Bill Nicolak · Jason Nissen · Brady Olsen · David Ouderkirk · Kathy Pecjak · Roland Portelance · John Power · Neil Power · Muriel Praught · Michael Pugliese · Matthew Rae · James Rae · Carrie Rawlins · Victoria Reedman · Emily Rowell · Nicholas Roy · Quinn Rozario · Jason Ruby · Chris Rudge · Andrew Saunders · Melanie Schwartz · Mark Shanahan · Derek Shorey · Ciprian Silaghi · Tova Silverman · Jack Sim · Neil Skelding · Mark Sluban · Andrea Smith · Steph Smith · Rona Smyth · Justin Sparkes · Micheline St. Clair · Bob Storey · Matthew Stratton · Megan Sutherland · Maria Toris · Shanaki Tufford · Dinah Turola · Ena Ujic · Lisa Kimberly Ulloa · Carolyn Vanden Hoek · Luc Villeneuve · Stephen Wagenaar · Daniel Wall · Craig Wallwin · Edwin White · Richelle Williams · Kelly Wilson · Alexander Young **62** Ambrose Adam · Brenda Amos · Anne Arksey · Susan Arnold · Jodie Auckland · Jennifer Babuska · Nancy Bailey · Melanie Banville · John Beaucage · Guy Beaudry · Dina Bell-Laroche · Lisa Bentley · Emily Bergeron · Summer Bly · April Bonia · Adam Bruno · Cathy Brydon · H. Michael Burrell · Liza Campbell · Mark Carlson · Linda Chaput · David Chernushenko · Elisa Coates · Doug Collins · Stacey Collins · Melanie Coulson · Wendy Cousineau · Ken Cronmiller · Sara Curwen · Sean Davis · Austin De Ste Croix · Patrick Delaney · John Dooley · Julie Doppido · Hugh Dore · Erin Down · Ann Dreger · Kirk Dudtschak · Jennifer Duffin · Jeff England · Robert Esmie · Kara-Leigh Ferlatte · Martine Feuer · Scott Forbes · Christian Fortin · Nicholas Fung · Olivia Goodfellow · Madelaine Govan · Stephen Graham · Heather Hackney · Rob Janoska · Chris Jeffkins · Robyn Jennings · Jason Karsh · Rebecca Kilpatrick · Jeffrey King · Robyn Klinkman · Jessica Knowlton · Bruce Kruger · Michael Kwiatkowski · Deirdre Laframboise · Clinton Lahnalampi · Claire Laviolette · Donald Leavens · Ryan LeBlanc · Christopher Lee · Doug Leigh · Caresse Ley · Jane Little · Nathan Loken · Jim MacLachlan · Don MacLean · Doug Malin · Danielle Malo · Celeste Mannila · Joe Marcello · Tracy Marshall · Mary Joanne (MJ) McCann · Rob McCann · Dave McLean · Douglas McRae · William Mekers · Terry Morin · Ralph Moulton · Michelle Newlands · George Nickerson · Danielle Norrie · Shari Orders · Marc Paquette · Andrew Peddle · Brandon Pludwinski · Ameet Pradhan · Amy Ramsay · Tricia Rande · Kathleen Reid · Cathy Rennie · Ryan ReYnolds · Taylor Robertson · Paul Ruppel · Tony Ryma · Michael Samoszewski · Katelyn Sander · Stephen Seewald · Tom Sharpe · Traci Shepheard · Wyatt Simcoe · Steve Simms · Winston Smith-Badger · Greg Smyth · Brett Solmes · Darlene Squibb · Nikki Storr · Helen Stoumbos · Bruce Stroud · Beth Stroud · Bill Stuckey · Sue Stummer · Beata Tomczyk · Paul Tomlinson · Bill Trayling · Anna van der Kamp · Jessika Vey · Steve Wallace · Allysha Wassegijig · Tim Westin · Tricia Zakaria · Robert David Zalewski **63** Erica Armstrong · Alain Audet · Tommy Auger-Cadieux · Jean-Philippe Bastien · Gaston Bélanger · Luca Bertucchi · Les Birta · Shelby-Lyn Bouckley · Neil Burnside · Eileen Byart · Deanna Caldwell · David Canning · Jack Ceaser · Tara Chevrier-Lavigne · Chantal Chirgwin-Popp · Barry Clout · Edith Cloutier · Andre Cloutier · Dennis Colley · Tyler Colley · Theoren Commanda · Graham Conti · Stuart Craig · Steven Dengler · Katherine Denis · Sylvain Denis · Rachelle Denomme · Riley Denver · Mary Deschatelets · Dylan Desmarais · Adrienne Dewsberry · Gabriel Dionne Desbiens · Brian Duval · Brian East · Nathalie Faucher · Dave Felsher · Judith Fitzgerald · Raymond Fortier · Kate Gajosik · Taylor Giovannini · Virginie Guegan · Cliff Guillena · Darine Haddad · Joan Hale · Richard Hamel · Nicole Havers · Beth Hawken · Ryan Heckert · Jacob Heroux · Alison Herst-Jackson · Teagan Iverson · Denyse Julien · Jen Kentfield · Renee Lachance · Lynda Lachapelle · Mathieu Lafond · Renée Lafrenière · Dominic Lalonde · Melodie Lanoix · Briana LeBlond · Amélie Lefebvre · Marc-Andre Lepage · Sophie Lovell · Candice Maloney · Mélissa Maloney · Yvette Mantha · Aura Margison · Erik Margison · Emily McAllister · David McMillan · Bob Morin · Wendy Murphy · Nadine Ogonowski · Brian O'Shaughnessy · Manuel Osoria · Kijeba Papatie · Miguel Paquin · Rene Pennell · Andrew Pisaric · Andrew Pittman · Paul Pittman · Jeff Reinhart · Chelsea Roisum · Steeven Roy · Janet Ryk · Avril Sanguinetti · Addison Sayewich · Heidi Schellhorn · Jeff Simpkins · Nancy Sturino · Charles Sullivan · Kyle Tarini · Peter Thivierge · Olivier Toupin · Kiefer Uuksulainen · Alexandra Wilson · Vicky Wilson **64** Brandon Aitchison · Madison Allick · Monty Averall · Brianna Barkell · Laura Benitez-Ek · Tyler Benson · Angele Bouchard · Karissa-June Boulay · David Brown · Annie Chartier · Emma Chaylt · Angela Chiasson Fox · Ian Clermont · Warren Crowder · Bryden Daoust · Monica Davis · Samantha Desjardins · Lionel Ducharme · Michelle Dupuis · Danny Frontczak · Marc Gagnon · Christine Girard · Rachel Goard · Ashley Grossinger · Rocco Guarnaccia · Laury Guarnaccia · Don Harris · Tracy Hautanen · Paul Herring · Michael Hill · Ken Hulme · Sharon Jones · Lyne-Sue Kistabish · Tyler Klockars · Riley Kolisnyk · Samuel Krnac · Karlee Laberge · Leo Lafleur · Eric Landreville · Debbie Legrow · Anne MacDonald · Jordan Mathieu · Isabelle Mayrand · Emily McCracken · Andrea McDonald · Elizabeth Mesarosch · Danelle Messier · Clint Monaghan · Francois Munger · Neeraj Murarka · Daniel Nissenthall · Brenda Paco · Franco D. Pittui · Xavier Poce · Ed Pupich · Michelle Rougerie · Aaron Seabrook · Leah Shorrock · Kevin Silver · David Sim · Matthew Small · Sharon Speers · Stephanie Steele · Eric Studholme · Taigen Sullivan · Chris Sweeting · Cindy Sweeting · Michelle Tonner · Jean-Claude Tremblay · Samuel Tremblay · Jean-Francois Turcotte · Shania Twain · Marc Veilleux · Paige Weller · Syndy Withers **65** Patti Bartolucci · Alex Baumann · Lorna Bell · Helen Bobiwash · James Bot · Donald Bretzlaff · Valerie Bullock · Mark Burgess · Joseph Burke · Edgar Burton · Nicholas Callaghan · Ethan Campbell · Jennifer Cawley Caruso · Nathan Coombs · Meagan-Ann Cornelson · Tom Davies · Doug Daybutch · Claude Denker · Mark Devitt · Valerie Domm · Susanna Doucette · David Doucette · Robert Drolet · James Ewing · Michael Falcone · Natasha Floyd · Caray Ford · Bryce Ford · Rob Gallinger · Lindsay Gilbertson · Pete Goodmurphy · Larry Grand · Deanna Hagan · Justine Halvorson · Mark Hamill · Julie Hancin · Cheryl Haney · Ian Harris · Jeffrey Higgs · Bonnie Huang · Carole Hunt-Ford · Dereck Hurley · Joe Iachetta · Shaylene Kern · Colton King · Ryan Lafraniere · Stephen Lajambe · Alexis Lajambe · Karli Lee · Margaret (Peggy) Lemieux · Karen Luczak · Brian Martin · Adam Mauntah · Thomas McGibbon · Duncan McKenzie · Zachary McKillop · Erin Miller · Marina Moffatt · Jennifer Muir-Birtles · Hayley Oikari · Lesly Reid · Judy Ritza · Justin Roberts · Marva Schlueter · Marjorie Smith · David Tischhauser · Brandon Trotter · Jessica Tuomela · Marc Vaillancourt · Stephen Webb · Seth Whitley · Kristen Winkel **66** Tom Alexander · Janice Birch · Richard Boon · Richard Brosseau · Ashley Buchanan · Chris Carlson · Jim Carr · Dom Commisso · Edith Commisso · Cosimo Commisso · Gerry Couturier · Matthew DeGagne · Pat Dingwell · Robert Duguay · Fiona Duncan · Robert Edwards · Sam Elliott · Carol Elliott · Michael Erko · Karen Figliomeni · Deana Figliomeni · Sal Figliomeni · Domenic Figliomeni · Kim Figliomeni · Mario Figliomeni · Gerry Figliomeni · Shawn Figliomeni · Diana Figliomeni · Phil Figliomeni · Cosimo Filane Figliomeni · Philippe Forget · Mike Garavaglia · Paul Gratton · Pat Halonen · Jenna Hill · Craig Hodgson · Kailie Kernaghan-Keast · Judy Kett · Brian Kett · Lindsay Killen · Tanya Kim · oe Kootenay · Jyles Leboeuf · Genevieve Lefebvre · Ian MacDonald · Larry MacGregor · Carole Maucieri · Joey McColeman · Ron Michaliuk · Jack Myers · Judy Nagy · Richard Nichols · Elora Oades · Andrew Oosterhoff · Jane Palahnuk · Bradley G. Peacock · Jaime Profeta · Stephen Ray · Thomas Ries · Kayla Rutenberg · Dakota Sagutch · Jean Savard · Frederick Schwertner · Chris Sheldon · Dale Shippam · Elaine Sideco · David Stezenko · Loïc Théberge · Caroline Tierney · Alain Vachon · Katie Weatherston · Gunther Wirtz **67** Michelle Arseneault · Pat Bagshaw · Anthony Bergamo · Louise Carleton · Liv Carter · Brenden Condie · Rosemary Cox · Chris Cumbers · Dalton Demerah · Roxanne Derouard · Grant Duchesne · Mike Farley · Nathalie Ferguson · Wayne Ficek · David Garrow · Daniel Gervais · Annick Harvey · Chris Holland · Robyn Alexis Houle · Randall Jacobs · Andrea Johnson · Tommy Johnson · Brandon Kearney · Michael Kelso · Jason Klukas · Jason Komoski · Brian Kowalczyk · Frank Kowpak · Jasmyn Kozlowsky · Brad Krampp · Nicole Labelle · Heidi Langman · Nicole Le Dressay · Meggie Lesage · Brooke Lindsey · Katharine Lough · Denis Maltais · Aaron Martyniw · Linda Mcnally · Randy Mehagan · André Navarri · Lisa Prost · Anne Renaud · Margaret Rooney · Stephanie Rowan · Michelle Simone · Debra Teelucksingh · Alexandra Tremblay · Simon Vermette · Kevin Waara · Melissa White · J. Brad Yeo · Mavis Zhiha **68** Carina Adsbol-Nielsen · Ernie Allen · Ryan Anderson · Rob Anderson · Maddy Arkle · Russel Audet · Lloyd Axworthy · Nicole Baker · John Barillier · Rebecca Bayes · Karin Beauchemin · Ray Beauchemin · Donna Bell · Marc Bissonnette · Desiree Blackmore · Rick Buffie · Rita Burgess · Dwayne Carter · Barry Catt · Rielle Chwartacki · Sebastian Clements · Mario Clouatre · Fernie Conrad · Ambrose Cox · Doug Dealey · Gary Dear · Rachelle Demetrioff · Wayne Demkey · Peter Dick · Marla Dueck · Danielle Dupas · Robin Dutton · Brian Dwyer · Alyssa Emond · Randy Faseruk · Laura Forrest · Susan Gerlach · Morgan Glasgow · Chris Goethals · Patrick Gordon · Graeme Green · Alison Hall · Jennifer Hamilton · Pamela Hamm · Gary Hansen · Rod Hansey · Vincent Hartigan · Amy Henderson · Candice Homewood · Deborah Hopwood · Jeffrey Illchuk · Richard Ivey · Kymm Johnston · Tasha Jones · Sarah Kanceruk · Heather Kemkaran-Antymniuk · Megan Kilvert · Victoria Knapp · Darius Konotopetz · Gerald Koroscil · Kurtiss Krasnesky · Sally Kukko · Joe Landreville · Thibaut Lauwers · Adelaide Law · Kathleen Leathers · Brian MacLean · Sarah Mandamin · Rachel Martel · Georgia Martell · Jason Mayert · Errol McKay · Derek McLennan · Vivek Menon · Steven Muise · Jim Nemeth · Andrew Nixon · Kenneth O'Connor · Donna Ogal · Miguel Ordonez Marin · Charlie Paille · Noah Palansky · Ian Pitre · Lennie Plett · Brett Rach · Rohil Rajagopalan · Grant Ritchie · Courtney Robinson · Clayton Sandy · Edward Scully · Richard Sherby · Tony Sliwiany · Mark Smith · Florian Soble · Scott Solmundson · Phil Starnes · Allison Stefanyshyn · Don Streuber · Donna Sutherland · Janelle Tarnopolski · Kaitlan Taylor · Brent Trepel · Harvey Tschetter · Michele Tumber · Kathleen Turk · Brian Unger · Brooke Amber Vandekerckhove · Ashley Waller · Michael White · Angel Williams · Sean Wilson · Garth Wintle · Joe Woitas · Robyn Wolfe · Alison Yakel · Dennis Yakimenko · Thomas Yarduk · Kevin Young · Cheryl Zealand · Cheryll Zembik · Colton Zembik · Darren Zembik · Greg Zembik · Teigen Zembik · Madison Zienkiewicz **69** Robin Armstrong · Shannon Bailey · Millard Barteaux · Larissa Best · Braedon Borschawa · Jean Louis Carrière · Ray Carter · Cailyn Cheasley · Louis Dauphinais · Rachel Epp · Janelle Flaten · Leah Gair · Shane Haney · Tim Ireland · Edward Kennedy · Nicole Kerbrat · Lynn Kolba · Brandon Kopochinski · Ashley Newman · Kyle Norquay · Kyle Prince · Greg Selinger · Brandon Stamm · Twylla Stamm · Michelle Stamm · Meaghan Sternat · Kiinnan Stevenson-French · Ryan Wehrle · Gio Wickett · Terina Wickett **70** Phil Adamo · Shauna Arnott · Gail Asper · Lindsay Baker · Curtis Bamford · Kylie Bard · Tyler Bargen · Ian Bawa · Ian Bell · Diane Bell · Rick Bent · Don Binne · Israel Binnun · Jodi Bodnarchuk · Chelsea Bothe · Dustin Boyechko · Lucy Brancati · Kevin Branch · Denis Brodeur · Aimee Carvey · Brad Chambers · Jody Champagne · Kris Cherewyk · Irene Chomiak · Gail Cielen · Mireille Collet-Lachance · John Coutts · Randall Craddock · Tracy Czoch · Lynley Davidson · Sheryl de Leon · David Deighton · Jennifer Denesyk · Karen Doell · Angela Doerksen · Josh Eagle · Eddie Edwards · Danielle Ethier · Ronald Grant Evans · Daryl Fagnan · Sheila Flemmer · Stephanie Foy · Raymond Friesen · Steve Friesen · Kimberly Friesen · Tiffany Froese · Gene Gelmich · Caitlin Genaille · Kaili Gilroy · Robyn Goodwin · Philip Grandmont · Darren Hall · Amy Hampton · Brent Hill · Caleb Hofer · Todd Hughes · Paul Huntington · Cory Jackson · Mike Kananoja · Edward Kaulbach · Lauryn Keen · Jeff Kerr · Cheryle Knutson · Marianne Korhonen · Kim Krahn · Djahl Kristjanson · Robert Kudajczyk · Sylvia Kuzyk · Bennett Laurel · Ken Leslie · Dylan Loucks · Maria-Aileen Madden · Leonard Magill · Andrea Malcolm · Bryce Malcolm · Joel Marcon · David Mark · Billy Martens · Elizabeth McCallum · Marina McGlenen · Jo-Anne McRae · Rosa Menjivar · Guy Moffat · Ross Naringahon · Chris Newman · Robert Obirek · Alvin Ogilvie · Regina Olazo · Kevin Olszewski · Brandi Parnell · Dylan Passaggio · Charlotte Pennell · George Petranick · Stephen Pratt · Catherine Prusak · David Rew · Andrew Rhoden · Dwayne Richard · Norva Riddell · Debbie Ritchot · Dan Robertson · Tyler Rody · Alexandre Ross-Gautron · Glenn Rossong · Cathy Sauder · Michael Saunders · Nikole Schoenborn · Daljit Singh Sidhu · Edmund Smith · Orville Smoke · Coleen Soos · Jamieson Stock · Diana Stout · Leanne Straker · Laird Sutherland · Jennine Thaddeus · Jayme Tully · Tyler Warden · Matthieu Webb · Trevor Westwood · Marg Wilson · Frank Wilson · Patricia Woodman-Hooker · Colleen Zacharias · Munther Zeid **71** Brad Alexander · Richard Amann · Jim Anderson · Brandon Ashcroft · Donald Askeland · Warren Beleyowski · Jean-Paul Bellamy · Jessica Biggs · Michael Blatherwick · Jonathan Tyler Blatz · Chelsea Braybrook · Debbie Burkart · Michael Burns · Paul Caines · Drew Caldwell · Matt Chartrand · Bernie Chrisp · Meghan Classen · Leo Collins · Chris Coppinger · Ryan Coward · Nina Crawford · Adam Cyr · Chad Dedelley · Cheryl Dixon · Andrew Evans · Kara Falkowski · Doug Fansher · Grace Farmer · Elaine Feniuk · Sheri Fisher · Phillip Fontaine · Marla Fontaine · Justin Ford · Tom Foster · Dale Fust · Muriel Gamey · Bonnie Glasman · Patrick Gross · Barry Hales · Lowell Haugen · Carmen Henry · Karen Hickman · Jovan Hofer · Harold Isfeld · Julie Joannette · Dale Kasper · Debra Kasprick · Benjamin Kay · Johnathan Kelly · George Kennedy · Glen Kirkland · Oleksandr Kondrashov · Ken Koots · Marcus Krinke · Grace Krinke · Paige Krueger-Trottier · Janelle Lafantaisie · Murray Lang · Marco Lauzon · Marc Lavoie · Maria Leach · Lise Leflour · Elorie Macchia · James Mackenzie · Allison Manning · Jaime Manser · Thomas Mauthe · Jamie McKinley · Michael McNabb · Don McNabb · Billy Meeches · Roger Merrick · Candace Mundy · John Nelson · Jason O'Neill · Sean Osztian · Joshua Pashe · Arden Pashe Jr. · Mark Pelletier · Kris Prior · Kenny Proden · Patrick Rae · Peter Reid · Stephanie Reling · Orlando Sanchez · Jaimee Schmidt · Kristjana Schure · Ken Shepherd · Allison Snezyk · Kaitlyn Spulnick · Wade Strand · Denise Tinkler · Michael Tintor · Eryn Wiebe · Gregory Wiebe **72** Evan Ashdown · Teajin Barkley · Shirley Bell · Jason Bender · Roger Bierwagen · Grace Bjarnason · Larry Breault · Aida Brenneman · Ian Brown · Roger L. Brown · Vicky Chahal · Sheila Coles · T. Terry Cooney · Tony Cote · Jody Culic · Dan Davidson · Kerri Davies Geisel · Jessie Doan · Tyler Eftoda · DAve Einarson · Andrea Fahlman · Janet Flash · Lucie Gautier · Clayton Gerein · Kevin Granrude · Amber Hack · Zara Hanson · Danette Harrison · Brady Hotain · Don Hull · Doug Hunt · Jasmine Jackman · Dianne Jamieson · Tanya Johnston · Darren Johnston · Lee Jones · Alyssa Kaiswatum · Tom Keep · Derek Klaassen · Billy Kot · Deb Kusniak · Jeff Livingstone · Deanna MacDonald · Dan MacDonald · Donald MacKay · Don Martin · Brandon Masson · James McDonnell · Harvey McEwen · Daynen Kyle McKay · Sheena Metzger · Alexander Miller · Rick Minett · Callie Morris · Jeff Moyer · Lori-Ann Mundt · Peter Nabholz · Dale Nixon · Patti Jo Nixon · Tamela Lynn Olafson · Kurt Olafson · Paula Orecklin · Courtney Oyka · Rhonda Pillsworth · Kristy Rasmuson · Wayne Ruhr · Richard Schwan · Tannis Schwean · Mike Schwean · Barry Sharpe · Quinn Skulmoski · Kimberley Smith · Jodi Smith · Devon Soltendieck · Jason Taylor · Caleb Taylor · Laura Toews · Shayne Tucker · Crystal Vankoughnett · Veronica Wenc · Stacy Wolitski · Melanie Wood · Penny Woods · Min Qiang Wu · Oksanna Zwarych **73** Nicole Agar · Herb Alkerton · Ashley Barron · Jan Betker · Lorna Billan · Kelsey Bohachewski · David Boudreau · Natalie Brons · Stephanie Buckley · Kia Byers · Kelsey Calder · Roland Card · Wayne Chura · Don Clearihue · Adrien Cozart · Allen Davey · Laura Dean · Gilles Desjardins · Denis Desjardins · Peter Dragan · Katie Durant · Peggy Ellis · Shannon England · Bob Fahlman · Cheryl Feader · Erin Fisher · Roberta Fonger · John Fortune · Amy Funk · Marcel Gagnon · Paul Ganes · Rhonda Girard · Regan Gorski · Marcia Gudereit · Mike Hall · Angelique Haysom · Janet Heatcoat · Jennifer Heggie · Ryan Higgins · Harvey Jakubowski · Ted Jaleta · Dwight Jensen · Bonnie Johnson · Peggy Junek · Brittany Karst · Danica Kindrachuk · Debra King · Mark Kirkpatrick · Daylynn Knodel · Lee Kormish · Mike Kozun · Sharon Krogsgaard · Chethan Lakshman · Heather Leduc · Brenda Lepine · Lionel Li · David Lyons · Scott MacDonald · Zang Mah · Brett Marchand · Rod Markewich · Nick Martin · Brian McGillivray · Jamie McLaren · Claire McLellan · Mykaela Mennie · Rocio Mijangos Urbina · Michael Milani · Len Mintenko · Susan Murray · Dean Myers · Helen Napadaljo · Garnet Bruce Neill · Robert Neufeld · Reginald Newkirk · Biata Ngalula · Bert Olson · Vincent Ostryzniuk · Holly Paluck · Carole Picklyk · Cody Pilsner · Darlene Poole · Debbie Porter · Doreen Prescesky · Stephanie Ramsay · Lee Reaney · Lisa Reimer · Hazel Robertson · Lee-Ann Ross · Erwin Sandejas · Michael Savory · Trina Schiml · Tyson Schmidt · Kim Scott · Andrew Shenouda · Richard Sibbald · Greg Simpson · Jenna Smith · Kristina Spate · Victor Standish · Angela Stumph · Matthew Teevens · Shawna Teles · Diane Therrien · Kelly Thompson · Leanne Thoroughgood · Cindy Tokarchuk · David Treanor · Nicholas Valcamp · Robert Vanderhooft · Marc Velasco · Franc Wagener · Frank Watkins · Thomas Welch · Gerald Welsh · Joshua Whincup · Regan Wickett · Monique Wiens **74** Vanessa Agira · Anne-Marie Allard · Brady Anderson · Nathan Baldwin · Elllot Baldwin · Nolan Benesh · Jason Bettin · Ruebin Bignell · Bobby Jo Kenneth Bodnar · Perry Boeker · Frank Bojkovsky · Denise Bortis · Cassidy Braun · Gordie Broda · Damara Brown · Vince Brule · Robert Burns · Philippe Candeloro · Corinne Carey · David Carnegie · Robin Chambers · Erin Cumpstone · Faysal Dlikan · Ilana Duff · Rhonda Dunfield · Warren Dungen · Lynette Epp · Danika Ethier · Daniel Fahlman · Jana Fisher · Rose Fleury · Christine Foth · Giselle Frank · Carol Friesen · Trevor Funk · Kyle Gareau · Stanley Gladys · Katie Gray · Leo Guigon · Greg Hamm · Patricia Hankey · Roy Hanson · Rhea Hartl · Kent Hartshorn · Kelly Herriges · Eldon Hill · Angela Hodgson · Rebecca Jalbert · Rochelle Jalbert · Sarah Jean · Rebecca Jean · Samantha Johnson · Veronica Jubinville · Jackie Juson · Jim Kinnear · Dean Klassen · Todd Kropinak · Aaron Krywicki · Steven Lam · Jacqueline Lavallee · Jonathan MacDonald · Richard Marr · Natasha McLean · Meghan Mercer · Laura Millions · Donna Mindiuk · Blair Morgan · Karen Neumiiller · Erik Paquette · Keith Parker · Crystal Parton · Rob Pederson · Tyson Poulin · Brandy Pyle · Mark Regier · Shawn Rempel · Jayme Riley · Debbie Rodger · Mark Rogstad · Murray Sackmann · Sydney Sawka · Miela Schlekewy · Lia Sorensen · Brianna Spenst · Larry Spratt · Susan Stene · Aaron Storos · Kay Tarleton · Derrick Thomas · Nora Tinant · Ken Tralnberg · Brent Trickett · Bruce Trimbee · Janaya Trudel · Treva Veilleux · Dustin Whitney · Taylor Woloshyn · Sam Xu · Viola Yanik · Michelle Young · Asia YounGman **75** Israr Ali · Racheal Ananas · Tim Archer · Franklin Arthurs · Josephine Awasis · Darrell Balkwill · Chelsea Behn · Darcy Bellamy · Anthony Bidgood · Felix Bisson · Kayla Blanchard · Bonnie Bond · Ruth Bond-Martinson · Robert Chow · Lynn Colyn · Howard Edward Cook · Danielle Cross · Courtney Crush · Montana Daniels · Lisa Davis · Travis Dumont · Laurie Eddleston · Brian Edey · Rowena Epp · Wendy Ewanik · Rilley Fiolleau · Rick Flaman · Ian Gamble · Tanisha Gardypie · Alysha Gaudry · Ross Gregory · Glen Hadland · Chris Harris · Marc Hauser · Sarah Head · Dale Hrynuik · Curtis Hunter · Matthew Huynh · Kirsten Jones · Cody Kahpeaysewat · Crystal Kainz · Carson Kalyn · Dione Kardynal · Wade King · Sydney Kirychuk · Dwain Krissa · Uta Kvaratshkelia · Gabe Lafond · Shelley Lang · Nicole LaRocque · Stefanie Lawton · Frances Grace Mangahas · Mervin Mann · Cresida Masson · Corey Matthews · Glenda Mcintosh · Cyndie McIvor · Sandy G. A. McVittie · Paul Melnikel · Allison Morrison · Emily Motoska · Terry Nielsen · Vienna Ochuschayo · Khrystina Okemaysim · Josephine Olivieri · Kent Page · Michael Palmer · Shaun Pawluk · Russell Pawlyk · Craig Peterson · George Pietersma · Timothy Popp ·

Robert Potter · John Radostits · Horace Ratt · Mary Renard · Roxanne Reynoldson · Christopher Ross · Faridullah Safi · Tessa Schwan · Derrick Sellka · Dakota Smallboy · Fiona Smith-Bell · Tim Squire · Pat Stewart · Tim Strom · Lacey Sutherland · McLaren Taylor · Brandon Thomas · Tashynna Tipewan · Anita Torbert · Shailin Tournler · Brenda Urton · Lynette Vey · Don Walchuk · Trona Wheaton · Brian Whincup · Andrea Wiebe · Heather Wielgoz · Cody Windels · Kyle Wong · Tyler Young **76** Robert Adams · Teri-Lynn Adams · Belle Alexis · Lucas Alexis · Carol Anne Alloway · Don Anderson Jr. · Bradley Armitage · Murray Badger · Allan Bailey · Tim Berrett · Tevin Bird · Robert Bliss · Kenneth Block · Lindsay Bosch · Alexandrea Brand · Scott Brattly · Shelley Brennan · William Brese · Larry Brewster · Karen Brown · Mike Buell · Ahmet Ceylan · Selina Chan · Colleen Christie · Cory Claeys · Erin Clark · Kimberly Clowery · Corey Colling · Carla Coubrough · Alanna Craig · Lisa Cross · Ryan Cusveller · Don Dart · Steven Diachuk · Anne Douglas · Donna Doyle · Kim Duke · April Dunkley · Daniel Edwards · Bill Elkington · Curtis Englot · Lorna Fife · Ellen Finn · Mary Fraser · Ross Garbe · Heather Gardiner · Cheryl Gibson · Randall Gladue · Rosh Goonewardene · Nicholas Govias · Adam Hamilton · Erika Hannem · Krysta Hendrickson · Dale Henwood · Perry Hilden · Colton Hippe · Jim Hole · Samantha Houle · Lori-Lee House · Linda Hrycun · Dietrich Humbke · Gabrielle Humbke · Twyla Istace · Trina Nicole Jackson · Gerry Johnson · Dmitry Kaplan · Robert Karwacki · Wayne Katchur · Brooke Kootenay · Joseph Kootenay · Gail Kormish · Angie Kosch · Stephen Kushner · Michael Kwan · Tony Lenarcic · Lise Anne Lepage · Ghislaine Lessard · Tina Leung · Stephanie Levitz · Dana Lindal · Jamie Michelle Linington · Stefan Litalien · Donna Lux · Casey MacDonald · Kevin MacIntyre · Robert Mackin · Blake Mantovani · Christopher Marler · Erin Marsh · Stiel Masse · Alice Mawdsley · John McCann · Mike Medicoff · Karl Meissner · Karina Miller · Alasdair Mills · Carlone Mitchell · Nicholas Monfries · Wenonah Morin · Aaron Moser · Brendan Murphy · Cara Neale · Vivian Ng · Warren Nordin · Tammy Nousek · Lisa O'Brien · Marjorie O'Connor · Lois Ough · Celine Ozirny · Mark Palman · Desmond Papin · Steve Parent-Korbie · Rick Payne · Kristy Payne · Jonathan Pearson · Danielle Peers · Janelle Peister · Isabelle Phaneuf · Darlene Pon · Owen Procter · Rod Proudfoot · John Pun · Pat Quinn · Celeste Rain · Katerina Rain · Daris Rain · Daron Rain · Christian Rain · Marie-Josee Rancourt · Robert Reeves · Anna Reyes · Shasta Rudyk · Doreen Delores Ryan · Rosanna Saccomani · Indira Samarasekera · Tatiana Sandoval · Conner Scheu · Guy Scott · Lori Seemann · Christine Selinger · Wayne Shillington · David Shultz · Sue Simpson · Brandon Solyom · John Stanton Jr. · Jack Stonehocker · Derek Sung · Jammie Swap · Irene Tang · Norm Thorsen · Tristan Threefingers · Tyrone Trapper · Jason Tusor · Alisha Ushko · James Van Dyke · Sheldon Wagner · Darren Weeks · Theresa Wells-Taylor · George Whyte · Cheryl Williams · Brett Yakimetz · Darlene Ziegler **77** Day off / *Congé* **78** Graham Adam · Janet Adams · Cole Anderson · Barbara Armbrust · Erika Pearl Asuncion · Steve Banks · Terri Baptiste · René Barakett · Rebecca Beals · Chole Besse · Meagan Big Snake · Tara Bond · Danielle Brown · Carolyn Brown · Norma Button · ShaughN Butts · Michael Carroll · Meagan Carroll · Mike Caza · Sherman Chan · Johnny Cherwick · Byron Chikinda · Junho Choi · Kevin Claerhout · Barbara Clark-Parolin · Riley Collins · Isabelle Colmers · D'Arcy Costello · Steven Cox · Carleigh Crane Big Plume · Kendal da Costa · Lui Dasilva · Swami De Leon · Kenneth Delahoussaye · Kristie Derkson · Cody Desjardine · Deidra Dionne · Joanne D'Lugos · Christie Dominiuk · Sean Dunn · Alex Ebhardt · Amelia Falk · Carla Farnesi · Shauna Filtz · Sandi Fleury · Cindy Forbes · Joseph Frank · Lindsay Franz · Lucas Gabriel · Garry Gibson · Christina Giese · Matthew Grant · Agnes Griffiths · Caitlyn Hagen · Landon Haigh · Barbara Haley · Elaine Halina · Linda Hampton · Lamya Hanna · Katie Hansen · Lois Hansen · Kelly Harke · Aliisa Victoria Hodgson · Walter Hoffmann · Brad Hussey · Susan Hutchison · Dianne Ingle · Jessee Johns · Robert Jones · Kevin Kobi · Bryn Kowalchuk · Michael Kozuska · Chris Lacher · Patrick LaForge · Kim Langmaid · David Lauscher · Richard Lelacheur · Jessica Lieffers · Wilton Littlechild · Deanna MacDonald · David MacTavish · Robert Mast · John McGee · Becky Mercer · Frances Gail Miller · Abi Mitchell · Sarah Mosaico · Cary Mullen · Usama Nasrullah · Philip Nicholls · Ray Nielsen · Terry Nimetz · Victoria Northrup · Dana Olstad · Donald Padget · George Perry · Carrie Petasky · Miles Poliak · Les Powers · Dennis Preshing · Rhiannon Prince · Sylvain Prud'homme · Ximena Ramos-Salas · Tim Roulson · Clayton Rowney · Carly Rumley · Boris Rybalka · Luanne Sawatzky · Curtis Setso · Arya Sharma · Kate Storey · Lindsey Sutherland · Jim Szautner · Sarah Taylor · Niek Theelen · Ivan Todosijczuk · Elenita Torres · Jen Tucci · Kristy Vest · Glenna Walsh · Joel Ward · Brad Weaver · Peter Weddell · Sherry White · John Whitney · Chris Wilkes · Ashley Wilton · Karen Woodley · Ron Woodward · Wei Wu · Jacqueline Zellner · Charlene Zilinski · Pavel Zvonov **79** Bill Anderson · Barb Baker · Vanda Balsys · Glen Barrow · Carter Brady · Charlynn Branton · Rick Brink · Amber Brown · John Bruch · Wyatt Calf Robe · Diana Carlson · Alanna Cellini · Ashton Coultman · Jade Coultman · Josee Desjardins · Steve Dougherty · Gerald Eberle · Harold Exner · Colleen Feeney · Tara Furger · Daniel Germain · Shannon Giebelhaus · Robert Glover · Megan Gough · Pamela Goyette · Tony Hansen · Dave Harris · Albert Hoffarth · Natalie Holloway · Patrick Jarvis · Deborah Johnson · Gerry Kaluzniak · Jenson Kerr · Lori Kirchner · Kevin Kobelka · Lidia Kocovski · Sylvia Kyriacou · Jean-Philippe Lacroix · Ravinesh Lal · Michele Langer · Helene Larway · Ellena Lawrence · Keith Leong · Stephen Lo · Liam McFarlane · Martin McSween · Ken Merritt · Marc Michaels · Kelsey Amanda Moore · Drew Morris · Louise Mosier · Staci Muller · Ronald Noel · Melissa Oberman · Nico Papanikolaou · Brodie Parker · Jordan Phillips · Sarah Plishka · Elizabeth Rae · Moira Rainville · Darren Reilly · Beverly Reimer-McAndrews · Shauna Richard · Les Richardson · Brady Richardson · Josie Sciangula · Harold Smallbones · Jacey Lea Solway · Michael Stefanyk · Gillian Bryn Storey · Todd Strong · Marnie Thomas · Shelley Waite · Laurie Wallis · Scott Wallis · Gary Wicentowich · Nancy Wilson · Daniel Wourms · Reid Yester **80** Dylan Assen · Jose Barbieri · Dianna Barry · John-Scott Beaton · Dr. Gerald Beckie · Rob Bernshaw · Twylla Bexte · Diane Bird · Steve Bohan · Norm Brennand · Kim Brinkhaus · Andrew Britton · Michelle Buchanan · Rick Burry · Gordon Bussey · Dayenera (Dayna) Bythell · Domino Cahilig · Coleen Campbell · Noah Cappe · Brayden Carriere · Bob Chabay · Joanne Chilton · Ismail Choulli · Elisabeth Collins · Nicholas Colyer · Rylan Cooper · Dawna Coslovi · Dan Crews · Darlene Dallard · Catherine Dalton · Tess Danielson · Mackenzie Dawson-Agnew · Miriam Deitz · Riley Dow · Chantelle Dubois · Dave Exley · Matthew Frank · Brooke French · Pat Friesen · Caleb Fuller · Kathleen Gallant-Schwab · Sarah Gibbons · Laura Giroux · Michael Gray · Pete Gronemeyer · Roberta Gwinner · Heidi Halstead · Grayson Henderson · Drew Herauf · Cody Herrell · Gabriella (Gabby) Hopfner · Steven Hull · Kara Hurkens · Patricia Jamieson · Alisha Janiga · Darrel Janz · Michael Jones · Edith Kish · Christopher Klassen · Danielle Koch · John Koot · Vidya Kowshik · Karen Kristianson · Erin Leahy · Allen Leitert · Alonya Lewis · Ashley-Ann Loewen · Cathy Love · Madison Luif · Jason Manning · Jacinthe Marion · Melanie Mazereeuw · Linda McDonald · Kaitlin McKendrick · Roslyn McMann · Shad Milligan · Nelson Millman · Hailey Mizera · Allison Nitchke · Evan Oliver · Taija Olszewski · Brenna Pavan · Matteo Picone · Clara Piedalue · Karen Priest · Evan Pyett · Jill Quirk · Harpinder Rai · Logan Rakai · Julie Raw · Kristin Raychert · Donna Rickard · Raelyn Riley · Erica Ritch · Ken Rogers · Haralambos Roussinos · Jessica Royan · Jessica Royer · Blaise Russell · Conor Sandford · Catherine Scott · Kimberley Sharkey · Nathan Shedd · Arden Shibley · Scott Sibbet · Joel Skulsky · Wendy Slavin · Diane Starrenburg · Sarah Stickel · Wayne Street · Lynn Sutherland · Jessica Taylor · Mark Tewksbury · Paul Tichelaar · Taylor Todd · Ziya Tong · Darrell Turner · Megan Tyner · Desiree Unvoas · Jill Van Gunst · Jack Van Norman · Pauline Van Roessel · Giftin Varghese · Imtiaz Vira · James Zanoni · Ivanka Zecevic · Tracey Zehl · Christopher Zottl **81** George Agapeyev · Robyn Ainsworth · Jason Alexander · Benjamin Allen · Sami Amery · Gail Amundrud · Linda Arksey · Celeste Austring · Wil Bacalso · Calvin Barks · Beverly Beaulne · Mark Bellstedt · Graham Besse · Racey Big Snake · Shelley BilLinghurst · Daniel Breau · Diane Burnett · Elizabeth Burns · Donald Cameron · Dr. David Chalack · Clay Chattaway · Allan Chief Body · Daniel Chow · Paul Clark · Jordan Coldham · Silvia Paola Contreras · Shelley Cooke · Chelsea Davidson · Marci Dedul · John Demerchant · Patricia Doyle · Darcy Dyck · Mike Fleck · Ashleigh Ford · Dagmar Fortmuller · Ron Freiburger · Emily George · Catherine Gibbs · Greg Gibbs · Jeremy Gillespie · Gordon Godfrey · Ian Gordon · George Gosbee · Corey Goulet · Sarah Gregory · Chris Grimes · Douglas Gurney · Marc Halas · Gavin Hamilton · Lana Harbin · Crystal Hardy · Ian Harris · Bertha Harris · Mark Harris · Douglas Hartl · Trevor Haynes · David Hendricks · Jonathan Herbert · Keil Hillis · Tanya Hogue · Bill Holmes · Paul Howden · David Humble · Jungle Jim Hunter · Matthew Jordan · Chuck Juergens · Danielle Kelly · Patrick Kelm · Leigh Kelm · Corrina Kennedy · Ashlee Kephart · Fadwa Khourieh · Vern Kimball · Casandra Knooihuizen · Mia Kofoed-Kristiansen · Darren Kuprash · Sandy Layton · Taylor LeBaron · Alison Lerner · Carol Lethaby · Steven Lopez · Camila Louzada · Hope Lowe · Richard Luhning · Wendy Lumby · Jason Lynn · Bruce Mackenzie · Mac Makenny · Cindy Martin · Lindsay Mason · Kelly McGuire · Ryan Midtdal · Lisa Miller · Donavon Miller · Kim Mitchell · Lyle Moline · Matthew Murray · Jim (Bearcat) Murray · Bruce Neve · Claire Noble · Ashley Nordstrom · Brian Noronha · Sean Notenboom · Colin O'Leary · Rich Pal · Bill Patrick · Allison Pegg · Emily Phernambucq · Elizabeth Pitura · Belf Quon · Darcy Randa · Tom Richards · Margo Ruigrok · Melissa Ruigrok · Jonathan Ruigrok · Jamie Ruigrok · Jacquelyn Ruigrok · Nicholas Ruigrok · Kevin Rusteika · Dave Rutherford · Sherali Saju · Kathy Salmon · Bob Sartor · Katie Saunders · Tasha Schindel · Mayo Schmidt · Jed Selkowitz · Alexandria Sham · Kyle Shewfelt · John Sidhu · Alex Smith · Rowan Sommerfeld · Donna Spencer · Erin Stanford · Trent Stangl · Ron Story · Michael Strikes with a Gun · Shannon Taylor · Troy Thieman · Kelcie Thomas · Jamie Topping · Alysha Tubera · Danielle Vielle · Laura Webber · Kathryn Wilson · Brett Wilson · Sarah Wingfield · Samantha Wright · Danke Wu **82** Gus Adolf · Timothy Alford · Dianne Allen · Stephen Ames · Bernie Anderson · Len Anderson · Faye Anderson · Susan Arnison · Jason Ashton · Susan Auch · Chris Avelar · Marie Bandao · Karen Bannick · Nick Bass · Yvonne Bergmann · Amanda Bichai · Tannis Judy Lee Boudreau · Patrick Breen · Daniel Brown · Michael Bruce · Claire Buffone-Blair · Shane Burleigh · Patrlcia Byron · Kaitlyn Chana · Dorothy Christoperson · Robert Church · Aidan Cornhill · Shirley Cottick · Trudy Coucill · Lori Crawford · Blake Crossley · Adil Damani · Elisea De Somma · Michelle Dickie · Ross Douglas · Susan Eaton · Sadaf Eghtesadi · Kathleen Engel · Brent Ferster · Debra Fisher · Marla Forth · Audrey Forzani · Jamey Frank · Marty Gaffney · Frank Galloway · Ann-Marie Giannetti · Chantelle Gill · Russ Girling · Kaitlin Gordon · James Greig · Jatinder Grewal · Kristina Groves · David Guttman · Nicole Hare · Steve Herlehey · Suanne Hesse · Shane Hewitt · Zach Hiebert · Barb Higgins · Matt Hindle · Rachael Hoppins · Elizabeth Hughes · Sharon Jeckells · Vyvyan Dawn Jenkinson · Joanne Johnson · Shawn Johnson · Diane Jones Konihowski · Anna Maria Kaufmann · Joseph Kavanagh · Frank King · Brian Krausert · Tasleem Kurji · Talia Leman · Hank Levine · Craig Lindsay · Ed Loo · Denise Ludwig · Leonard Luke · Sam Lum · Barbara Macleod · Jonathan Magat · Patricia Malatesta · Matthew Marshall · Doug Martineau · Christopher Matthews · Jeff McCaig · Bryce McCormick · Laura McIntyre · Marc Melnic · Cheryl Merritt · Tricia Minions · Lois Mitchell · Dayna Morgan · Sandi Morley · Reid Morrison · Bryce Motley · Carol Mulder · Chuck Mulvenna · Curtis Myden · Nora Myra · Elizabeth Nabel · Tracey Nameth · Dylan Olsen · Judith Palfrey · Walter Pang · Stan Papulkas · Jake Parker · Mark Parkman · Ranbir Parmar · Sheena Parris · Jessie Pavlinac · Susan Amanda Payne · Stevie Peacock · James Pivarnik · Gregg Planert · Jen Prosser · Tom Quinn · Amal Remu · Joshua Riker-Fox · Ralf Russell · Lance Sandberg · Marc Saunders · Emile Saurette · Tania Schesnuk · Rob Schram · Dennis Scott · Amanda Seliga · Michael Shaw · Brian Sloan · Shanice Smith · Greg Smith · Dwayne Sorobey · Coralie Sorochuk · Cassandra Spencer · Jo Ann Stimpson · Douglas Stitt · Maureen Sutka · Erin Tang · Sam Taylor · Wayne Thomas · Mary Townson · Cyrus Tsu · Lillian Turner · Karl Unger · Kristen Vardy · Claire Verhagen · George Vilven · Marika Wagner · Brent Wallln · Ted Waltho · Allison Warkentin · Steve Warme · Ken White · Heather Wicksted · Chuck Wielgus · Dan Winiski · Kyle Yoshida · Ashley Young · Keghan Youngpine · Robert Zazuliak **83** Alana Adams · Maurice Allard · Elliot Allen · Nelli Azayeva · Jim Bagshaw · Sarah Bain · Alex Barton · Susan Black · Anatoli Bogovik · Chantel Boone · Jim Boyde · Ray Busby · John Byrne · Joan Carson · Maria Catala · Conrad Chala · Chris Chernuska · Joseph Clohessy · Karen Connellan · Logan Coutts · Sarah Czechowskyj · Nlcola Davies · Arthur Davis · Karl Dawson · Jaimie Dawson · Kevin Dawyd · Yukon De Leeuw · Melanie Dechant · Rhonda Delong · Heather Edwards · Llewellyn Edwards · Gene Edworthy · Christa Enns · Josh Epstein · Emilio Fantin · Mitch Fennell · Adriano Fisico · Leeanne Gagne · Kirsten Gillett · Tasha Giroux · Leslie Gurba · Stuart Harden · Natasha Harvey · Tracy Hecker · Josephine Heiland · Robert Herritt · Peter Hicks · Ryan Hildebrandt · Michael Hilton · Carly Holland · Jessalyn Holodinsky · Kelly Houston · Tom Howard · Mike Huxley · Kara Iginla · Veronique Jeggo · Gordon Jewett · Madelyn Kelly · Naomi Kennedy · Konrad Kiss · Gary Klaudt · Yvette Kobylnyk · Sam Kolias · Carol Korec · Ricardo Kramer · John Krasnodemski · Lorna Kuhn · Janell Lautermilch · Sandy Lecour · Shirley Leung · François Lord · Jonathan Ma · Paul MacKenzie · Michael MacLean · Joseph MacLellan · Tyler MacRae · Cherith Mark · Donald Matthews · Elaine Maytwayashing · Jean McAllister · Stewart McDonough · Ryan McIntosh · Sarah McLean · Margot Micallef · Richard Morrison · Ward Morton · Matt Mosteller · John Murchie · Terry Napper · Chloe Neil · Stephen Neveu · Erik Nielsen · Bob Niven · Michael Norris · Larry O'Brien · Sidrean Okeymaw · Kimberly Parke · Kelsey Pellerin Isbister · Steve Penny · Karen Percy-Lowe · Steven Perron · Dan Phelps · Ron Pierce · Rhyan Pietromonaco · Luke Praught · Dave Rees · Micheal Rioux · Danijel Ritz · Scott Robertson · Melonee Rose · Cindy Ross · Matthew Rowley · Jacqueline Ryan · Ken Sallows · Eric Sawyer · Jeffery Schmalenberg · Cindy Seibel · Wanda Shaw · Russell Sherman · Jan Simonson · Eric Smith · Christina Smith · Tony Spoletini · Terry Steinkey · Matt Strum · Kim Tew · Jane Thomas · Geddes Thurton · Catherine Truong · Terry Underschultz · Vickey Volk · Shane Wagstaff · Jamie Ward · Geoff Waylett · Irene Welton · Christopher Wilson · Angela Wittig · Roni Wolach · Richard Young · Neil Younger **84** Abbas Ahmed · Carol Allendorf · Adrienne Asp · Kenneth Bahadur · Pam Barg · Alexis Beamer · Terry Bourne · Patrick (Wally) Buono · Colin Buschman · Malcolm Campbell · Don Carruthers Den Hoed · Manuel Chavarriaga · Suzette Cooke · Monica Cormier · Robin Cox · Nathaniel Day · Elijah Dixon · Christopher Doig · Howard Evans · Syd Feuz · Zack Fowler · Meaghan Garvie · R. Michael Giuffre · Noel Grisdale · Karen Howorko · Ronald Kustra · Carolyn Lane · Tzu Kuang Lee · Daniel Lefebvre · Florence Legros · Charlie Locke · Holliston Logan · Elizabeth Logan · Edgar Peter Lougheed · Jun Lu · Dianne Maier · Fiona McLean · John Mcleod · Brandy Miller · Ruslyn Nanan · Steve Neary · Kayla Neudorf · Maeve O'Beirne · Natascha Okimaw · Carmen Oszust · Nicole Pacas · Fred Parafina · Erik Petursson · Thomas Rockwell · Paul Sceviour · Eric Schmadtke · Sirish Shah · Sean Smith · Susan Smith Halak · Renato Soria · Myra Stevens · Wendy Tink · Nadine Tratch · Phillip van der Merwe · Elisabeth Vathje · Danielle Vrielink · Karl Wagner · Kevin Wasko · Patrick White · Sarah Williams · Verna Yiu **85** Scott Adams · Joe Ambrosio · Erik Andersson · Margaret Beckerjeck · Matthew Bennett · Beverly Berenson · Adrian Bergles · Rebecca Bermel · Ross Bidinger · Brianna Bock · Marc Boisvert · Justyna Boon · Judy Boucher · Randy Brash · Barbara Brown · Tasha Bukovnik · Michael Bumstead · Dwayne Burgoyne · Faro Burgoyne · Dion Burgoyne · Shane Caldwell · Brenda Caldwell · Kyle Casault · Justin Casimer · David Cavers · Herrick Cheung · Miles Chisholm · Marguerite Cooper · Alisa Cooper · Scott Cowan · Michelle Cramton · Daniel Crossley-Wing · Ashley Daigle Stevens · Sara Daigle Stevens · David Das · Andre De Champlain · Prem Domingo · Kerry Ellingboe · Sasha Eugene · Judith Ewashen-Slapak · Kathleen Foreman · Shirley Fu · Terry Gagnon · Doriann George · Sat Gill · Whitney Goold · Bill Goss · Jay Hamilton · Jeff Hodgson · Wendy Hogg · Robert Honsberger · Patrick Hughes · Bob Hunter · Randall Jackson · Roger Jackson · Lora Janzen · Jessie Jewell · Cheyenne Jimmy · Elisha Jimmy · Pierre Jimmy · Jerry Johnson · Jessica Jones · Kelly Keating · Megan Kinley · Shawna Larade · Ray Le Clair · Ingrid Liepa · Paul Livingston · Marvin Lupango · Scott MacDonald · Jennifer MacKay · Ronald Mannix · Herman Mauthner · Jon McDonell · Sam McIlwain · Christine McManus · Sean McMaster · Lisa Melo · Gayle Michel · Linda Michel · Tracy Monaco · Krisy Myers · Hanako Nagao · Chris New · Sara Ng Thomson · Joseph Nicholas · Jesse Nicholas · Aaron Nicholas · Michael O'Halloran · Angie Palmer · Karin Penner · Harry Pering · Rob Pettigrew · Annamay Pierse · John C. Ratcliffe · Susan Renney · Brian Rogers · Margaret Judy Rogers · Jamie Ross · Janet Ruzycki · Narinder Sabharwal · Skyla Sam · Stephanie Sam · Faith Saunders · Peter Schill · Colleen Sharp · Lorne Shovar · Shane Siemens · Jessica Smith · Darrell Smith · Stanford Smith · Dieter Soellner · Sandy Storey · Simon Sutcliffe · Megan Sweet · Rhonda Teneese · Marilyn Teneese · Danilo Terra · Hans Terstappen · Arden Thacker · David Thanh · Koby Thibeault · Erin Thom · Zachary Thomas · Bradley Tipper · Dolores Varga · Dawn Voysey · Delilah Wajchina · Yusef Washington · Lyle Wilson **86** Jennifer Ahlefeld · Gaetano Ambrosio · Kiwan Anderson · Ron Antalek · Cera Atherton · Courtney Babcock · Lisa Beaulac · Manon Beliveau · Robert Bell · Blaine Beranek · Lindsey Black · Linda Blair · Philip Boulton · Donovan Brekke · Lawrence Brennan · Justin Brown · Crystal Browne · Alex Buczewski · Ken Butler · Michael Butorac · Susan Buttnor · Marlene Callfas · Brenda Campbell · Keven Cann · CJ Caputo · David Charlton · Matthew Chenard · Trish Chernoff · Sierra Chilton · Brian Conrad · Rhonda Cook · Glen Cunningham · Andrew Davidoff · Leona Dimock · Matt Dixon · Mabeth Donaire · Shawn Downey · Keith Eismann · Shawn Ellis · Gary Fenton · David Ferraro · Dean Ferraro · Eriki Filipe · Stephanie Findlater · Toni Frisby · Rod Giles · Sunny Gill · Colton Grolla · Glenn Halliday · Melissa Hamm · Kyle Hansen · Brennan Harder · Ferg Hawke · Valerie Hes · Ryan Hewitt · Lindsey Hill · Tom Hong · Chris Hultin · Jim Hunking · Dave Irwin · Joel James · Janey Johnson · Kenny Johnstone · Craig Jones · Brandon Jung · Wafa Kadri · Chad Katunar · Kelly Kelland · Kim Kennedy · Blake Kirkham · Shelly Kochorek · Allen Kuffert · Colleen Lakevold · Theresa Langellotti · Trudy Lawson · Mike Lazzaroni · Michael LeBlanc · Brandon Liljenquist · Tom Liljenquist · Peter Lim · John Reginald Lovett · Travis Ludwar · Erin MacDonald · Zara MacDonald-Markham · Kere MacGregor · Hallie MacLachlan · Sean Maktaak · Jordan Marshall · Ryan Martin · Ron McAnaugh · Justin McArthur · Matthew McArthur · Stephanie McComb · Bill McDonnell · Colton Meaden · Catherine Meeks · Kevin Misurak · Irving Mitchell · Patti Mitchell · Brody Moen · Jennifer Mortimer · Darrell Mott · Linda Mott · Johanna Mulder · Kris Munoz · Dennis Munroe · Daphne Neal · Alex Nilsson · Robert Norum · Gideon Pangestu · Jeannie Phillips · Gloria Preston · Tony Prophet · Andrea Purcell · Ann Purdy · David Quinn · Amanda Racher · Spud Ronnquist · Ben Rutledge · Miriam Saville · Oscar Schmidt · Joe Schwartz · Sherry Shrieves-Adams · Mark Sirges · Brittnay Sopko · Judith Stead · Ellen Stronach · Rob Stuckey · Bradley Sutton · Scott Swiston · Marc Symbaluk · Kim Tassone · Keith Tellier · Nancy Van Oosten · Rob Vickers · Brock Ward · Melinda Watson · Ron Weaver · Guy West · Trevor Whalley · Daphne Wing · Erika Wood · Donnamarie Young · Chao Zhang · Brad Zubick **87** Nick Ahlefeld · Bill Allan · Sheri Allarie · Tim Austin · Glen Baber · Ryan Bail · Cynthia Baker · Peter Bambridge · Tony Batista · Dmitri Belotchkine · Bradley Berg · Sohen Biln · Mark Brown · John Cantin · Mark Cecchini · Jose Luis Chavez · Axel Chore · Sang Chun · Diane Clement · Murray Cockburn · Jean Cockburn · Blair Cooper · Gloria Darud · Bryan Dumas · Scott Dundas Sommerville · Maureen Duwors · Chris Elia · Peter Elliott · Dayna Esson · Benjamin Fischer · Christopher Gaze · Karyn Giesbrecht · Chantelle Gilbert · Cheryl Grant · Tim Haberstock · Aaron Haines · Katie Hammill · Lorne Hansen · Gill Harding · Rob Harkness · Jenna Harrad · Susan Heaton · Linda Henniger · Deborah Hicks · Karie Hildebrandt · Ben Hindle · Alysha Hinecker · Cathy Honor · Samuel Idler · Christopher Ius · Valerie Jerome · Mark Johnston · Brittany Jones · Tara Kettner · Trisha Keywood · Richard Koo · Gina Kwan · Doug Kyle · Robert Kyle · Carol Kyle · Connor Labossiere · Lesley Leithead · Stan Levenson · Richard Lewis · Jeffrey Louis · Carmen Lucich · Jackie MacDonald · Jock Mackay · Rhonda Mann · Cathy Manson · Dodie Manuel · John Marsh · Audrey Maxwell-Polovnikoff · Mary McCracken · Ernie McCullough · Sue McCullough · Juleen McElgunn · Frank McFadden · Suzan McKortoff · Gordon McLeod · Gordon Menelaws · Andrew Merringer · Ken Money · Rita Montgomery · Chris Moorhead · Gerry Moro · Mariah Morris · Tracy Noseworthy · Bob Patton · Jennifer Pendleton · Andrea Perrier · Kent Peterson · Diane Pew · Thierry Poirier · Catherine Pollock · Cheri Poznikoff · Gerry Rempel · Miles Ritchie · Derek Robbins · Gordie Robertson · Vanessa Rogers · Charlene Rothwell · Jaclyn Salter · Alice Simicak · Dennis Skulsky · Laird Sloan · Lance Sloan · Sharman Thomas · Curt Tingley · Jo-Ann Tisserand · Terry Tobacco · Margaret Tosh · Robert Travers · Charles Truscott · Linda Tynan · Dominic Uyede · Colin van der Kuur · Valdis Vilks · Joy Wallace · Peter Webb · Blair Weston · Elijah Whalen · Eric Wharton · Charles Wieder · Susi Wilkinson · Doug Wong · Charles Wood · Teresa Wright · Victoria Yehl **88** Michaela Ashbee · Kelly Atamanchuk · Ellissa Avila · Richard Baptiste · Dean Barrett · Butch Bautista · Chantel Bayliss · Henry Beesley · Leah Benazic · Joshua Bergstad · Don Bertoia · Michelle Bessette · Paul Best · Barton Bigford · Frank Biro · Christina Borring-Olsen · Bob Brander · Gregory Breedveld · Merylen Bunnage · Colin Burns · Amy Buzikievich · Tobi Byrne · Robert Cable · Al Cade · Jason Caissie · Melissa Calvert · Scott H. Campbell · Marg Caravetta · Hailey Causton · Harriette Chang · Barb Coble · Chris Cochrane · Michael Conlin · Sam Corea · Elizabeth Corrigan · Kathy Coutts · Viola Creasey · Nick Curalli · Bob Daly · John Dampf · Jim Daniels · Nicole Darveau · Marvin Dean · Sean Dexter · Harley Dickinson · Wenhua Ding · Vicki Dreger · Barrita Durward · Nelson Dutra · Kevin Ellis · Teresa Engel · Ken Ferguson · David Ferguson · Wilhelmina Findlater · Karen Flavelle · Angela Fleming · Rich Floersch · Carla Fowler · Scott Frandsen · Katrina Gallagher · James Gamblen · Bob Gibney · Navpreet Jolly Gill · Ron Gorman · Mike (Monas) Haidar · Jessica Halina · Kent Hawkins · Ashley Hayes · Ron Hayman · Vili Heczko · Jeri-Lynne Hickling · Bob Hissink · Norman Houle · Melissa Howey · Carlton Huber · Ashley Hughes · Stephanie Hughes-White · Nora Hunt-Haft · Jay Ingram · Ron Jackson · Aliesha Jacobs-Tobias · Brenda Jmaeff · Morgan Jmaiff · Matthew Johnston · Kayla Johnston · Kristine Jones · Jaxon Jurome · Andrea Kardos · Emerson Kirby · Stephanie Klym · Sharon Koch · Bob Kraemer · Jordon Krause · Vanessa Lameiras · Marlene Lang · Paige Laroche · Meghan Lee · Anna Leitch · Kathleen Linley · Daniel Litchinsky · Cambria Little · Luis Lizardo · Clarence Louie · Lindsay MacEachern · Brent MacGregor · Sarah Mackay · Robin MacMillan · Daniella Macri · Mark Manton · Aly Marson · Paula Martins · Brian McDonald · Jack McPherson · Phil Meggison · Andrea Messing · Natasha Montgrand · Joseph Morelli · Sue Morrison · Brett Mottershead · Kenneth Naylor · Jonathan Alford Neitsch · Marissa Nelson · Trish Nixon · Alexander Norman · Debbie Olafson · Alex Ortega · Rick Papineau · Pawan Patil · Jesse Peacock · Kayden Peters · Kendall Pew · Hayley Pipher · Ken Poulin · Will Pratt · Trevor Prior · B. Prokop · Ye Quiao Bo · Ross Rebagliati · Stephen Reynolds · Kristi Richards · Jay Rittinger · Andrea Robertson · Michael Ross · Stacey Rotheisler · Jean Saul · John Saunders · Paul Savage · Katrina Scarlett · Luc Schingh · Leesa Schlenker · Mitchell Segal · Katie Semenoff · Margaret Shapiro · Tom Siddon · Kelly Lynn Soros · Devin Spence · Erin St. Jean · Adolf Walter Steffen · Jessica Stewart · Anthony Stewart · Wade Stolz · Scott Storle · Tom Suitor · John Swanson · Dianne Taft · Stacey Takenaka · Chris Taneda · Laura Terness · Jarrod Thalheimer · Kaden Thomas · Renee Tremmel · Cadence Trites · Tracy Turcotte · Andy Van Ruyven · Martin Vandervelden · Paul Varian · Mark Versfeld · Miguel Angel Viedma Lloreda · Shane Vogelgesang · David Walker · Nadine Weiss · Gene Wells · Susie Welsh · Gary Werschler · Prescott Wick · Elizabeth Williams · Robert Woodbury · Lorraine Wylant · Glen Yule · Kirk Xiao Zhou **89** Roxana Adams · Rob Adolph · Leonard Anderson · Dylan Armstrong · Judy Armstrong · Adam Ashton · Gary Athans · Gurjit Aujla · Beatrice Austrom · Dave Bachmier · Albert Baldeo · Michael Ballingall · Theodore Barfoot · Camille Bartsch · Graeme Bekker · Rosetta Bernava · Bodan Boggs · Art Bonney · Shane Bourbonnais · Molly Brewis · Michael Burke · Maryssa Camacho · Mark Cameron · Jan Campbell · Marcus Carberry · Alexandre Cardoso · Georgina Chin · Grant Chu · Ronald Coleman · Catherine Comben · Paige Conlin-Mouat · Jimmy Corbett · Richard Crowley · Trish Dalcourt · Velma Davies · Peter Devries · Rod Eaket · Elaine Embury · Brittany Evans · Eli-Marc Fattal · Lynne Findlay · Janet Fisher · Susan Foisy · Chris Fraikin · Sam Frese · Diana Friend · Tere Friesen · Carole Gariepy · Pat Gerk · Ian Gordon · Curtis Grainger · Christie Gray · Lynn Hadfield · Frank Halperin · Tian Hannah · Kimberly Hardy · Brenda Harvey-Jones · Boyd Hayes · Bob Hazell · Lachlan Hicks · Ron Hohner · Chris Holmes · Steve Holmes · Cairy Holtby · Brent Horii · Benjamin Horne · Lannie Houle · Jake Huff · Peter Hughes · Ross Hyde · Alison Ibbotson · Laura Ingram · Blair Ireland · Caroline Ivey · Trent Jensen · Harvinder Johal · James Johnstone · Steve Jones · Kilian Jungen · Sylvia Jurys · Doug Kelly · Angela Klein · Linda Kynoch · Brooke Kynoch · Nelson Lanza · Barry Lapointe · Rob Leach · Darlene Lee · Ben Lee · Paul Longden · Chief Robert Louie · Peter Lutsky · Lauren Lypchuk · Chelsey MacBride · Gordon Mackie · Georgia Manhard · Reg Marte · Niomi Mattioda · John McInnes · Cheryl McKinnon · Terence McKinty · Michael McKnight · Linda McLaren · Maggie McLeod · Adam Medrek · Kelly Megyesi · Dave Merklinger · Jennifer Miller · Joanna Morris · Sarah Newton · Angela Nordin · Judith Ouillette · Daniel Ouimet · J. Michael Pennington · Ross Pickard · Sara Pieper · Robert Pringle · Darren Prowse · Justin Radermacher · Debbie Ranger · Carl Rankin · Stefanie Reutgen · Carl Richard · Dave Roemer · Mike Sawisky · Michelle Scabar · Jory Schlitt · Mary Jo Schnepf · Nicole Shaver · Kelcy Sherbank · Justin Sigal · Auburn Sigurdson · Christine Silver · Lawrence (Lawrie) Skolrood · Brian Spence · Bill Stanbury · Constance Stephany · Terry Stevens · Corey Sturgeon · Glen Thayer · Janet Tietzen · Luci Tremblay · Darren Tseng · Olivia Vardabasso · Robert Vorotinskis · Tristyn Waechter · Cam Walton · Craig Warner · Ann Whitman · Christine Wiebe · Josephine Wilder · Natasha Dawn Worby · Shayne Wright · Randy Zahara · Gerry Zimmermann **90** Sandra Abernethy · Garry Andal · Paige Archie · Byron Ashton · Parmjit Bal · Melissa Baptiste · Amanda Barrett · Kaitlyn Baskerville · Colleen Bell · Jo Berry · Rebecca Blow · Jennifer Bonar · Ari Bruns · Karen Buemann · Elijah Buffalo · Catlyn Cameron · Dwayne Clark · Isabel Clark · Stephen Cousins · Cody Crocker · Rebecca Cullum · Wendy Cummer · Janet Daoust · Marlene Deans · Christine Devries · James Dickie · Indira Doman · Darren Donas · John Dormer · Randy Dudka · John Dumbrell · Ann English · Michael Farrington · Joel Feenstra · Kyle Flatman · Donna Flatman · Marina Flatman · Marshall Flukkinger · Leah Foreman · Jennifer Fossum · Amanda Frayne · Jason Freund · Lisa Fuller · Melvin Galloway · Joe Gavin · Shylah Gibb · Matthew Graham · Rob Graham · Fred Green · Jesse Grist · Thomas Hardy · Jesse Heckrodt · Jacob Heigers · Callie Hill · Davin Hofmann · Spencer Jackson · Amanda Jackson · Ross Jardine · Sandra Jenkins · Ky T. Johnny-Charters · Suzanne Joly · Rachel Jonat · Sklyer Jones · Marleigh Kallhood · Erikki Keski-Salmi · Jacob Kitchen · Silken Kleer · Frederick Parker Knox · Demetra Koutsopodiotis · Neills Kristensen · Leanne Kujat · Melinda Kunhegyi · Farhan Lalji · Eric Lam · Kim Le · Ed Leduc · Les Lindhout · Bobby Lipsett · Kashtin Mair · Diane Mann · Jonathan McCullough · Lorne McNeilly · Malcolm Metcalfe · Terry Michell · Vivian Morris · Jeff Murphy · Fernando Pardo · Gregg Patterson · Petronella Peach · Catharine Pendrel · John Perrin · Diana Peterson · Kerry Phelvin · Sergio Pike · Debra Podruzny · Kevin Poole · John Pritchett · Don Quilty · Nancy Raine · Mark Recchi · Kate Richardson · Donna Rozinkin · Adrian Rufo · Roy Sakaki · Jeff Sandmoen · Tracy Sankey · Heather Savage · Gur Sharan Singh · Ranbir Singh · Alyssa Skaalid · Clive Smith · Kevin Smith · Gordon Sonier · Reese Stone · Barb Tetrault · Susan Thompson · Jacques Trudel · Adrienne Underhill · Carmen Underhill · Brenda Walch · Cliff Wale · Phil Wallensteen · Dorien Wamelink · June Wayslow · Lynne Welock · Shawn Wenger · Crysta Westoby · James Whitehead · Annie Woodhurst · Todd Woon · Leanna Yip · Josee Zimanyi **91** Juan Jose Aniceto Porcar · Adrian Archie · Cassian Archie · Katleen Archie · Mike Archie · Tom Charles Barr · Riann Batch · Tricia Beauvais · Gabriel Bergen · Cheyenne Blackbird · Justin Bosher · Lance Boyce · Alex Bracewell · Alvina Cameron · Claire Cathro · Jody Charlton · Melissa Christopher · Alyssa Christopher · Deanna Christopher · Amber Christopher · Taisa Cole · Steve Cook · Betty Cosens · Terry Cunning · Calvin Daling · Rachel Daniel · Evan Daniels · Tanya de Dood · Matt Defouw · Kristy Dejong · Korah Dewalt · Kalei Dixon · Marcia Dixon · Tillia Dixon · Kaitlyn (Ryna) Dixon · Marty Dixon · Massimo Dossetto · Joel Eccleston · Rachael Elliot · Susan Emile · Collin Emile · Tammy Ferris · Margaret Findlay · Chantel Frank · Jenny Ann Frowd · Shelley Ganchar · Danny Gilbert · Keith Gordon · Barbara Gordon · Leslie Hall · Peter Hamilton · Megan Harstad · Brenda Hartley · Werner Heine · Beth Henschel · Mark Howkins · Sandra Howkins · Amanda Huynh · Gwen Ireland · Ava Kibalian · Shirley Kwan · Stephanie Lindal · Austin Llewellyn · Kristina Luke-Airey · Jimmy Lulua · Kelly Marce · Chris Matthews · Breanne Mcclusky · Mark Monroe · Daryl Moore · Tom Nowak · Kaitlin Olson · Gerry Olund · Walter Orb · Julie Palmantier · Will Parei · Kate Parker · Linden Paul · Donna Petri · Lynda Price · Deb Radolla · Britta Rempel · Kaja Salovsky · Marta Sanfeliu · Miles Sanoy · William Sellars Jr. · Scott Simson · Linda Skelly · Darlene Slobodian · Linda Smerychynski · Josie Spence · Marty Spreacker · Nanci Taylor · Maribel Thorimbert · Gordon Thorsteinson · Arnold Tobler · Teresa Wallace · Darrel Warman · E. Karen Williamson · Ali Zentner **92** Jolene Agabob · Lisa Allen · Stacie Anaka · Kevin Cruz Antunes · Patty Apps · Melissa Arkinstall · Karen Aubichon · Christopher Baker · Dennis Baptiste · Laurie Bare · Lynne Bent · Jeanne-Anne Bentham · Daniel Bilotta · James Bourque · Blair Browning · Hazel Burns · Kathaleen Buxton · Tim Carmack · David Carmichael · Marcel Chalmers · Pat Cheung · Lisa Coltart · Amber Cooper · Sherry Daniels · Cora David · Tanya Davoren · Marta De Sousa · Pal Dhadly · Brian Dohler · Craig Douglass · Julie Duckworth · Gary Ducommun · Natasha Dudoward · Rod Duncan · Barbara Durau · Jim Dyer · Gilgamesh Eamer · Victoria Feistmantl · Kary Fell · Betty Fisher · Chad France · Dale Freschi · Kimberly Friesen · Brad Gamble · Rylan Gaudet · John Giannisis · Nancy Giesbrecht · Thomas Guillemaud · Robert Hedges · Erin Henderson · Lois Herrick · Michelle (Tuppy) Hoehn · Brandy Hoglund · Phil Horton · Marie Jensen · CHantelle Jimenez · Paul Kainth · Laurel Katernick · Valerie Kidd · You Seung - Austin Kim · Bryan Kineshanko · Donna Koning · Keith Laboucan · Malonie Langthorne · Joey Laquerre · David Law · Brian Le · Nicholas Leatham · Luella Long · Davish Longe · Mary Ann Lyall · Caitlynn MacDonald · Ed Mah · Leah Malo · Gordon March · Melissa McCall · Renee McCloskey · Mikey McDonald · Myrna McDonough · Dayle McKinnon · Chad Munro · Peggy Myhre · Joanne Nguyen · Marlies Olson · Louella Pacaide · Carol Paynter · Rodger Peterson · Darcie Petuh · Sheri Preissler · Rick Publicover · Lis Quinn · Helen Ramsay · Steve Raper · Kirsten Reimer · Adelle Rennie · Rick Rhodes · Nicole Rishaug · Dirk Robson · Colleen Rose · Colleen Ruddy · Colin Sanderson · Gayle Sayese · Angelina Schafer Gauthier · Dorrie Sharcott · Dakota Stone · Lisa Stuart · Ginette Thomas · Jennifer Thompson · Tracey Thornhill · Collette Trudeau · Dean Trumbley Trumbley · John Tymofichuk · Shirley Walker · Alix Wells · Inge Wiggins · Dave Wilkinson · Todd Wilson · Burke Wittenberg · Andy Wong · Kanil Youngman **93** Tracy Arrowsmith · Colleen Black · Lisa Brise · Emily Cavallin · Brenda

Chinn · Lee Coxford · Angela Cudlipp-Lehr · Zul Dahya · Darcy Dennis · Alexandra Dickson · Isabella Dinh · Maciek Dobrowolski · Jonathan Dunn · Catherine Elliott · Logan Erickson · Devon Flynn · Joann Francis · Andrew Gregory · Richard Harrison · James Hedalen · Francis Holland · Carol Huynh · Ross Hyam · James Ingle · Heidi Jakubec · Ed John · Norman Johnson · Pennie Jones · Stacey Joyce · Barbara Kennedy · Allen Kessler · Colin Kinsley · Nicholas Krizmanich · Oleh Kuzma · Laryssa Kuzma · Yvette Labatte · Joshua Larson · Kohen Leslie · Jordana Luggi · Joan MacGillivray · Kaileen McCulloch · Amy McGuire · Raye McMeeken · Marcel Melanson · James Michell · Vanessa Moore · Tyler Mutch · Floyd Naziel Jr. · Saja Noor · Brian Pepper · Robin Raymond · Ryan Rounce · Glenn Rupertus · Tracy Sam-Stephens · David Scheer · Dean Scott · Marilynne Shanks · Travis Shaw · Evelyn Shenk · Matthew Skinner · Kirsten Stephen-Barnes · Ray Sturney · Robson Swift · Judy Thomas · Ceejay Turner · Laurel Vaadeland · Keith Van Tine · Tyler Wardrop · Carrie Wardrop · Darren White · Derrick Williams · Thelma Wright · Ryan Yasayko **94** Bryanna Birks · Doug Bloom · Dan Bouillon · Erin Bow-Noskiye · Rita Bryant · Annette Burridge · Cole Calliou · Larry Campbell · Don Chahley · Samantha Davis · Lauren Dohler · Doris Duchesneau · Greta Goddard · Cyril Hannon · Jenn Harcourt · Charles Helm · Mohammed Janief · Trevor Kolkea · Kirk Laboucan · Dolphus Laboucan · Clarissa Laboucan · Lana Laboucan · Jamie Lee · Liz Logan · Tristan Loonskin · Francine Loonskin · Rodrica Loonskin · Shelly Loonskin · Nadia Loonskin · Ross H. Maclean · Hazel MacMillan · Barry McKinnon · Coleman Mercereau · Emilda Nanooch · Tylene Neary · Laverne Norris · Steve Oliver · Robin O'Reilly · Calvin Osterlund · Charlotte Pardely · Elaine Peterson · Rebekah Posthuma · Andy Ribbonleg · Vincent Ribbonleg · Connie Richter · Jory St. Arnault · Joey St. Arnault · Susan Stark · Caren Tallcree · Lonny Tallcree · Darryl Tegart · Kashtin Wilson · Kathryn Winter **95** Mike Ambach · Jason Arsenault · Justin Barton · Cheryl Beattie · Donald Blanchard · Marl Brown · David Robert Brown · James Casey · Kristina Csondes · Robert Cuthbert · Mario Desjardins · Theresa Fincaryk · Laurie Gallant · Carmen Gemmell · Amarjit Grewal · Diana Gryckiewicz · Sierra Harrold · Ali Howard · Dave Jephson · Katherine Taneille Johnson · Otto Kamenzin · Norma Kerby · Greg Kingdon · Margaret Kujat · Kwan Ping Law · Ian Maxwell · Wilma Maxwell · Kevin McKay · Shantelle McLean · Justin Mercer · Kelly-Ruth Mercier · Lindsay Mickelson · Matthew Mills · Robert Munroe · Ken Newman · Sarah Peden · Ted Pellegrino · Laurence Robinson · Charlotte Rowse · John Ryan · Benedict Sabal · Heidi Siebring · Jesse Smith · Grant Spelsberg · Linda Spouler · Robert Thompson · Jane Treweeke · Michel Valois · Bill Walker · Jordan Wesley · Patrick Whidden · Mike Wu · Alex Wyder **96** Randy Arsenault · Chad Bell · Mike Bell · Brayden Belleville · Doug Bondue · Malcolm Browne · Riley Browne · Tyson Cadwallader · Adam Carlson · Collette Child · Darryl Coon · Tyren Dustin · Terry R. Eissfeldt · Clayton Ellis · Brittany Falconer · Rod Hikida · Wilfred Humchitt · Ali Hunt · Nick Klein-Beekman · Riley Mathieson · Curtis McCarrick · Rene McCarrick · Rod (Mehrad) Nikmaram · Brandon Pelletier · Justin Powell · Todd Ringness · Chantel Rompfer · Liam Ryan · Antonio Saavedra · Coltton Slater · Cliff Starr · Christina Stauffer · Greg Stenmark · Corey Swain · Don Tite · Brett Walker **97** Paula Aldersey · Gemma Avila · Robbie Bailey · Erika Barker · David Benton · Miranda Berney · Tara Beuk · Amanda Birtig · Mat Bodie · Steve Boneham · Reid Campbell · Finnigan Canadensis · Joyce Carlson · Christopher Co · Jamuga Cook · Carmen Correia · Justin DaSilva · Adele De Wit · Darren Dean · John Dejong · Sandra Dyer · Brenden Forbes · Brandon Formosa · Matt Garbowsky · Michael Garteig · Liza Grant · Jordan Grant · Susanne Green · Christine Gullstrom · Patricia Hawley · Kathy Hodgins · Darcy Huisman · Phyllis Jones · Klay Kachur · Cathy Kirby · Mitchell Labreche · Deb Leger · Abby Lloyd · Lucinda Louie · Sherry Masengarb · Jenny McCormack · Alex McDougall · Gordon Meehan · Jean-Paul Modde · Chad Niddery · Mariann Paice · Jade Palm · Braden Pears · Andrew Pettitt · Ben Schmidt · Carter Shinkaruk · Taylor Soper · Gavin Texmo · Erynn Tomlinson · Stuart Wild · Jason Yee **98** Patrick Adiba · Ken Bagshaw · Brian Barnes · Barbara Behan · Sue Belbeck · Melanie Bird · Jim Boner · Mackenzie Booth · Adrienne Bouris · Pat Brand · Caroline Brunelliere · Sandra Campden · Rachel Canning · Frances Casey · Shiloh Cashin · Jerry Causier · Olga Chernosvitova · Rick Chisholm · Gary Coblenz · Hal Coleman · Kimberly Coonfer · Craig Cusick · Darrick Cusick · David Deally · Caroline Depatie · Trent Dixon · Sarah Doherty · Susan Doyle · Rosey Edeh · Gwendolyn Edwards-Hooley · Erin Eidsvik · Andy Evans · Bonnie Fairbairm · Kevin Flynn · Marlowe Fraser · Cameron Fyles · Olivier Gendron · Ross Gentleman · Esther Gilichensky · Jaeten Gosal · Sandra Hale · Phillip Hamel · Colleen Hamilton · David Hamilton · Mark Hatfield · Jiang Heping · Jim Hoggan · Sonia Jacoboni · Maria Jedrejcic · Lakota Joe · Keith Julius · Lynn Kanuka · Effie Karapidakis · Gus Karvelis · George P. Kavouras · Douglas Kennedy · Jim Kenney · Effie Kerasiotis · Peter P. Kletas · Ferdinand Lagadi · Bruce Daniel Lane · Toby Lau · Dan Lecours · Shirley Lewis · Nick Liapis · Thomas Liaskas · Julie Lingley · Jeannette Lucas · John Macleod · Anastase Maragos · Maria Maragos · James Martin · Kristin McBride · Bill McCormick · Thomas McLaughlin · Henry Metzler · Mary Miles · Bernard Miranda · Chris Moldenhauer · Trina Moldenhauer · Darren Murphy · Daniel Muzyka · Jessica Neilson · Kai Nestman · Chad Neufeld · Mark Nishiguchi · Wendy Northwood · Valerie Oakes · Jane Ostashek · Nick Panos · Konstantine Papageorgiou · Harry Parslow · Dwayne Paul · Daphne Pay · Deverell Pelletier · Hailey Perry · Kade Peterson · Jocelyn Pettit · John Phillips · Jason Plank · Pierre Plourde · Sassan Pourfar · Travis Ramsey · Stephen Reid · Randy Schisler · Brittany Sheppard · Herb Simak · Jared Siminoff · Norm Singhavon · Terry Sklavenitis · Lauren Storoschuk · Laura Sukorokoff · Pam Tattersfield · Jennifer Tester · John Thiessen · Denice Thompson · Kenneth Tran · Fotis Tsonis · Wanda Turner · Cassandra Whelan · Mary Winn · Carolyn Ann Wray · Demetri N. Zambus **99** Scott Aldrich · Cameron Alexander · Gordon Alexander · Tyler Allison · Houshang Amiri · Roberta Andrus · Geoff Appleton · Gerald Arksey · Donald Arnold · Mary-Sue Atkinson · Barbara Bain · Michelle Beland · Tzeporah Berman · Stuart Bird · Brenda Bjorkman · John Blok · Erin Boisvert · Larissa Braganza · Gail Bremer · Brian Brodie · Rob Burgess · Carmen Bustillo · Mark Butschler · Kathleen Cadenhead · Michael Cadman · Robert Carter · Romilly Cavanaugh · Vivian Cheung · Joe Chidley · Charles Coffey · Mike Creery · Mark Crossman · Eric Crowe · Marcella Cusano · Charles Davis · Erik Davis · Arthur De Jong · Rob Drygas · Karine Dubreuil · Kevin Ducharme · Maria Durham · Sarah Dusanj · Kathryn Kary Firstbrook · Stephanie Fleckenstein · Matthew Friesen · Brad Fritz · Alex Gershon · Joey Gibbons · Stephen Giblin · Robert Gibson · Penny Ginsberg · Jim Godfrey · Darlene Goetz · Mike Golbey · Kim Gordon · Chris Graham · Arthur Griffiths · Michael Guenter · Roger Handling · Jim Harris · Sandra Hartley · Neil Hastie · Jan Heath · Andreas Hestler · Evan Hilchey · Nicole Hillis · Bob Hindmarch · David Hindmarch · Mark Hoag · Fred Holst · Alexandre Horobjowsky · Victor Huckell · Robert Hulyk · Andrew Kadziola · Don Kajiwara · Zornitsa Kaneva · Christopher Katsuleres · Matthew Kauffman · Michael Kealey · Mac Kennedy · June Kleban · Michael Landsberg · Maya Lange · Lauren Law · Vince Lee · Rachel Leverton · Chase Lewis · Michael Lincoln · Elaine Lui · Margaret MacBeth · Bill Mackie · Naomi Manley-Casimir · Lisa McDougall · Drew Meredith · Anton Mitsyuk · Jim Moodie · Shannon Murphy · Robyn Murray · Julia Murray · Saranaz Navabi · Holly Nelson · James Ng · Minh Ngo · John O'Brien-Bell · Heidi Oetter · Evanka Osmak · Jessie Oswald · Kelly Oswald · Alexander Owen · Atenea Pallares · Zichun Pan · Avtar Parmar · Jason Patchell · Jim Pattison · Heather Paul · Max Peiffer · Ellen Pekeles · David Pike · Deborah Pink · Matt Pinsent · Steve Podborski · Patrick Postrehovsky · Andrew Pringle · Valerie Pringle · Richard Prokopanko · Roy Purssell · Frank W. Quo Vadis · Jagdeep Rana · Ben Remocker · Benoit Reneault · William Roberts · Cierra Rohde · Robyn Ruholl · Suzanne Marie Rutherford · Waldemar Sambor · Dillon Sampson · Jayne Sandilands · Robin Scholefield · Mark Schonfeld · Joanna Schwarz · Benjamin Sears · Wendy Shard · Mark Sherman · Bryce Shoemaker · Sharon Shore · Cary Skidmore · John Smart · Shannon Smith · Akanksha Stevens · John Stibbard · Harvey Strecker · Gavin Stuart · Eko Suharto · Mitch Sulkers · Donald James Taylor · Alison Taylor Robb · Suan Teo · Ken Thicke · Ann Thur · Michelle Tice · Lesley Tomlinson · Rebecca Tran · Augustus Charles Tugade · Shannon Turner · Andrea Unger · Dominique Vallee · Karen Vinnedge · Remy Warren · Georgina Wheatcroft · Victoria Whitney · Deb Whitten · Ron Wilson · Karl Wilson · Joanne Young **100** Roger Adolph · Rick Aleck · Seataesca Andrew · Keegan Andrews · Talisa Antone · Murray Atherton · Aiden Baker · Kelly Bartlem · Jason Beukens · Grégory Bonfils · Kayla Boston · Rusty Brewer · Ryan Scott Bystrom · Peter Campbell · Jan Charlie · Marco Chiaramonte · Susanna Chow · Brooks Coble · Payton Dan · Linda Dan · Treanna Delorme · Jordan Demeulemeester · Kelsey Dennison · Alan Ding · Courtney Downey · Cora Dunlop · Channelle Edwards · John Egan · Andrea Elliott · Carter Faulkner · Robert Finlay · Tanya Goertzen · Bram Goldstein · Raj Gondara · Anne Hale · Ian Hanomansing · Dominick Harry · Kelly Haws · Lindsay Hubley · Justin Hui · James Jennings · Taylor Joe · Kwimtsxn John · Ryan Johnston · Shari Jonker · Kemal Khan · Reg Krake · Alan Kristmanson · Marion Lay · Alexis Leech · Jean Leiper · Hayden Leo · Alexandria Leon · Megan Marsh · Chelsie Mccutcheon (Mitchell) · Greg McDonnell · Gabriel Moody · Cheryl Morch · Donnie Morris · Susan Nattrass · Tishyna Ned · Rob Needham · Dominique Niyonizigiye · Scott O'Hara · Jazzmin Pascal · Logan Pehota · Dalton Pehota · Randall Phillips · Darcy Porter · Inderjit Randhawa · Alex Read · Jonathan Redman · Cora Renaud · Alicia Ann Rhodenizer · Sarah Richter · Jarnail Sahota · Stevie Scott · Tyler Seitz · Bob Sheridan · Perry Solkowski · Dan Sorotschynski · Joyce Sparks · Kayla Spencer · John Patrick Sta.Maria · Bobbie Stager · Jacqueline Stewart · Levi Swaenepoel · Bonnie Swanson · Christine Tallon · Walter Terry · Delanie Thorlakson · Sara Tronson · Andree Vajda Janyk · Maria Villar · Holly Watkinson · Cate Webster · Peter Webster · William Wiltse · Heather Zoller **101** Don Adams · Salimkhan Ahmed · Bernice Albert · Dan Alvo · Betty Andres · Mia Angus · Myia Antone · Lise Arsenault-Goertz · Sarah Ayton · Paula Barchard · Barbara Barlow · Timothy Barrington · George Bartel · Shelby Bay · John Belanger · Rex Blane · Brooke Bobb-Reid · Jared Bogdanovich · Annie Bottiglieri · Dana Britton · Shauneen Bruder · Mike Bugden · Noelle Bunn · Isabella Burczak · Lisa Byrne · Maria Calalang · Jonathan Calvano · Justin Cathcart · Debra Cerny · Ada Chiu · Ann Colasimone · Christine Couturier · Heather Cowie · Duncan Cronkhite · James Currie · Cassie Cutajar · Duane Dahl · Mary-Jane Dahl · Diana Dampier · Ron Day · Shelley Deacon · Alanna Dean · Charles Dehelly · Joelle Derulle · David Dufault · Blair Elder · Razia Esmail · René Fasel · Patrick Flanagan · Pauline Foster · Daniel Frankel · Carol Fulcher · Chanea Gabriel · Brennan Gademans · Candace Garbo · Denise Gariepy · Eli Gershkovitch · Satinder Gill · Bill Goerzen · Beth Grant · Frederic Gueissaz · Christine Hartnoll · Patrick Hergott · Carl Hoath · Drew Hollingworth · Chantell Horel · Kirk Illingworth · Pharid Jaffer · Hans Jeschek · Mark Jiles · Brian Johnson · Jamie Kerenko · Jacek Klonica · Dorothy Kostrzewa · Bindi Kullar · Guy Laflamme · Angela Laws-Peel · Emil Lee · Frank Letkeman · Andy Lin · Javier Lopez · Dane Low · Melissa Luther · Tony Lyons · S. Peter Malek · Roxanna Malek · Tim Maloney · Bernard Manuel · Adrienne Marsh · Pierre Yves Martin · Michel Matifat · Rob Mays · Jason McLean · Deena McNeill · Pam Mills · Nicole Mirante · Myles Mitchell · Maya Molander · Pierre Morin · David Munro · Neil Munroe · Aaron Myales · Megan O'Leary · Jacqueline Onagi · Rob Pankhurst · Derek Peddlesden · Desiree Petersen · Merrell-Ann Phare · Ken Phuah · Jim Playfair · Allison Prieur · Matt Pryde · Pete Quevillon · Poppy Quinlan · Rob Quiring · Lorri Ratzlaff · Douglas James Reimer · Michelle Rempel · Sandro Ricci · Andrew Richardson · Brieanna Robotham · Tracy Ronmark · Roman Rovensky · Allan Sanders · DJ Sandhu · Erin Sanford · Benjamin Seeley · Carrie Serwetnyk · Andy Amandeep Sidhu · Fred Snooks · Dave Stephen · Barry Stewart · Gerry Swan · Mitch Syberg-Olsen · Derek Takahashi · Nick Taylor · Karen Thompson · Linda Tom · Ashley Topnik · Gary Tosh · "Danny, Kai-Hsien" Tseng · David Urban · Koji Ushikubo · Laurens Van Vliet · Jennifer Velthujzen · George Walker · Elisabeth Walker-Young · Shannon Wheeler · Mike Williams · Peter Williams · Joern Winkler · Gilbert Yeung · Scott Young · Susan Yurkovich · Kate Zabell · Anna Zampieri · Joanna Zipser-Graves **102** Philip Alalouf · Stephanie Albiston · Gilles Allemann · Magnus Alvarsson · Jessie Anderson · Lee Anderson · Steve Armitage · Gordon Armstrong · Debbie Armstrong · Diane Askin · Daina Augaitis · Rapinder Aujla · Thomas Bach · Isaiah Baldissera · Lauren Barwick · John Bear · Graeme Benn · Miro Bezjak · Jody Bialowas · Alex Blaby · Claudia Bokel · Mike Bos · Keary Bott · Valaree Braaten · Christopher Brearton · Pat Brethour · Taylor Briggs · Jesse Briggs · Michelle Brown · Sergey Bubka · Burt Burdett · Gerry Burgess · Susan Caley · Ken Carlsen · Alfonso Castillo · Lekie Chand · Janice Chisholm · Coleen Christie · Susan Cline · Alaura Chantelle Emily Ellis Collet · Chantelle A Anne Boulay Lafontaine McCormick Kelly Victoria Collet · Marlys Cory · George Coucopoulos · Brian James Coxford · Gloria Cuccione · Yvonne Curry · Fenton Davis · Robert Davison · Deborah Dickson · Chris Diersch · Andrea Digby · Greg Durrell · Darren Dutchyshen · Lisa Edwardson · Rory Fatt · Joe Fauchon · Guillaume Felli · Jill Ferrie · Martin Gifford · Pam Glass · Leslie Goldsby · Bill Good · Bob Gray · Matthew Gray · Harbans Grewall · Sergio Grossi · Mandy Hadfield · Bill Hallett · Sarah Hannigan · Teresa Hardie · Andrew Harvey · Lauren Hearty · Kathleen Heddle · Rhonda Hildebrandt · Sally Hinksman · Sheila Hogan · Brent Holliday · Kevin Hong · Jenny Hong · Jim Hubbeard · Elizabeth Hughes · Chi Ho Hui · Tricia Hunt · Jeff Hutcheson · Daniel Igali · Danny Jakobs · Ben Jan · Cornelius Jansen · Bernard Jaquier · Doug Jensen · Nancy Jensen · Ajit Johal · Satnam Johal · Meghan Johnson · Brian Johnston · Bill Jolly · Marilyn Jourdain · Quamar Jutt · Aman Kahlon · Pawan Kang · Jesse Kaufman · Robert Kerr · Margaret Krieck · Rachael Lafreniere · Adana Lagerstrom · Margaret Langford · Clarissa Larsen · Chris Lasher · Seanna Lasher · Mireille Lavoie · Joy Ann Lois Lee · Kurt Louie · Don Lowry · Chris Luff · Austin Machholz · Fraser MacRae · Mark Madryga · Maryam Malekyazdi · Matt Malenstyn · Lorne Malinowski · Rick Manuel · Raymond Martin · Anne Martin-Lederrey · Colleen Mathieson · Ryan Mathieson · Robert Matichuk · Bruce Mavis · Thomas (Tom) Mayenknecht · Vernon Mazerolle · Stephanie McCann · Ramona McClymont · Mark McGaire · Gerald McGhie · Jim McGregor · James McKechnie · Ian McMaster · Josh McNutt · Saul Gabriel Merino · Darko Mihajlovic · Tracy Minor · Pete Mitchell · Carole Morin · Doug Mossey · Ali Nanji · Rupa Nanubhai · Stephen Neal · Michael Nell · Jamie Nelson · Gale Neumann · Robert Neumann · Richard Nilson · Dan Nugent · Patty Nugent · Dave Olafson · Dave Orr · Terri Orser · Catherine Ortelli · Sue Paish · Dave Parker · Linda Pauls · Dan Pederson · Hedy Pemble · Alexandre Pera · Celia Pereira · Alan Peretz · James Pitblado · Stefano Podini · Jérôme Poivey · Kiya Posthumus · Keith Prefontaine · Terry Prefontaine · Brittany Reimer · Bob Rennie · Laurel Richardson · Phil Riffel · Yumilka D. Ruiz Luaces · Scott Sagmoen · Rod Sangala · Jeff Schulz · Aaron Seguin · Ana Shapiro · Hayley Shay · Jay Sher · Shawn Siak · Jagjit Singh Rai · Anastasia Skobkareva · Danny Sng · Terry Snutch · Milford Sorensen · Patrick Stalder · Chris Steunenberg · Marsha Taylor · Wilfrid Taylor · Suzanne Ten Haaf · Bev Tennant · Joanne Thember · Marc Theriault · Lisa Timar · Brenton Toderian · Kavie Toor · Steve van der Leest · Maximillian Vanry · Marco Varnier · Gordon Vitkay · Dan Voetmann · Lisa Wade · Pascal Waeber · Andrew Walsh · Brody Watkins · Jennifer Watts · Patrick Watts · Theresa Watts · Robert Watts · Brad Waugh · Andrew Wight · Brian Wilks · Katherine Williamson · Cyndi Willis · Ronald Wilson · Rebecca Wyse · Pedro Yang · Eddie Pui Lun Yuen · Renato Zane **103** David Alexander · Scott Allen · Chamila Anthonypillai · Bob Archambault · Pauline Aveyard · Julian Barrera · Olive Bassett · Adam Beaudin-Ball · Arlene Beitel · Jeanne Beker · Lisa Belanger · Scott Bell · Alfred Bennett · Hawley Bennett · Don Benson · Ralph Berezan · Maria Bernardo · John Betts · Shirley Blair · Mark Blundell · Janeen Brodie · Russ Brummer · David Bullock · Shannon Butler · Elaine Campbell · Steve Capus · Sherry Carter · Caleb Chan · Peter Chen · Susan Chen · Blake Choquer · Serah Chow · Darian Chustz · Joanna (Jody) Clark · Yajaira Collante · Shannon Cordingley · Andrea Cotter · Warren Cruickshank · Jessi Cruickshank · Laura Cuthbert · Adrien D'Andrade · Akber Dhanjee · Baltej Dhillon · Pravesh Dookun · Francine Grace Dyksterhuis · Chris Eastman · Bob Elton · Sarah Evanetz · Jennifer Ferguson · Christopher Fryer · Carole Gair · F. Greg Garnett · Shaun Garvey · Mary Gazetas · Jacob Gebrewold · Caleb Gebrewold · Patricia Genereaux · Steven Goguen · Bob Goody · Ron Green · Eric Greenwood · Mike Grieve · Matthew Griffeth · Delaney Griffiths · Sara Groenewegen · Matthew Gu · Toby Guidry · Nicholas Gurniak · Rick Hansen · Brian Hartley · Wendy Hempstock · Gary Hilton · Kuan Ho · Annette Holloway · Monika Hope · Jennifer Hopp · Adam Hori · Lucia Tanja Hrgovic · Dorian Huang · Daylan Hughes · Jonathan Hui · Jackie Humber · Robert Hurst · Bill Jaffe · Gordon Janzen · Dan Jeffries · Li-Kuo (Cody) Jen · Damon Jones · Lloyd Jones · Daryn Jones · Len Jordan · Brittany Kachur · Will Kalutycz · Grant Keogan · Peter Khakh · Mike Killeen · Seul Kim · Jim Kojima · Andrey Kolesnikov · Sabrina Kolker · Cynthia Kumar · Olivia Lam · Michael Lehnert · Daniel Levy · Axel Lewenhaupt-Cash · Jackson Li · George Liakopoulos · Jim Lightbody · Don Lindsay · Margie Lo · Adam Loewen · Denise Logan · Fontaine Ma · Bruce MacLaren · Phil Mahre · Mike Marcoux · Cheri McCuaig · Michael McDaniel · Stuart McDonald · Heather McGrath · Sheryl McMillan · Tod McNab · John Mills · Brent Mizell · Marina Moslenko · Peter Motzek · Scott Muirhead · Robert Mukai · Jennifer Ng · Christy Nicolay · Daniel O'Hearn · Shirley Olafsson · Jacqueline Oostergo · David Ostrom · George Paleologou · Tim Palmer · Taylor Ann Parkinson · John Pasin · Chad Pederson · Paul Plimley · Andrea Pont · Michael Pratt · Melissa Preddy · Thomas Prigl · Shareen Rai · Monty Raisinghani · Doris Reach · Mike Ridley · Sheila Riggs · Kathryn Elizabeth Robertson Delisser · Ashley Roed · Karissa Roed · Melinda Rogers · Ann Rothe · Jacqueline Roy · Vincent Ruan · Jordan Ruegg · Nicholas Rutckyj · Peter Ryan · Kalwant Sahota · Alan Sakai · Brendan Sallis · Tony Sandhu · Shamir Santosh · Mary Saunders · Jeff Schiebler · Kyle Schofield · Kerri Seaman · Danielle Shack · Dylan Shaw · Jeremy Shaw · John Sherman · Nick Shular · Navjot Sidhu · Dylan Siegle · Robyn Sigalit · Gurwant Singh · Kelly Smith · Brian Smith · Scot Smythe · Anna Solnickova · Harolyn Stefanik · Bill Stewart · Angelina Stiglich · Andy Stilin · Alanna Stockford · Tyler Stolting · Lisa Stratton · Julie Sullivan · Cory Sutton · Novell Thomas · Paul Toom · Jack Traa · Clara Van Meel · Jimmy Van Ostrand · Denis Vandal · Kelly Vanderbeek · Mickael Vinet · Anisha Virk · Diana Vuong · Sue Wallace · Bethany Wallis · Alex Warner · Sharon Watkins · Brian Webb · Kevin Webster · Rayne Williams · Kristi Wilson · Walter Wu · Frank Xiao · Brian Yip · Jordan Yuen · Lang Zhou · Martyn Ziegler **104** Kluane Adamek · Raynald Aeschlimann · David Aisenstat · Bruce Allen · Rosie Ander · Mark Andrew · Christina Anthony · Susan Archibald · Constance Baechler · Kirsten Barnes · Kathleen Bartels · Kerri Beattie · Neils Bednarczyk · Erica Bell · Diana Bennett · Oliver Bock · Jasmeen Boparai · Trevor Boudreau · Patricia Branch · Vikram Singh Brar · Kathy Bremner · David Brodie · Cassandra Brondgeest · Chloe Brown · Warren Buckley · Victor Buholzer · Cathy Butler · Leanne Butler · Orysya Bykowa · Colin Campbell · Corrie Carlile · Melissa Carr · Jose Castillo · Dan Caten · Dean Caten · Clifford Chan-Yan · Maxine Chapman · Chelsea Charlie · Peter Chen · Ken Chen · Amanda Cheong · Angela Chung · Amber Church · Veronica Church · Ryan Clarke · Mark Clayton · Francis Cloiseau · Jessica Coe · Yvonne Coelho · Michael Coleman · Robert Couzens · David Cross · David Culbard · Andrea Cunningham · Victor de Bonis · Andy Demeule · Fiorella Di Liberto · Yuming Ding · Arnesa Duldulao · Tyler Dumont · Brian Eby · Kristina Egyed · Nawal El Moutawakel · Scott Ellis · Susan Espin · Laura Fielding-Vandergaag · Joel Finlay · Richard Fosbury · Frank Fredericks · John Gartland · Dayle George · Leonard George · Kalila George-Wilson · Graeme Gerlach · Olive Gilmour · Alberto Gonzalez · Jason Grad · Virginia Greene · Jeffrey Groberman · Ethan Gugliotta · Valerie Hahn · Brian Harlow · Loan Ho · Blair Horn · Rick Horne · Carolyn Hubbard · Troy Hutchinson · Ocean Hyland · Gary Jackson · Austin Jang · Kelli Jennings · Russ Jones · Tewanee Joseph · Mike Jusiak · Stacey Kahn · Neil Kamide · Adriana Kapelan · Kim Kavanagh · Jill Kelly · Tiko Kerr · Lisa Kershaw · Margaret Kettlitz · Olga Kotelko · Victor J. Kraatz · Kathy Kreiner-Phillips · Reem Sabah Kubba · Frank Kurucz · Alice Laberge · Baljit Lalli · Justin Lamoureux · Kevin Lawrence · Alison Lewis · Michael Lynch · Courtney Maddocks · Julia Madigan · Karen Magnussen-Cella · Clint Mahlman · Rafia Mahzabin · Aaron Marchant · Pamela Martin · David Martin · Daniel Martin · Sarah Massey · Mark Mattson · Heather McAlpine · Mark McCarthy · Bob McCormack · Don McGregor · Stuart Mclaughlin · Jim McPherson · Dino Mehmedi · Barbara Melamed · Russell Meszaros · Jinny Milligan · Benn Millman · Carol Millman · Bailey Moznik · Aishah Muhammad · Albert Nagel · Maurice Nahanee · Aarthika Nakanthiran · James Naknakin · Brendan Ng · Janie Nguyen · Ryan Nickerson · Bojana Nikolic · Kerry Nyhan · Fiona O'Brien · Noel Oco · Devon Okrainetz · Shawn O'Sullivan · Heather Owen · Chelsea Padley · Robert Pellatt · David Podmore · Richard W. Pound · Wynne Powell · Kathryn Precious · Doug Querns · Randall Rae · Alan Rae · Kennedy Raine · Sam Ramsamy · Tasreen Rana · Troy Reeb · Jon Rees · Kelly Revell · Thomas Riedel · Kelly Ringstad · Scott Rintoul · Michael Rose · Kenneth Ross · Patricia Sahlstrom · James Sandover · Johan Sauer · John Schlueter · Frank Shan · Sohail Shariff · Michael Shaw · John Shinnick · Jennifer Sine · Avilgayle Sine · Kader Si-Tayeb · Graham Smith · Lina Smith · Stephanie Strube · Ashley Sullivan · Sierra Tasi-Baker · Nihat Tetiker · Cheryl Therriault · Fallon Thomas · Erica Thompson · Candy Tran · Alexandra Tran-Nguyen · Kim Trowbridge · Ralph Turfus · Gary Turner · Irit Uzan · Rosamund van Leeuwen · Mike Vargas · Aliaksandra Varslavan · Eric Vuong · Thurid Wagenknecht · Roland Wahlgren · Andrew Warfield · Justin Webb · Karen Wells · Roger Williams · Brett Wilson · Larry Witherspoon · Francis Wong · Holly Wong · Ken Woods · Anthony Wright · Xiangdong Wu · Cassie Xiong · May Xu · Ernest Yee · Rowena Younes · Kenneth Young · Amanda Yuen · Ellia Zhong **105** Atesh Akbay · Johnnie Allan · David Altman · Doug Alward · Andy An · James Andruski · Rick Antonson · Paolo Aquilini · Jann Arden · Peter Armstrong · Janet Austin · Gary Bass · Maya Beaudry · Jenna Beaudry · Emily Beggs · Sarah Bell · Karen Bertram · Kristi Blakeway · Gabrielle Bloomfield · Brian Bogdanovich · Jeff Bohnen · Robert Boisjoli · Adam Borean · Jennifer Botterill · Fraser Boyer · Rick Brace · Veronica Brenner · Richard Brodeur · Chantal Browne · Michael Buble · Amy Bunnage · Janice Burns · Steve Cahillane · Richard L. Carrión · Jim Chan · Selina Chen · Emily Chen · Simon Chevalier · Pierre Choquette · Jeff Clark · Rick Cluff · Brian Commons · Bob Costas · Titus Cusiak · Helen Cvitanovich · Lori Cyr · Jason Davenport · Ross Davidson · Bruce Deacon · Henry Dejong · Bruce Dewar · Paul Dmytriw · Sean Dolynski · Tim Donegan · Thomas Donnelly · John Downs · Josh Dueck · Evan Eichler · Patrick Elliott · Colby Fackler · Arlena Farley · Christian Farstad · Ivan Fecan · Joy Fera · Ian Ferguson · Joy Foo · Gord Forbes · Natalie Forster · Carey Fouks · Leah Frome · Laura Fudge · Balbir Gill · Jack Gin · Neil Golden · Carol Greaves · Bob Guerin · Monice Gustafson · Gina Hahn · Matthew Hall · Heinz Haller · Melanie Hameluck · Kevin Harasymchuk · Tatiana Hassenstein · Gerhard Heiberg · Derek Heidt · Brian Hill · Tara Hluchy · Mike Hopkins · John Clyne Horton · George Hungerford · Ismaaciil Idiris · Marisa Luvancigh · Debbie Jackson · Richard Jalbert · Azim Jamal · Maana Javadi · Sana Javaheri · David Jennings · Andrea Jensen · Zoya Jiwa · Raman Johal · Wendy John · Ben Jung · Greg Jung · George Kallas · David Kam · Colton Kerfoot · Katherine Kim · David Klein · Wayne Kwan · Karen Kwok · Lauren Kyle · David Labistour · Liesa Lang · Matt Lauer · Catriona Le May Doan · Keith Lee · Robert Lee · Jack Leigh · Wilfried Lemke · Lily Li · Li Lin · Trevor Linden · Lena Ling · Crispin Lipscomb · Wendy Lisogar-Cocchia · Brandt Louie · Juan R. Luciano · Gerry Lush · Kevin Luther · Ken Lyotier · Anna MacDougall · Betty MacLeod · Mike MacNeil · Yan Yan Man · Carrie Lee Marshall · Marc Marshall · Takashi Maruyama · Matthew Mathison · Mèlanie Mathon · Jim McCarthy · Clare McCormick · Dave McGregor · Bob McKay · Donald McKenzie · Sarah McLachlan · Tanya McLachlan · George McRae · Tracey McVicar · Charlie Meszlenyi · Deb Miller · Nina Miller · Katy Milne · Kyle Mitchell · Justin Morneau · Fran Mulhern · Steve Nash · Sarah Nelson · Agnes Ng · Ser Miang Ng · David Nichols · Brent Nichols · Arjang Nowtash · Manabu Ogawa · Linda Oglov · Chris Oosthuizen · Denis Oswald · Adrian Pape · Jessica Park · Catherine Patterson · Cianna Pawluk · Lynda Perovich · Mario Pescante · Joel Pineau · Brittany Point · David Porte · Frank Pozzobon · Rita Quicho · Shayne Ramsay · Dabir Rashid · Lisa Redmond · Craig Reedie · Vicki Reese · Maeve Reynolds · Chris Rinke · Laurie Rix · Ed Robertson · Peggy Robinson · Gayle Roodman · Ken Rooke · Tamara Roughead · Randi Roy · Dan Russell · Amornthep Sachdev · Antony Scanlon · Dr. Charles Scudamore · Brian Sears · Lauren Senft · Natalie Shantz · Anoop Sharma · Bill Sheedy · Jenniffer Sheel · Nicole Shum · Joanie Kaur Sidhu · Taya Smith · Shannon Smyth · Hugh Smythe · Yang Song · Cindy Sparrow · Terry Sparrow · Mark Stoklosa · Marvin Storrow · Joe Strasser · Robert Swannell · Scott Tabachnick · Tamara Taggart · Malik Z. Talib · Trevor Tamplin · Rick Tarala · Michael Tchao · David Thomson · Charles Tobin · Tia Town-Schon · Brit Townsend · Sebastian Troen · Ka Chun Joseph Tsang · Meikaela Tumber · Charles van der Lee · Borvonan "Obi" Vattanawong · Giuseppe Venturoli · Kimberly Weatherspoon · Brooke Webber · Tania Webster · Matthew Wemple · Darren West · Chris Wilson · Chip Wilson · Julia Wilson · Tracy Wilson-Kinsella · Jody Wilson-Raybould · Paul Winston · Shaylene Wiseman · Arnold Witzig · Brendan Wong · Ming Wong · Rokin Wong · Jennifer Wong · Cheryl Wong · Chrissy Young · Zaiqing Yu **106** Suzanne Allard Strutt · Jose Armario · Leonard Asper · Harjot Bains · Geoffrey Beattie · Sylvia Bedwell · Sam Belzberg · Daniel Berardo · Jackie Bevis · Brian Bovencamp · John Brock · Scott Browning · Beverley Burmeister · Julie Bussiere · Judy Caldwell · Judy Campardo · Mahisha Canagasuriam · Dmitry Chernyshenko · Marc-Andre Choquette · Doug Clement · Seb Coe · Jacqui Cohen · Chantal Coschizza · Cindy Crapper · Malcolm Crawford · Charmaine Crooks · Patricia Cross · Cheryl Cruickshank · Craig Cunningham · Chastity Davis · Ashley dela Cruz Yip · Permjoat Dhillon · Kini Do · Peter Dolman · Ken Downie · Ann Duffy · Jacob Emerson · Kathy Ensor · Amanda Feng · Hugh Fisher · Shirin Foroutan · Rolly Fox · Julie Francis · Dan Frewing · Michael Gannon · Andre Gerolymatos · Javier Goizueta · Larry Gold · Nancy Greene · Walter Gretzky · Wayne Gretzky · Ric Handren · Rick Hansen · Andrea Hill · Maria Hobson · Paul Hollands · Sarah Howard · Chi Yan (Terry) Hui · Yuen Lam Hui · Kau Mo Hui · Patti Jackson · Kamini Jain · Karen James · Carol Jillings · Tania Joukova · Jodie Judd · Barbara Kendall · Janice Ketcham · Dave Kimpinsky · Jeff Kirkland · Hugo Kotar · Ed Kry · Wendy Lai · Catriona Le May Doan · Matt Lee · Pam Leech · Bob Lenarduzzi · Morgan Leung · Wallace Leung · Alice Lin · Paula Liveris · Elias Loukas · Ryan Maillet · Jay Malinowski · Jordan Marcia · Colleen Marsel · Keith Martin · Andrew McFadyen · Hayley McLeod · Hassan Merali , Robert C. Meredith · Ed Michayluk · Roderick Mickleburgh · Natalia Mihai · Robert Milton · Nadir Mohamed · Dae Sung Moon · Patricia Moreno · Bob Morrell · Michelle Myring · Maria Nagi · Steve Nash · Marion Olivieri · Lui Passaglia · Jan Peace · Murdie Pollon · James Praught · Gareth Rees · Rogelio Reyes · Dal Richards · Adam David Robinson · Teerath Sandhu · Mark Schnarr · Arnold Schwarzenegger · Concettina Scorda · Peter Scott · Beckie Scott · Garry Senecal · Turner Seward · Masoud Shafie · Anil Singh · Allison Smith · Celestina Smith · Stan Smyl · Erik Stevenson · Mac Stewart · Sam Sullivan · Krysta Sutton · Ronald Suzuki · David Takahashi · Eddie Tang · Stephanie Tang · Susan Tatoosh · Kristian Tocher · Jordan Tolton · Ian Tostenson · Albert Tsang · David Turcotte · Robert Ryan Tyrell · Wayne Verch · Al Vogt · Jason Warren · Michael Watts · Pernilla Wiberg · Bobbe Wood · Rob Wynen · Chris Zimmerman

PRESENTING PARTNERS PARTENAIRES PRINCIPAUX

SIGNATURE SUPPORTERS SUPPORTEURS OFFICIELS

SIGNATURE SUPPLIER FOURNISSEURS OFFICIELS

HOST COUNTRY PAYS HÔTE

HOST PROVINCE PROVINCE HÔTE

VISA     CANWEST

THE GLOBE AND MAIL     CTV

Editor-in-chief / *Rédactrice en chef* : Alison Gardiner
Creative direction / *Direction de la création* : Ben Hulse
Art direction and design / *Direction artistique et conception* : Greg Durrell
Lead photography / *Photographie principale* : Rick Collins
Colour correction / *Correction des couleurs* : Vairdy Andrew and/et Ben Hulse
Cover design / *Conception de la couverture* : Ben Hulse

Supporting photography / *Photographie secondaire* :
Kevin Arnold (p.142)
Sandra Behne, Getty Images (p. 156)
Derek Baxter (p. 143)
Gabrielle Beer, Image Media Farm Inc. (p. 36, 41, 42, 43, 124, 125, 138, 174)
Luca Bertacchi, Image Media Farm Inc. (p. 6, 8, 16, 17, 38, 44, 45, 104, 106, 124, 134, 145, 146 174)
Greg Durrell (p. 41, 42, 43, 44, 45, 46, 48, 49, 50, 52, 55, 56, 58, 118, 122, 123, 124, 134, 176)
Richard Heathcote, Getty Images (p. 160)
Harry How, Getty Images (p. 156)
Ben Hulse (p. 15, 153, 154)
Jasper Juinen (p. 157)
Sean Kilpatrick, The Canadian Press (p. 76)
Mélanie Kimmett (p. 20)
Streeter Lecka, Getty Images (p. 156)
Randy Links (p. 142, 143)
Oreon Mounter (p. 83)
Lorenzo Negri, Image Media Farm Inc. (p. 20, 51, 138)
Steve Simon (p. 68, 69, 70, 71, 76, 77, 78, 88, 102, 103, 108, 110, 111, 112, 124, 129, 134, 164, 166)
Cameron Spencer, Getty Images (p. 156, 158)
The Hospital for Sick Children, Graphic Centre (p. 79)
Nicholas Tsikourias, Getty Images (p. 10)
Jeff Vinnick, Getty Images (p. 20)

Project management / *Gestion de projet* : Tina Morabi
Production management / *Gestion de la production* : Sarah Hancock
Project leads / *Chefs de projet* : Alison Maclean and/et Monica Netupsky
Text and captions (English) / *Texte et légendes (anglais)* : Lianne Kerr
Copyediting and proofreading (English) / *Travail éditorial et lecture d'épreuves (anglais)* :
Andrew Tzembelicos and/et Holly Munn
Translation (French) / *Traduction (français)* : One World Translations
Copyediting and proofreading (French) / *Travail éditorial et lecture d'épreuves (français)* :
Marie Pierre Lavoie, Maryse Désaulniers, Sarah Duchesne-Fisette, Annie Frenette and/
et Tina Sarazin

Special thanks to / *Nous tenons également à remercier* : Teena Aujla, Pamela Boyde,
Karen Bryan, Dave Cobb, Dave Doroghy, Vidar Eilersten, Sharon Fisher, John Furlong,
Chris Gear, Andrew Greenlaw, Bryn Isaac, James Jermyn, Denyse Johnson, Mélanie Kimmett,
Margaret Ko, Jeanette LeBlanc, Heather Maciver, Salman Manki, Julie Morgan, Shawn Parkinson,
Daniel Perez-Valencia, Christiaan Piller, Suzanne Reeves, Jim Richards, Chris Shauf,
Andrea Shaw, Jennifer Smith…and the rest of the Vancouver 2010 Torch Relay team and
others who helped with this book in countless ways. / *…ainsi que tous les autres membres
de l'équipe du relais de la flammé de Vancouver 2010 et les personnes qui ont participé
de maintes façons à l'élaboration de ce livre.*

Extra special thanks to Leo Obstbaum (October 26, 1969 – August 20, 2009) whose passion, brilliance and heart guided the Look of the Torch Relay, the torch design and this book, long before the Olympic Flame was lit.

*Un merci très spécial à Leo Obstbaum (26 octobre 1969 – 20 août 2009) dont la passion, l'intelligence et le cœur ont guidé l'identité visuelle du relais de la flamme, la conception du flambeau et de ce livre, bien avant que la flamme olympique n'ait été allumée.*

NORFOLK COUNTY PUBLIC LIBRARY